Stefansson and the Canadian Arctic

Vilhjalmur Stefansson (1879-1962) was Canada's greatest modern Arctic explorer, theorist, writer, and pioneer ethnologist. For the first quarter of the twentieth century his ideas captured the imagination of Canadians and gave them a sense of Canada's northern destiny. However by the mid-1920s he had become persona non grata in Canada, although he remained an acknowledged Arctic expert elsewhere in the world. Even today Stefansson's character is the subject of debate. His admirers consider him a prophet and visionary; his critics consider him a charlatan, a manipulator, and, in some instances, a liar. In this award-winning book Richard Diubaldo explores the controversy surroundings Stefansson and his achievements and the reasons Canada rejected one of its biggest supporters.

Stefansson's contributions to Arctic exploration are immense. He discovered some of the world's last major land masses in the Arctic and his hydrographic soundings outlined, for the first time, the continental shelf from Alaska to Prince Patrick Island and revealed the submarine mountains and valleys beneath the Beaufort Sea. While in the Arctic he lived with the Inuit, learning their habits and language, and kept a detailed record of early Inuit society.

However some of Stefansson's deeds, and the motives behind them, garnered reproach. In one instance Stefansson was accused of abandoning ship just before the ship was crushed in the ice, a heinous act for the leader of an expedition. On another occasion, following a disastrous expedition to Wrangel Island during which great numbers of the party died, Stefansson was accused of deliberately misleading members of the expedition and lying about the perils that faced them. The affair caused Canada to become embroiled with the United States and the Soviet Union, and many argued that Stefansson was more concerned with personal fame and financial gain than people's lives.

Was Stefansson a prophet or a profiteer, a victim or a villain? *Stefansson and the Canadian Arctic* reveals the truth about this fascinating personality.

RICHARD J. DIUBALDO is professor of history and director of the Centre for Continuing Education, Concordia University.
Winner of the John Lyman Award and a CHA Regional History Certificate of Merit

Richard J. Diubaldo

STEFANSSON AND THE CANADIAN ARCTIC

McGill-Queen's University Press

Montreal & Kingston • London • Ithaca

© McGill-Queen's University Press 1978
ISBN 0-7735-1815-0
Legal deposit third quarter 1978
Bibliothèque Nationale du Québec

Reprinted in paperback 1998

This book was first published with the help of a grant
from the Social Science Federation of Canada,
using funds provided by the Canada Council

McGill-Queen's University Press acknowledges the financial support of
the Government of Canada through the Book Publishing Industry
Development Program for its activities.
We also acknowledge the support of the Canada Council
for the Arts for our publishing program.

Design by Julia Harris

Canadian Cataloguing in Publication Data

Diubaldo, Richard, 1940–
Stefansson and the Canadian arctic
Includes bibliographical references and index.
ISBN 0-7735-1815-0
1. Stefansson, Vilhjalmur, 1879–1962. 2. Arctic regions – Discovery and
exploration – Canadian. 3. Canadian Arctic Expedition (1913–1918).
4. Canada, Northern – Discovery and exploration. 5. Explorers – Canada –
Biography. I. Title.

G635.S7D58 1998   910'.92   C98-901148-8

To my Mother and Father

CONTENTS

INTRODUCTION TO
THE 1998 REPRINT

Vilhjalmur Stefansson was the most important figure to explore this country's Arctic regions in this century. He was only nominally Canadian (he was born here but his parents moved to the United States when he was an infant), but because he led the Canadian Arctic Expedition of 1913-1918, spent the better part of twelve years in the Arctic, and discovered more new land there than any other Canadian, he is a central figure in the history of this country's north. Stefansson is a perfect subject for a biography, for his was an extremely strong personality and his life had many contradictions. On the one hand he was a member of a small band of Arctic pioneers who had the wisdom to adopt Inuit technology and survival techniques, and as a result was able to live in the region in relative comfort and safety. In the purely physical aspects of exploration he was triumphantly successful. On the other hand he was a tireless promoter, both of the Arctic and of his own interests, and some of his schemes went badly (and in one case fatally) wrong, to the serious detriment of his reputation. As a result of this, and also of his own shortcomings in dealing with people, those who knew him were divided into two camps: those who admired him intensely, and those who loathed him with equal intensity.

Stefansson's personality was an unusually magnetic one, and like a magnet, it both repelled and attracted. Of the several books that have been written about him, all but this one are almost uniformly laudatory, perhaps because writers find the "man of action" a compelling subject. D. M. LeBourdais, who was a personal friend of the explorer, published *Stefansson: Ambassador of the North* in 1963, a year after its subject's death; his book is unashamedly hagiographic. The approach E. P. Hanson took in *Stefansson: Prophet of the North* (1941) is made clear in the title. William R. Hunt, in his *Stef* (1986), tried hard to be detached from his subject but ultimately failed. He dealt with the controversial episodes in Stefansson's life, trying hard to present a balanced view, but the great man's magnetism proved too much for him, and he invariably ended up by agreeing with his subject and defending his interpretation of events.

In *Stefansson and the Canadian Arctic* Richard Diubaldo has done his work in the published and unpublished sources, but has gone beyond them to interview a number of people who knew Stefansson and worked with him at the height of his fame (not all of them admirers). He has taken a more balanced approach than Stefansson's other biographers and has concentrated in this book on the years Stefansson actually spent in the Arctic, rather than on the last half of his life, which he spent in trying to promote his vision of the north to an international audience.

In the twenty years since this book was first published, the remaining characters in the controversies that dogged Stefansson's life have died, and the passionate views, favourable and unfavourable, that once marked any discussion of his career have faded into faint echoes. What remains is the man himself and his remarkable accomplishments as well as his failures, all of which are lucidly and fairly analysed in this book.

W. R. Morrison,
University of Northern British Columbia
Prince George

ILLUSTRATIONS

MAPS

CHART

PREFACE

This book is a study of an important, though never thoroughly examined, side of Vilhjalmur Stefansson, Canada's greatest modern-day explorer, pioneer Eskimo ethnologist, arctic writer, and theorist. The period covered stretches, roughly, from 1906 to 1926, when Stefansson was most active in Canada. The book, however, does not presume to trace once again his heroic feats of arctic travel and endurance; rather, this work focuses on a curious reversal in the fortunes of Stefansson. Here was a man whose northern work and ideas about Canada's northern destiny had fired the imagination of Canadians. Yet by the mid-1920s he had been unofficially ostracized from Canada and, for all intents and purposes, has been forgotten here. His fame and reputation, though, survived in the United States and the world at large. This book then is about the rise and fall of Stefansson in Canada.

In such a short space it is exceedingly difficult to give proper due to those who helped make this study possible, for there are many to whom the author owes a considerable debt. The writer wishes to thank Professor Morris Zaslow at the University of Western Ontario, for his unlimited patience and ideas. As well, Professor Richard Wilbur made many helpful suggestions on style and approach. The University of Toronto Press has allowed me to include a slightly revised version of my article "Wrangling Over Wrangel Island," which appeared in the September 1967 issue of the *Canadian Historical Review*. I must thank the following individuals and institutions for making available information which was vital to the book: Mrs. Evelyn Stefansson Nef of Washington, D.C., for allowing me to examine the correspondence of her late husband, Vilhjalmur Stefansson, in the Stefansson Collection; Mrs. Dorothy A. Smith of Carp, Ontario, for allowing me to use the papers of her late father, Rudolph M. Anderson; Mr. W. P. Chipman for permitting me to quote from the private diaries and correspondence of his father, the late K. G. Chipman; the late Dr. Diamond Jenness, for several interviews; and Mr. C. T. W.

Hyslop for permitting me to use active files of the Department of Indian Affairs and Northern Development. Wonderful archival and library assistance was given by the staff of the Public Archives of Canada; and especially Mrs. Erika S. Parmi, librarian, Stefansson Collection; Miss Marion E. Brown, now retired, of the Thomas Fisher Rare Book Library, University of Toronto library; Mr. John Bovey, former archivist of the Department of Indian Affairs and Northern Development and now with the Archives of Manitoba; Mrs. Robin Smith, assistant archivist, the American Museum of Natural History; Mrs. Katherine B. Edsall of the Peabody Museum of Archaeology and Ethnology, Harvard University; Miss Lynn S. Mullins, assistant librarian, American Geographical Society; Miss Nora Corley, formerly of the Arctic Institute of North America library when it was located in Montreal; Mr. George Crossette of the *National Geographic* magazine; Sergeant Sanderson of the Royal Canadian Mounted Police; the Theodore Roosevelt Association and Harvard University library. The Social Science Research Council and the Department of History and Faculty of Arts of Concordia University provided the much-needed financial assistance. The author owes a great deal to a very special person: Joan, patient wife and helpful critic, who provided the incentive to continue.

Two final notes. First, unusual spelling of words, misspellings, lapses in grammar and punctuation in quoted material have been left, more or less, in their original state. Secondly, although I prefer the term "Inuit," I have used the word "Eskimo" throughout simply because it was the expression universally accepted during the period this book covers.

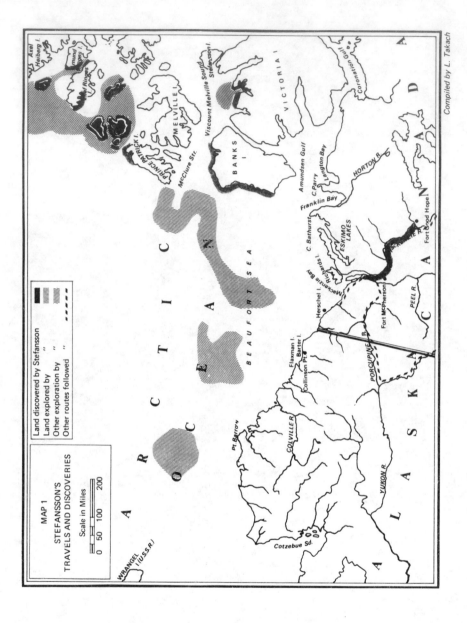

MAP 1
STEFANSSON'S
TRAVELS AND DISCOVERIES

Scale in Miles

0 50 100   200

Land discovered by Stefansson
Land explored by   "
Other exploration by   "
Other routes followed   "

A   R   C   T   I   C

O   C   E   A   N

WRANGEL I.
(U.S.S.R.)

Pt. Barrow

BEAUFORT SEA

COLVILLE R.

Flaxman I.
Barter I.
Collinson Pt.

Herschel I.
Mackenzie Bay

YUKON R.

Cotzebue Sd.

A   L   A   S   K   A

PORCUPINE R.

Fort McPherson

PEEL R.

Axel
Heiberg I.

mund
I.

PRINCE PATRICK I.

MELVILLE I.

McClure Str.

Viscount Melville Sound

Stefansson I.

BANKS I.

VICTORIA I.

Amundsen Gulf

C. Parry
Langton Bay

C. Bathurst

Franklin Bay

ESKIMO
LAKES

RICHARDS I.

Coronation Gulf

HORTON R.

MACKENZIE R.

Fort Good Hope

C   A   N   A   D   A

Compiled by L. Takach

1

Introduction

On 3 August 1969, a distinctive sculpture by Walter Yarwood created in memory of Vilhjalmur Stefansson was unveiled at Arnes, Manitoba, together with bilingual plaques erected by the government of Canada. The Historic Sites and Monuments Board of Canada had recommended in October 1964 that Stefansson be declared an "eminent Canadian" and the inscription on the plaque outlines the essentials of his contribution:

> VILHJALMUR STEFANSSON, NOTED
> ARCTIC EXPLORER AND ETHNOLOGIST,
> WAS BORN AT ARNES, MANITOBA, IN
> 1879. IN MAJOR EXPEDITIONS IN 1906–
> 07, 1908–12 AND 1913–18, HE GREATLY
> EXTENDED KNOWLEDGE OF THE ISLANDS
> AND COASTLINES OF THE WESTERN
> ARCTIC, AND OF ITS PEOPLE. STEFANSSON
> WAS AN EARLY EXPONENT OF THE IDEA
> THAT EXPERIENCED ARCTIC TRAVELLERS
> COULD LIVE OFF THE LAND AS THE
> NATIVES DID. AS AUTHOR AND LECTURER
> HE BECAME A PERSUASIVE ADVOCATE OF
> ARCTIC DEVELOPMENT. STEFANSSON
> ISLAND PERPETUATES HIS MEMORY. HE
> DIED AT HANOVER, NEW HAMPSHIRE,
> IN 1962.

Stefansson was, and is, more than an eminent Canadian. He was one of the most widely known personalities in the Canada and the world of the 1920s. His explorations and discoveries won him the thanks of the Canadian government expressed in an order-in-council in 1921, and the coveted, prestigious gold medals of the American Geographical Society, the National Geographic Society, the Philadelphia Geographic Society, the Chicago Geographic Society, the Geographical Society of Paris, the Explorers Club of New York, the Geographical Society of Berlin, and the Royal Geographical Society of Great Britain. In the United States, where he spent the bulk of his years, he is regarded as a folk hero. His early life, for example, has been made the subject of a primer in the Childhood of Famous Americans series intended to educate and inspire young Americans.[1] The Soviet Union, which has translated many of his works, officially recognizes his greatness and considers him a friend of the Soviet people: "In his predictions and in his long, tireless propaganda as to the meaning of the north he strove to destroy the deep-rooted misconceptions about the environment and living conditions of this region. This is where he best deserves his praise. The rapid settlement, growth, economic assimilation and the increasing interest in the North not only in our country but others as well, are all indicative of Stefansson's insight into the great future of the northern areas."[2]

Between 1906 and 1918, Stefansson's explorations were monumental by any standard. In that time, more than ten years were spent in the Arctic. During the Anglo-American Expedition of 1906–7 he spent eighteen months with the Eskimo of the Mackenzie Delta learning their habits and language. From 1908 to 1912, he remained in the north for fifty-three months, mainly on the western arctic coast where he added to our general knowledge of the region. It was on this expedition that Stefansson's reputation became worldwide with the news of his discovery of a group of Eskimos who had never seen a white man, the so-called "Blond Eskimos" (Copper Eskimos) of Victoria Land. His diaries and books have left us with a detailed record of what primitive Eskimo society must have been like; they remain a rich source of data and observations for generations of anthropologists and archaeologists.[3]

His greatest exploits came during his third and final expedition, which stretched from 1913 to 1918 and was the first entirely under the auspices of the government of Canada. In those five years, he discovered some of the world's last major land masses—Brock, Borden, Meighen, and Lougheed Islands—bringing full circle a process his Viking ancestors had begun almost a thousand years before. Stefansson delineated and redefined for map-makers many of the coastlines in the west-central Arctic. His hydrographic soundings made while he was drifting dangerously on ice floes outlined, for the first time, the continental shelf from Alaska to Prince Patrick Island, and revealed the submarine mountains and valleys beneath the Beaufort Sea.

In those twelve years, Stefansson travelled more than 20,000 miles by sled and dogteam, exploring roughly 100,000 square miles of arctic territory. Part of this time, Stefansson managed to live exclusively by foraging, using acquired Eskimo techniques and his rifle, in areas where not even the Eskimo believed a man could survive.

Stefansson created more interest in the Arctic among Canadians than any other individual of his time. His books remain exciting testimonies to his Canadian career, for their scope goes beyond the mere record of dogged exploration and a stubborn will to survive. They reveal a far-ranging, ever-inquiring mind. He was to become, for example, a recognized and respected authority on the problems of diet, particularly the now popular high-protein low-carbohydrate diet.[4] He was one of the first, also, to advance the view that tooth decay had been virtually non-existent in societies which had subsisted primarily on animal products, a theory sustained by parallel investigations of the Eskimos' changed eating habits.[5]

More importantly, Stefansson became an arctic theorist, an expert commentator and analyst on things northern. Here he was at his best. His message was short and simple: the Arctic was not a bleak, frozen waste, a land of perpetual snows, but a region of habitable climate which must eventually be civilized and developed. He carried his concepts to his audiences using personal experiences and anecdotes coupled with seemingly airtight logic that only fools—or "illiterates" to use Stefansson's word—would dispute. Not only was he controversial and provocative, but in many respects he was right.

The "great circle" routes of today's major international airlines, the spectacle of nuclear submarines surfacing at the north pole, the possibilities of using gigantic submarine tankers to transport the riches of the untapped resources of the arctic archipelago, the use of drifting ice floes for scientific platforms—all had their origin in Stefansson's vision of a polar Mediterranean, his brilliant concept of a commercial empire of the Canadian North. He talked of using airplanes and submarines in exploring and exploiting the north at a time when such mechanical contrivances were in their infancy. By some he has been called the "Prophet of the North,"[6] and this is the title that appears on his gravestone in Hanover, New Hampshire.

Stefansson's books can still fill the reader, Canadian or otherwise, with a sense of romance and imagination about the destiny of Canada and its higher latitudes. His exploits and writings, we are told, have inspired young men in all countries to explore the unknown arctic reaches.[7] One thing is certain, however; his works added vigour to a traditional and persistent Canadian theme, "The True North Strong and Free."[8] Yet, one could safely say that Vilhjalmur Stefansson was, and is, better known outside Canada than he is in the country of his birth, the country of his breath-taking adventures and explorations. Canada, the country he hoped would develop its northern potential and become one of the leading nations in the world, simply does not know the man.

It is somewhat strange, indeed, that the only tangible memories Canada has of this man are Stefansson Island, off the northeast corner of Victoria Island, the memorial in Manitoba, and a few scattered mentions in Canadian publications. Why should such a renowned individual have left so little mark on Canada? Why should he have been ostracized from Ottawa where, in some government quarters, his name was (and still is) akin to a dirty word? In many private circles "Windjammer" became Stefansson's nickname. Why have so many officials chosen to forget and, if possible, to obliterate his memory, and to challenge his achievements with unusual bitterness? A whole forty years had to elapse, for instance, before the Rideau Club of Ottawa would reverse its decision and accept Stefansson as a member, even though his original sponsor was the Right Honourable Sir Robert Borden, Prime Minister of Canada. Only in 1960 did the club's management committee consider that he had been unfairly rejected in 1921. To make amends they named him an honorary member, giving to Stefansson a privilege accorded to only three other persons: the governors general Alexander, Massey, and Vanier.

Why has Stefansson, who received accolades from around the world, received little recognition in Canada? What went wrong between Stefansson and Canada? Essentially, this book is an attempt to analyse the personal side of Stefansson's Canadian career from roughly 1906 to the mid 1920s. This period was for all intents and purposes his most formative and influential in Canada. Why was he *persona non grata* in Canada, especially in Ottawa? Traces of bitter recollections still linger, and the subject still arouses controversy. To his admirers, Stefansson remains a dedicated scientist and idealist; to his enemies, an unscrupulous adventurer who sometimes used cheap publicity tricks to advance himself and dupe the Canadian government and people. Bureaucracies, as well as individuals, have long memories and not even the passage of time has completely erased the debate about the role and the personality of Vilhjalmur Stefansson. Still, most of the active participants in the controversies of fifty years ago have left the scene, and one may hope that the intense passions are quietly dissipating.

This book does not seek to offer yet another biographical or geographical study of Stefansson's activities. These have been the main subject of his own writings and those of his biographers. Instead, it will try to look through and beyond Stefansson to examine the impact of the man and his ideas on the Canadian scene. Very little space has been devoted to the exploratory events of his various expeditions, except for the sake of clarification. One should not gain the impression that Stefansson's explorations are underplayed because these feats were negligible. Nothing could be further from the truth.

In Canada by 1905–6, unbeknown to Stefansson, who was not particularly moved by things northern at this time, the stage was being set for his participation. The creation of two new provinces, Alberta and Saskatchewan, carved from a portion of the Northwest Territories, brought a revival of interest in Canada's frontier. Just as important in focusing more and more attention on the remoter regions of the young Dominion were other developments in the previous decade. The finding of gold in the Yukon generated a fever which transcended the boundaries of Canada; the stories of the riches to be found in the streams of the Klondike had an electrifying effect. Never before had so much international attention been directed at this country and the possible mineral riches she possessed. The exploitation of the gold fields helped unleash the Laurier boom, but it also raised questions concerning the future of such areas, especially their administration and their status. The gold finds also had larger ramifications. In the area of international relations, the method of the final settlement of the Alaska boundary in 1903 with the United States shook Canadian complacency.[9] It was no longer considered politic, nor in the national interest, to have Canadian matters settled by policies emanating from London, which seemed to ignore Canadian sensibilities in favour of global considerations. The Alaska boundary settlement also accentuated a lingering uneasiness over the stability of some of Canada's other ill-defined boundaries and of her sovereignty in those northern territories, particularly the future of the arctic archipelago, lying north of the Canadian mainland.[10] Over the next two decades, Stefansson was to become intimately involved with such problems.

The Dominion's anxiety over its legal position in the archipelago stemmed directly from a confidential report, submitted in 1905 by W. F. King, chief astronomer of Canada, which concluded that "Canada's title to some at least of the northern islands is imperfect."[11]

In 1870, full title to Rupert's Land, the Northwestern Territory, was transferred from Britain to Canada, yet no exact definition of the limits of this area or of the Arctic Islands was given. In 1880, by an imperial order-in-council, the boundaries of Canada were extended to cover all British territories and islands in the far north of North America. But even the order of 1880 did not specifically describe the territory transferred to Canada and, to complicate matters further, Canada did not formally acknowledge the transfer. Not until 1895, fifteen years later, did the Canadian government issue an order-in-council which had the effect of notifying other states that all territory between 141° west longitude and a vague line running west of Greenland was under the jurisdiction of the Dominion. Three new districts were created—Mackenzie, Yukon, and Franklin—the last being assigned the land in question. A later amending order-in-council of 1897, which made the boundaries of the territories much more explicit, had further stated that the District of Franklin included all lands and islands between the 141st meridian on the west, and on the east, Davis Strait, Baffin Bay, Smith Sound, Kennedy Channel, and Robeson Channel. That pronouncement also specifically named the chief islands then known to exist within those limits, extending as far north as Ellesmere. Yet, according to King, it was possible that Canada's assumption of authority in 1895 would not have full international force.[12] King took his argument a step further: "Canada's title to the northern islands derived from Great Britain's—Great Britain's title rests upon acts of discovery and possession. These acts were never, prior to the transfer to Canada, ratified by State authority, or confirmed by exercise of jurisdiction . . ."[13]

King's report had been made in response to a number of developments. The Alaska Boundary dispute had shown the extent to which the United States posed a threat to Canadian territorial pretensions in the Arctic, for Americans had been active in the north, in one way or another, since the middle of the nineteenth century. The majority of the American expeditions to the northlands were privately sponsored, but they frequently built cairns, deposited written records, and raised their country's flag at the places they visited, though there were apparently few definite territorial claims in the name of the United States government.[14] Nevertheless, the Americans could argue that their nationals had been far more active than the Dominion's subjects in the north. Added to this was the regular presence of American whalers operating and wintering in and around Herschel Island and Hudson Bay, whose attitudes might threaten Canadian sovereignty. The alleged misdeeds of whaling crews, and the desire to collect customs duties, sell licences, and otherwise regulate fishing and whaling, were key factors in the initiation of investigation and patrol voyages by Canada in the 1880s in Hudson Strait and Hudson Bay, and afterwards in the arctic islands.[15] It was the reported lawlessness at the winter headquarters of the American whaling fleet in the Beaufort Sea (in 1896) that caused the North-West Mounted Police in 1903 to descend upon the western Arctic and establish a post at Herschel Island and another police operation on Hudson Bay.[16] Ironically, these successful attempts to bring the arctic whaling industry under Canadian government control and demonstrate that the Dominion possessed effective administration in these areas coincided with the declining economic importance of the industry.[17]

The most direct threat to Canadian control of the entire archipelago at the turn of the century came from Sweden and then Norway which, as a result of Otto Sverdrup's explorations between 1898 and 1902, could have claimed Axel Heiberg and the Ringnes Islands (later to be known as the Sverdrup Islands) on the basis of prior discovery.[18] King's report served to reinforce Ottawa's suspicions: Canada was in danger of losing complete and unquestioned control over some of the arctic territories unless she could demonstrate that she could exercise effective occupation.

Some Canadians were patently alarmist. Captain Joseph Bernier (1852–1934) had been urging the Canadian government for a number of years to remedy the situation and make secure Canada's claims to the archipelago. From 1897, Canadian expeditions had been touching on arctic islands and making a point of raising the flag. Between 1906 and 1913— which covers the years of Stefansson's first two northern expeditions— Bernier, as a fishery officer and agent of the Canadian government in other capacities, carried out his government's instructions to demonstrate that Canada had the wherewithal and the interest to care for her northern territories.[19]

By the turn of the century, the Canadian government had embarked on a long range, though relatively low-key, program of finding out more about her northern territories, securing Canadian sovereignty, and advancing the frontiers of scientific knowledge. Stefansson, by then in his twenties, was soon destined to become one of the central characters.

In 1880, a year after Vilhjalmur Stefansson was born, his parents left Gimli, in what is now Manitoba, for the prairie settlements of the Dakota Territory. His Icelandic parents had moved from their island to the "Promised Land"[20] in 1875, but they were to find that, at this particular point in western Canada's history, the land held little promise. The Stephensons, as they became known,[21] were soon confronted with the bitter Manitoba winters, crop failure, floods, an epidemic, and the spectre of starvation. Two of their children perished as a result of these calamities.

Like many disenchanted Icelanders before them, the family pulled up stakes and trekked southward to the Dakotas.[22] "Villi" Stefansson was to spend most of his boyhood in the frontier wilderness of the North American plains and, during his later arctic exploits and adventures where self-reliance and ruggedness were called for, he made grateful references to his early pioneer and cowboy life. His log-cabin upbringing was enriched by his parents' Icelandic intellectual heritage[23]—tolerance, inquisitiveness, skepticism mysteriously combined with romanticism, a vaunted literary ability, and a profound respect for education. Though his primary education was spotty, twenty-seven months in all, Stefansson proved to be quick of mind. It allowed him to read aloud the Old Testament in Icelandic by age six; Icelandic sagas and a local newspaper, *Heimskringlia* (The Round World), would acquaint this youngster with history, literature, and politics.[24]

Actually, the years spent at the University of North Dakota, the University of Iowa, and finally Harvard, were to develop and reveal most of Stefansson's personal traits. Although Stefansson later saw his college career in a very rosy light,[25] that period of his life was one of more than the usual disillusionment and soul-searching, as well as of financial uncertainty. Stefansson was constantly having to make ends meet, from instructing with the International Correspondence Schools, to selling insurance for the Independent Order of Foresters, and speculating in Canadian land.[26] As well, the colourless academic routine seemed alien and meaningless to a young and brilliant individual who had long known his own abilities, and all of whose visions were underscored by the idea of personal greatness.[27] He was impatient with things as they were, and his impatience continually boiled up in outbursts of irreverence and iconoclasm —sometimes, one suspects, more for effect than substance. In curiously modern tones, he scoffed at the type of formal learning to which he was being subjected. As an educational process, it was stagnant and useless.

School learning hammered rules and outdated ideas into the students' heads. In the process, originality was discouraged and stifled by misguided teachers who considered their way to be the only way. Their idea of progress, Stefansson reasoned, was to mould another generation of close-minded individuals who would contribute little, if anything, to the advance of knowledge. Any serious person would gain more from independent reading than from formal schooling.[28] Stefansson's belief in a relatively unstructured education was only one early example of his lifelong adherence to, and promotion of, the so-called "school of unlearning." His mind, like his muscles, would grow weak without hard exercise. He felt nothing strengthened the mind as a fixed purpose. "Fix your eyes on a mark—a high mark—and never look back."[29] Lofty as some of his ideals were, these sentiments did not endear him to many people. On more than one occasion, precisely because of his efforts to be different, original, and stimulating, he was to find himself alone.

To assert himself, "Willy" Stephenson became Vilhjalmur Stefansson early in 1899—"thoroughly Icelandic."[30] To whet his appetite for more knowledge, he and his college companions spent many an evening discussing such "evils" as Robert G. Ingersoll, the American agnostic who attacked religion on "rational" grounds, and Charles Darwin, whose *Origin of the Species*, postulating evolution and natural selection, was upsetting the complacency of the second half of the nineteenth century, especially in fundamentalist mid-America. On one occasion, for holding forth too vehemently on such ideas, Stefansson was to lose his room and board. He soon found that the key to popularity amongst his peers was to excel in things academic while "playing lazy." In public he was a loafer, seldom attending his classes at North Dakota; secretly, he was an intense, hard-working student.[31] Such behaviour, along with a lighthearted disdain for all forms of authority, was to spell trouble.

His problems with the University of North Dakota administration are a key to understanding the young Stefansson at this stage of his career. Looking back on Stefansson's expulsion from North Dakota, ostensibly on the grounds of poor attendance and "failure to attend to his duties,"[32] Vernon P. Squires, his former professor in the Department of Literature, concluded that Stefansson "had settled the problem of life a little too decidedly and dogmatically" for one of his age and experience. Squires was certain that Stefansson had a bright future if he could only learn to be a little less egotistical and cocksure.[33] Stefansson's rather disdainful attitude prompted William Merrifield, president of the University of North Dakota, to spell out the establishment's position to the youthful skeptic. Rightly or wrongly, Merrifield had viewed Stefansson as an insubordinating influence; not only had Stefansson set authority at defiance, but he had incited others to do the same. Merrifield was willing to forgive and forget if the young turk would acquiesce and "be able to live as a loyal member of the community in which your lot may be cast." If he could not do so, the university would rather give up the relationship. "[N]o community can, or will, long tolerate a spirit of insubordination or defiance to its members. That spirit, of course, is anarchy, and everybody understands these days what anarchy is."[34] President McKinley had just been murdered by an "anarchist" in Buffalo.

Obviously Stefansson did not comply with Merrifield's conditions, for he soon moved on to the more congenial, less formalized, State University of Iowa, where he finally convinced the university authorities of his sincerity and speedily completed his undergraduate education. After this, he moved on to Harvard, probably the finest school in the country. True, he had had to register as a divinity student, on scholarship—but at least he was there. At Harvard, aside from the nagging financial worries, Stefansson felt at home among intellectual equals and more challenging teachers. Almost everyone who came in contact with Stefansson, Merrifield included, realized he had excellent ability. Stefansson, above all, was fully aware of his own capabilities, that he was made of the "right stuff" to succeed, and to succeed greatly. A determination to be successful, of course, was the ethic and drive of the time. While at Harvard he wrote a short article, originally called "Working Your Way Through Harvard," which, like many a beginning writer's efforts, was autobiographical, reflecting his own experience and assumptions about himself. Harvard, he pointed out, was not only terribly expensive, it was intellectually demanding—almost impossible—for the average, the mediocre: "[Harvard] is the place for the poor man who knows he is made of the right stuff, who has found by experience that he has more inferiors than superiors in ability and courage."[35]

Aside from this self-confidence, Stefansson had little to cling to in his early years. He entered college in 1898 a heartbroken young man; the girl he had loved had married someone else.[36] After this experience, Stefansson rarely concerned himself with women, except to give poetic notice to some short-lived flirtation or other.[37] More and more of his time was taken up with the academic life at Harvard, then one of the primary bailiwicks of Spencerian "Social Darwinism" in American thought.[38] Although by this time in its twilight and losing ground before the new, dissenting "social gospel," Herbert Spencer's application of Darwinian concepts to all facets of existence was being forcefully echoed in Harvard Yard.[39] Stefansson had encountered Spencer's *First Principles of Synthetic Philosophy* as a sophomore at Iowa, and had drawn from it a sweeping philosophical understanding of the universe.[40] Harvard was to reinforce this experience, and the view of the universe that resulted was to be one of Stefansson's major credos. Spencer applied evolutionary Darwinism systematically—if not always soundly—to mankind and his world. Along with the conception that all sound development must be slow and unhurried, Spencer stressed that the history of man's development depended on the persistence of force and natural evolution through the "struggle for existence" and the "survival of the fittest." Nature would ensure that the best competitors would win—and winning was the proof of being "best." The confusion of physical fitness with morally "best" can be seen in Spencer's extolling of such virtues as frugality and foresight, careful management, hard work, and profound self-sufficiency. Stefansson, looking to his own boyhood experiences, believed he possessed all of these virtues.

Stefansson preferred to study Spencer, Darwin, and Hugo rather than mundane subjects like geometry or political economy. To him, Spencer's formula of evolution was a masterpiece, a framework for the secrets of the universe. It had depth, breadth, and, above all, in Stefansson's words, "omnicomprehensibility." Kepler may have been the legislator of the stars, but, to Stefansson, Spencer was the law-giver and interpreter of the cosmos.[41] Stefansson appears to have adopted a Spencerian approach to many of his efforts, arctic or otherwise. His notebook-diary for 1904 records his reflections on the human attributes which contribute to human progress: remembrance, industry, adaptability, inventiveness, receptiveness, forethought. *Remembrance* and the treasuring of experiences was the first condition for human advancement. *Industry* was the effort to improve and strengthen all bodily and mental powers. In this way only could the environment be subjected. *Inventiveness*, to Stefansson, was self-explanatory. The fundamental attribute of all organisms, including man, was *adaptability* to the environment. Besides, individuals and nations must be *receptive*, must be willing to learn from each other. This could be accomplished by travel and comparative studies. The final attribute of human progress was *forethought*, the ripe fruit of intellectual development, man's ability to plan ahead, perhaps the most important distinguishing feature between uncivilized and civilized man.[42]

Stefansson had entered Harvard on a divinity scholarship of the American Unitarian Association. Initially, he was destined to become a Unitarian minister, but eventually the divinity school and the American Unitarian Association became convinced he was not suited to this career, and he was free to approach the graduate school of anthropology to continue his studies there. If anything, as Stefansson himself admitted, he undertook divinity studies so that he could be transferred to another faculty, anthropology, without having the requisite background.[43] As early as 1899, Stefansson had indicated a strong preference for sciences that dealt with life and society.[44] It is true that he did have a semi-religious concern. At the very outset of his Harvard career, he was able, much to his surprise, to convince both the university and the Unitarians that religion was folklore, hence a branch of anthropology. The Department of Anthropology had been impressed by Stefansson's ability and the intellectual prowess he had displayed in one of their undergraduate courses; it awarded him a fellowship.[45]

The life of a man of the cloth—if a Unitarian minister may be so described—had never really been Stefansson's goal, since for a long time he had had little use for organized religion. Life and society, as he saw them, had turned Stefansson into a singular pessimist about the future of man and his uncertainty about his own place in the scheme of things. He may have been self-confident about his abilities, but he seriously doubted that any talent had a purpose or value. His first great awakening came with his alienation from organized religion. Religion in all its manifestations was a worthless pursuit to occupy one's mind. In 1898, Stefansson attended a Unitarian convention in Boston as a representative of the Icelandic Unitarian Association. He came away completely disillusioned because of the petty doctrinal squabbles which abounded at the congress, and could not but agree with the observations of A. E. Morrison, his friend and adviser, that "any assembly of theologians is the best example we have of insanity reduced to a science, a systematic fraud, unconscious crime, of that system which wastes the life of man and shrivels up his soul." Everything in nature denied the existence of a personal god, and "yet this does not break on clouded minds, chained like slaves to tread the mills of toil, to make brick without straw."[46]

Stefansson expressed distress that the world was full of sheep who believed what they were told or read, who refused to explore beyond the dogmas that were so intimately bound up in their world view.[47] He was convinced that he had a special mission to remove the blind spot from humanity's eye, to let the world know, as loudly as possible, that the false assumptions it fancied were not eternal truths. The message in his poems are quite revealing on this score. He saw himself in an unending search for the holy grail, Truth, as one of a host of men in quest for the same goal. He would do his small part to challenge convention. Even if it meant martyrdom, there would be others who would carry on the fight.[48] Truth would win, and perhaps the surest way to bring about the "dawn" of truth was through science.[49]

But this ambition still did not solve his recurring doubts of his personal worth or the problems of his place in the scheme of things. A profoundly sensitive young man, he was given at times to pessimism about his fate, to feeling that his life—short as it had been—was a tragedy, that he was ruined, his dreams gone awry.[50] One gets the distinct feeling from his early writings that Stefansson would never be satisfied with the life of a common man. The brooding and pessimism had to find some release, some sanctuary, from the confusing hustle and bustle of a dehumanized brutal world.[51]

What was his sanctuary to be? Where was he to go? It is easy to suggest that his asylum was to be the loneliness and barren grounds of northern Canada, that the Arctic was to soothe his troubled being. This is only partly true. His real asylum was devotion to work, to drown himself utterly in hard tasks—whether in the Arctic or anywhere else.

Years later, in 1912, while on his return south from his second arctic expedition, an older (age thirty-two) and wiser Stefansson confided to his diary that he still had failed to find happiness and truth from his work. That May evening, Stefansson sat down and summed up his hapless plight:

> One reason for keeping one's emotions out of his journal is that any-one with imagination can guess what they are. They need only set before them a dreamer thrown among the hardest realities of our earth, one who longs for sympathy placed among people not un-sympathetic but as incapable of seeing the things that he sees as we are of seeing ultra violet light. . . . To my unfortunate mind nothing seems worthwhile—no success as seen by others, no success tho' I myself should have to admit it complete in every other respect would be to me worthwhile. I cannot picture for myself a heaven and no one has pictured a heaven for me that holds out the promise: "This will satisfy you." One heaven may be better than another and all may be better than hell, but none can satisfy. The best thing I can hope for is work. Work will drown sorrow better than any other thing I have tried — as yet I have not tried drink, and I shall probably never try it, for others have tested it and found its promises unfulfilled. The best to see hoped for is congenial work, and the work appears congenial after a fashion—I can think of nothing better and I am fit for nothing else by now. . . . My desire is to be able to keep abreast with my time. That they are flying now and could not when I left home is symbolical of what has probably happened to me generally—I am being left behind in the dark ages of my own creating. To be narrow in knowledge is bad; to be narrowed in sympathies is worse. Looking over such magazines as I have seen on my way west the last two months, I have found few things in them interest me. "So some of him lived but most of him died" seems to be my case.[52]

Apparently, his view of his place in the world had not been changed much by his first five years in the Canadian north. Despite his cocksure attitude in public, Stefansson was a sensitive man, given to moods of despair even when things did go to his satisfaction. One can imagine how he must have suffered from some of his later setbacks, how he summoned up the strength from within to pull himself together, to plunge ahead with his work. Constant and intense activity was not only his brand of personal therapy, but also a balm for failure—either real or imagined.

This glance into the "essential Stefansson," albeit brief, is requisite to understanding the qualities of the man who, by his mid-twenties, was soon to play a vital role in the history of northern Canada. He had had a chequered, and in some ways incomplete, university career; he was an aggressive and adaptive individual. Outwardly, a man who displayed a high degree of self-confidence and faith in his own star, he was occasionally plagued by self-doubts and feelings of insecurity that he kept strictly to himself. A man of action, Stefansson threw himself into demanding tasks, sure that hard work would aid his drive for personal success and greatness, and would bring him satisfaction in a world overly dependent on mis-guided tradition. As his Canadian career suggests, the will to survive despite the odds, to overcome obstacles, to be the master of the situation, and to ultimately win "the game,"[53] was a salient feature of Stefansson's drive for recognition and self-fulfilment.

2

Arctic Initiation

In 1903, Stefansson suggested to Frederick Ward Putnam, head of Harvard's Department of Anthropology, that he make a trip to Iceland, his ancestral home. Putnam was at first skeptical, but since the young graduate student was able to read the principal source languages, Icelandic and Latin, and because Putnam became interested in Stefansson's hypothesis of a possible correlation between tooth decay and the use of cereals in one's diet, funds were made available for a short trip.[1] The six or seven weeks in Reykjavik proved to be interesting, though not conclusive in proving the tooth decay theory. The following summer, under the auspices of Thomas Augustus Jaggar, "vulcanologist," funds were secured for a second trip to Iceland to study the island's volcanic activity. Stefansson was to have been Jagger's interpreter on this expedition, but at the last moment Jaggar went off to study Hawaii's natural wonders, virtually leaving Stefansson to his own devices.

Stefansson's work done in or about Iceland on this second trip resulted in the collection of a number of skulls which did much to convince him of the relationship between the consumption of cereals and tooth decay. Extremely important from the viewpoint of his later career was his article "The Icelandic Colony in Greenland," dealing with the disappearance of that colony. The article traced the discovery of Greenland and its subsequent colonization by Iceland, then a refuge for renegade Norwegian nobility, in the late ninth and tenth centuries. At first, contact between Greenland, Iceland, and the mother country, Norway, was very common, but by the early fifteenth century little or nothing was heard from the tiny outposts on the west side of Greenland. In the fourteenth century, contact between the European and the native population, the Eskimo, or *Skraelinger*, increased and this was followed by hostilities, burning, looting, and kidnapping on the part of the Eskimos who were expanding southward.

It was popularly believed that the remaining Icelandic colony in Greenland eventually had forsaken its true faith and mode of living, and had assimilated with the *Skraelinger*. Stefansson, on the other hand, concluded from the written sources, Eskimo oral tradition, and contemporary archaeological investigations that the Icelanders had been eradicated rather than absorbed by the Eskimo.[2] At the time, he placed little value on the article, but his later findings in the Canadian north were to be strongly coloured by what he had learned about the mystery of the Greenland colony's disappearance. And, though he had earlier shown little interest in the Canadian north, this article was to have an immediate influence in turning his gaze and imagination to the Arctic and making it his field of study.

Following his return from Iceland, Stefansson at first indicated no burning desire to do further anthropological work in northern latitudes. For one thing, aside from Peary's well publicized attempts to reach the North Pole, there was no great public interest in such activity; and the lack of such a market, in turn, discouraged financial backers, the pillars of the whole business of exploration. Besides, the turn of the century was to witness a profusion of expeditions to more exotic places, South America, Africa, and the unspoiled reaches of Southeast Asia—the last gasp of the imperialistic impulse of the nineteenth and early twentieth centuries. The appearance of such magazines as *National Geographic*, an outgrowth of the National Geographic Society (incorporated in 1888), was indicative of the appeal of romantic far-away places. The "Dark Continent" beckoned to the restive Stefansson, and he intended in 1906 to become a member of a British Museum expedition destined for Central East Africa.

These plans were changed when Stefansson was suddenly offered the position of anthropologist on the impressively named Anglo-American Polar Expedition, commanded by Ejnar Mikkelsen and Ernest de Koven Leffingwell. Apparently, Leffingwell, or one of his advisers, had read Stefansson's paper on Greenland[3] and surmised that Stefansson might be a suitably enterprising person, who would be willing to work for a small salary in exchange for the opportunity to become a member of the expedition. Forever hard-pressed for money, the Anglo-American Polar Expedition was on the lookout for inexpensive, qualified, scientific staff.

The purpose of the expedition was to explore the Beaufort Sea north of Alaska in an effort to find new land, if not a new continent. No one really knew what was in the Polar Ocean, but since the middle of the nineteenth century, attempts had been made to solve the mysteries of the Beaufort Sea. The captain and crew of H.M.S. *Plover* reported seeing land from the deck of their ship in 1849–50. During the winter of 1853–54,

Captain Collinson had attempted to sledge northward, but poor ice conditions and injuries to his party forced him back to his ship in Camden Bay, just west of the Alaska-Yukon boundary. Stories had circulated amongst Eskimos and whalers that mountains of this distant land had been sighted to the north of Camden Bay when conditions were right. A number of theorists, using the best scientific data then available, had concluded that land *had* to exist north of Alaska. The most prominent of these was Dr. Roblin A. Harris, a respected member of the United States Geodetic and Geological Survey in Washington.[4] From known tidal observations, from the heavy character of the ice which everyone assumed was stationary, and from data provided by the polar drifts of the *Jeannette* (1879)[5] and the *Fram* (1893–96)[6] Harris not only calculated the extent of this unknown land, but divined its exact position on contemporary maps. Harris's theory was hotly contested in some quarters, but it was generally accepted because people, Ejnar Mikkelsen included, wanted to believe it.[7]

There was "something," indeed, in the Beaufort Sea, but its discovery would have to wait a further forty years. In 1946, Colonel Joseph O. Fletcher (USAF), flying over the Beaufort Sea, picked up an unusual signal on his radar, made either by land or by an ice pack of gigantic proportions. It turned out to be an ice-flow of immense size (520 sq. kilometres), thicker and harder than the surrounding floes. The discovery of such a floating ice island, visible only from the air, was to be of major significance for the subsequent exploration of the Arctic Basin. From the ground, such islands could not be detected, but from a distance their hills, valleys, gravel, and huge boulders, shimmering across the ice, gave the appearance of land. Since these "islands" drifted imperceptibly with the current and meandered over the entire Arctic Ocean, it was highly likely that these were the explanations for the mysterious, fleeting reports of land in the Beaufort Sea, north of Camden Bay. No one at the time, not even the most experienced arctic traveller, could have uncovered the mystery.[8]

The plans of Mikkelsen's and Leffingwell's expedition were straightforward: a ship would skirt the Alaskan and Canadian coast to Minto Inlet, on the east coast of Victoria Island. There, Leffingwell hoped to carry out a geological study of the countryside, while Mikkelsen planned to make sledge trips to Banks Island and possibly Prince Patrick Island. From these advance bases in the Canadian Arctic, a comprehensive search of the western part of the Beaufort Sea would be initiated. In addition, the expedition was interested in the Eskimo tribes McClure and Collinson had seen in the Minto Inlet district in 1852. The financial support of one of their backers was dependent on their undertaking some anthropological work and, to meet this requirement, the commanders had "discovered" Stefansson.

Leffingwell was already impressed, and Mikkelsen, who made further inquiries, received strong recommendations to take Stefansson along. C. C. Adams, secretary of the American Geographical Society, thought Stefansson a fine fellow, a "splendid man" for the expedition. Stefansson's only reservation was his anxiety over the financing of the expedition.[9] Accordingly, upon the advice of Putnam, Stefansson insisted that he should go overland to Herschel Island, the American whaling station west of the Mackenzie delta, to conduct certain other projects and commitments of his own. Besides, Stefansson claimed that he did not relish the uncertainty of a sea voyage to the area in question, an attitude that Mikkelsen and Leffingwell were bound to resent. But it was made plain to them that Stefansson's employment was conditional on this, and time was running out. Unless Stefansson—or some other ethnologist—could be persuaded to join the expedition, there was the real danger that the financial backer interested in anthropology would withhold his money. With no other alternative, they agreed to Stefansson's terms.[10] Stefansson would travel from Boston to Edmonton and down the Mackenzie on his own to meet them at Herschel Island.[11]

The expedition had little money to spare for such a separate operation, but Putnam persuaded Harvard's Peabody Museum to advance Stefansson two hundred dollars in return for ethnological specimens. For his part, Stefansson also contacted the influential James Mavor, professor of political economy at the University of Toronto, whom he had met during his return from Iceland in 1905. The two, it seems, had become friends over chess and Mavor, then Canadian chess champion, was anxious to entertain Stefansson's ward and travelling companion, Bjorn Pallson, a chess prodigy from Copenhagen.[12] This contact was to be Stefansson's passport into Canadian business and political circles. Mavor induced Sir Edmund Walker, president of the Canadian Bank of Commerce, to donate three hundred dollars to the University of Toronto on behalf of the recently organized Royal Ontario Museum for Stefansson's project.[13] In return, the Royal Ontario Museum was to receive specimens and information—both Indian and Eskimo— gathered by the ethnologist as he proceeded down the Mackenzie.

Even the five hundred dollars he had now collected was munificent in comparison with the pittance Stefansson received from the expedition. Indeed the shaky financial position ought to have been a warning to Stefansson that the whole expedition was a dubious quantity. An aged schooner, the *Beatrice*, built in 1879, was secured and renamed the *Duchess of Bedford*, after one of their backers. Had Stefansson known that their ship cleared Victoria harbour with only twenty cents amongst the entire crew—not enough to pay a pursuing Chinese tailor, who sputtered and fumed from a nearby launch[14]—he might have abandoned the entire venture. Mikkelsen had continual problems in raising money for the expedition to get under way, and the search for further backers did not have the anticipated response.

Stefansson afterwards claimed he had been made wary of travelling by ship because he could foresee the possibility of the *Beatrice*, which had no auxiliary power, becoming trapped in the ice.[15] However, the agreement to go north, including Stefansson's separate operation, had been concluded before that particular vessel was purchased, or even considered. Nevertheless, Stefansson's overland trip and his determination not to twiddle his thumbs idly on board ship were amply vindicated by the failure of the *Duchess* to reach Herschel.

His northern journey really began in Winnipeg. From there it was on to Edmonton by rail and then to Athabaska Landing via a hard-seated open wagon. The trip took two bone-jarring days. At Athabaska Landing, Mavor had made arrangements for Stefansson to use the Hudson's Bay Company's fleet. On board a series of sternwheelers and scows, Stefansson and his fellow travellers, mostly fur traders and missionaries, ambled their way to Fort McPherson. Before Stefansson knew it, he was heading into the region that was to be his home for more than a decade, armed with a few books which, he hoped, would give him the necessary background for his encounter with the north and its inhabitants: Hanbury's *Travels*, the works of Hall, Wrangell, and Franklin, Kleinschmidt's Eskimo grammar, and four volumes of poetry. His only regret was that he had not provided himself with additional literature on the Eskimo—what little there was to be had.[16] It appears that, initially at least, Stefansson was totally unprepared for his encounter with the Eskimo, but so were most travellers who entered Canada's northern latitudes.

The first excursion into the Canadian north was to be a revelation for Stefansson. Soon after his arrival at Herschel Island, late in the summer of 1906, he was confronted with a number of unforeseen hardships. The ice conditions along the western arctic coast during the winter of 1906–7 were unusually severe. Consequently, the *Duchess of Bedford* had not arrived with the requisite "southern" supplies, forcing Stefansson to live as best he could. Even the whalers at Herschel Island were cut off from their own tenders. The Royal Northwest Mounted Police, with whom the novice

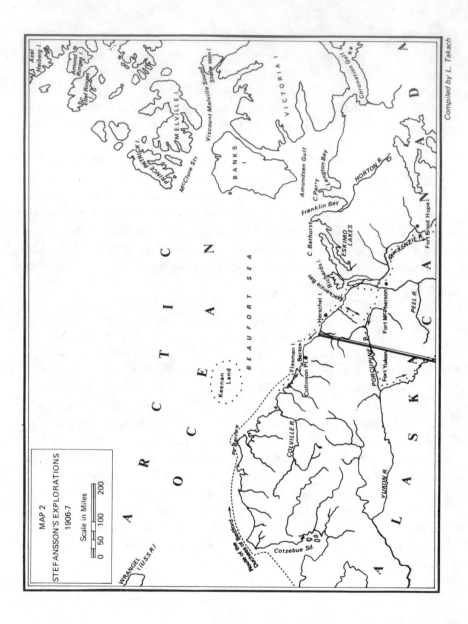

MAP 2
STEFANSSON'S EXPLORATIONS
1906-7

Scale in Miles

0 50 100 200

Compiled by L. Takach

explorer had been staying, were afraid some harm might come to him and denied him supplies in order to discourage his travelling. Stefansson tended to dismiss their warnings of starvation and "other horrors" if he remained in the north, and lost a good deal of respect for the Force. Finally, in a bid to frighten him off, the officers at Herschel told him that he "must expect no help from them in the provisions line (though they have plenty, getting one and half rations each when two-thirds of a ration is all a man can eat)." But the situation was not such as to warrant his running away from work that had to be done.[17]

Stefansson felt he had to stay. Alfred Harrison, a hardy gentleman explorer from England, who took an instant liking to the young man because of his powers of endurance and doggedness, offered Stefansson a share of his camp.[18] Stefansson declined, probably preferring not to become too friendly with a man who was in direct competition with the Mikkelsen-Leffingwell Expedition; only occasionally would he travel with and visit Harrison. The alternative, then, was to make the best of the situation—something natural to Stefansson's instincts.

The determined ethnologist chose to remain true to his task of studying the natives on their own ground. Since the coming of the whalers and the trappings of civilization in 1889, Eskimos of that locality had become extremely dependent on southern goods,[19] particularly foodstuffs. In 1906, however, owing to the non-arrival of the supply tenders, the natives were forced to revert to their traditional hunting practices and diet. Stefansson was able to observe them under conditions approaching their "natural" state. It was an exciting opportunity, for living with them was much better from an ethnological point of view than merely living amongst them, as other white men had done. Stefansson later conveyed the impression that his fare was exclusively Eskimo, and his diet, like theirs, varied between "flesh straight and an occasional hunger spell."[20] This was true perhaps of the two full months he spent alone in their company. But for a large part of his time in the north he lived on a mixed fare of Eskimo and southern food and usually he carried white-man's food wherever he went.

Initially, his provisions consisted of seven hundred pounds flour, one hundred pounds sugar, thirty-four pounds coffee, fifty pounds pork, ten cans baking powder, forty pounds oatmeal, twenty-five pounds beans, twenty-five pounds rice, and ten gallons coal oil for the camp stoves during the winter. In September 1906 he added a bit more to his supplies but by this time he was certain that the winter would not affect either him or his Eskimo help, because of the abundance of fish. This optimism may have been well for the early fall of 1906, but mid-November found Stefansson buying more supplies from the whaler *Narwal*: twenty-five pounds flour, three hundred pounds pork, and some molasses; there is no record of how much his own supplies had been depleted. Although he no longer feared starvation, it appears he was not going to take chances. Moreover, he confided to Putnam that he was anxious for a change from the Eskimo diet. He would either winter with Alfred Harrison, who was two hundred miles away at the south end of Eskimo Lake—if he had plenty of grub—and study the Eskimo, or buy from the Herschel Island supply steamer where goods could be bought at San Francisco prices. If neither of these was feasible, he would have to go back to the coast and live on rotten fish caught during the previous summer.[21]

If these supplies were not often used, it was still very comforting to know that they were there. This, of course, was only reasonable for a tenderfoot who had been bombarded by tales of starvation and woe. In later years, even with more arctic experience, Stefansson still felt the same way about being as well-provisioned as possible. None of this southern fare was to be eaten unless meat and fish were unavailable. The Eskimos, who had developed a craving for southern food since being introduced to it by whalers in the 1890s, agreed to this restriction. Such contingency food supplies were used for specific purposes such as the payment of Eskimos who sledded him from place to place, or for similar services. However, when on the road and not living in an Eskimo village, there should have been no need to use food for pay, since according to Stefansson a more sophisticated system of payment existed. On a promise of two hundred dollars per year, payable upon their discharge, the Eskimo would go any-where, provide the sled, dogs, and whaleboat, supply whatever game and fish they could catch, keep him in caribou and sealskin clothes. Cash was not needed, only a promissory note, "for on coming out, any of the whalers would trust me for a grub-order on their own stores which is fully as good as cash here, and the natives would take pay in ammunition, grub, etc., from the whalers."[22] Eventually, the company representing the whalers would present the note to Stefansson for cash redemption.

But, though Stefansson may have had well-meant intentions in keeping southern provisions away from the Eskimos, on occasion he found himself giving in to a mild form of blackmail. On one journey, his travelling companion, Roxy—a "sophisticated Eskimo"—insisted that the remaining food on the sled be divided immediately or he would go no further.[23] The novice had no choice but to acquiesce in order to preserve good relations and prevent his being abandoned. In fact, throughout his northern career, there were to be similar occasions involving even his white companions.

By January 1907, Stefansson's prospects of living with the Eskimo in a satisfactory way were considerably brighter "tho' more portable provisions would be [an] immense help." On hand were twelve sacks flour, fifty pounds rice, forty pounds oatmeal, plenty of tea and coffee, sixty pounds sugar, molasses, apples, syrup, salt, and spices. He was "very well off" indeed, although there was some concern over the party's inability to keep up with the pace of his dogs' consumption of the fish fodder.[24] By the end of January, he was off to Herschel to buy food, hopefully from the missionaries.[25] But it was a bad year for everyone and he could find no one interested in selling any substantial amounts. So Stefansson again settled down with only a few gastronomical amenities of civilization to live and work among the Eskimos.

When he had to, he adapted remarkably well. He could report back on occasion that "[a]ppetite and health always good, and always plenty to eat—cheerfully given. In fact about the best way of ingratiating oneself is eating hugely—which I seem always competent to do. The knife-fork-and-plate prejudices have left me and my fingers have been fork and dish for some time now. The fish diet does not pall at all."[26] He forgot his earlier lament about the inferior cooking of the Eskimo,[27] and before the year was out had even overcome his childhood aversion to fish. Eventually, the fish diet did not bother him and, contrary to his expectations, he did not "hanker" after salt, though he did find himself continually hungry for sugar.[28] On the whole, however, he had survived rather comfortably. He was no longer a tenderfoot. Even the winters were not discouraging or intimidating. The blizzard he experienced in November 1906 was, he considered, equal to an ordinary North Dakota blizzard, "but not a star performance."[29] His worst ordeal with an arctic storm came in February 1907, but that experience left him with nothing but minor frostbite.[30]

With so much time and effort being spent on making certain that food supplies and suppliers were adequate, Stefansson felt that the scientific results of his investigation were paltry, and was even ready to admit this privately to James Mavor. By late April 1907, although he had forwarded a few items (e.g. fish nets) to Putnam,[31] Stefansson conceded that "nothing I have found so far will enable me to bolster up any revolutionary theory and so distinguish myself."[32] The fact was, however, that he was learning much from his Eskimo companions and their way of life. Yet, there was one glimmer of success. As early as mid-August 1906, he had confided to Putnam that he had evidence of truly primitive Eskimos residing in Prince Albert Land.[33]

A ship, the *Olga*, driven east by thick ice during the winter of 1905–6, had wintered in Prince Albert Sound. In February 1906, the captain, "Charlie" Klengenberg, made a sled journey to Minto Inlet where he came in contact with two tribes of natives among whom he remained for several months. The natives apparently had never seen a white man, had never had any dealings with traders or whalers, nor even with the Eskimos to the south of them. They had no guns, only primitive spears and bows and other weapons made of copper. Klengenberg was told by his Eskimo guides that another group of these "wild people" sported red hair and beards. He passed along such tales, but not for a moment did the *Olga's* captain believe them.[34]

Stefansson, however, was keenly excited by the story. Both he and Roald Amundsen, whom he had met on board the *Gjøa* at the time of its arrival at Herschel Island, tried to buy Klengenberg's unique copper artifacts, soapstone curios, and musk-ox bows. Klengenberg shrugged them off.[35] It was normal for Stefansson to purchase such items if he could, for he was concerned that he would not be able to obtain enough artifacts for both Harvard and the Royal Ontario Museum.[36] The small "treasures" were tantalizing and Stefansson could hardly contain his enthusiasm. "This is encouraging—so also is the statement that game is plenty and driftwood obtainable—but," he lamented, "it is difficult to be unselfish enough to be glad so large a part of one's work has been forestalled." He was referring to the views of experienced whalers that Minto Inlet would be impossible to reach that particular year. He also feared that the commanders of the Anglo-American Expedition might therefore abandon the project of sailing to Minto Inlet. "In that event, I shall separate from the expedition," Stefansson decided. An Eskimo family would then be hired to take him to Coronation Gulf to see these strange people.[37] The planned visit to Minto Inlet never materialized. The unusual supply situation forced him to stay close to the Mackenzie delta and subsist on the generosity of the local Eskimos. Yet, despite the inaccessible ethnological "gold mine" on Victoria Island, this living-in with the natives was probably the most valuable experience he could have gained.

Stefansson may have had another reason for wishing to strike out on his own. The entire Leffingwell-Mikkelsen Expedition was in bad shape, continuously plagued by poverty, bad luck, and poor judgement, as Mikkelsen himself admitted. Its financial resources were depleted and projects could not be continued. Mikkelsen sent off frantic letters to former backers hoping to coax them into further support.[38] More money was needed, but none was to be found.

Stefansson could not be sure that he had the full backing of that expedition for this promising, once-in-a-lifetime, ethnological venture to Victoria Land. Before long, civilization in the form of numerous Klengenbergs might reach these isolated people and ruin his chances for original, ground-breaking work. "Contamination from the . . . vanguard of civilization—the hunter, the trader and missionary—is spreading so fast that, in most sections, ethnological work could be much more successfully carried forward now than ten years hence." The Eskimo arcadia was doomed. It would "not long escape the influence of the missionaries whom our spare pennies support in their work of 'carrying light to the dark places of the earth'."[39]

Stefansson severed his ties with the Anglo-American Polar Expedition in August 1907. Ostensibly, he returned to civilization to contradict the "shocking" and false report that Mikkelsen, Leffingwell, and their party had perished in the Beaufort Sea. It was a humanitarian gesture to offset an injury that such news might bring to Mikkelsen's ailing mother. His departure, though, has raised a few questions. His detractors would charge that he had abandoned the expedition to capitalize on the publicity attached to his reports that no tragedy had befallen Mikkelsen and the others.[40] As early as mid-July 1907, Stefansson apparently did agree to stay on another year.[41] Then, within a month, he had completely changed his mind. In the two or three weeks between deciding to stay another year and determining to leave, Stefansson must have concluded that the expedition was on the rocks and held nothing for him. What better chance to organize his own expedition? Stefansson stated later that Mikkelsen and Leffingwell had informed him that the expedition was "practically over," so he decided to "sever his connections" and organize his own expedition to study the people of Victoria Land.[42] On 6 August, he left the Anglo-American Polar Expedition to journey home.

Mikkelsen hoped, believed, or pretended to believe, that Stefansson would rejoin them. On 13 August, a full week after Stefansson had made his intentions clear and left for the outside, Mikkelsen sent out a report to the American Geographical Society to the effect that all was going according to plan. He reported that he expected to be dropped off at Banks Land, go out on the ice and follow the continental shelf as far as Herschel Island, presumably to verify what he had already discovered. "Mr. Leffingwell and Mr. Stefansson will go estward [sic] too, with another family to work around the Coppermine River and, if nothing unforeseen happens, wee [sic] will carry out the program laid out at the start. . . . If the money come [sic] you will please pay the wages out [of] that amount, and let Mr. Steafensen [sic] use what of it he needs for his expenses involved in coming back to the Arctic, and for other things he needs."[43] One must conclude that the commander was only bluffing and was trying to allay fears that Stefansson's departure revealed the sinking condition of the expedition's affairs. If further support for the research could be obtained before the truth were known, the expedition—and a few reputations—might be salvaged.

Even if Stefansson had given Mikkelsen grounds for believing he would return to the expedition, he had every justification for changing his mind. Despite Mikkelsen's good intentions, it was the expedition that had abandoned Stefansson. It still owed him seven hundred and fifty dollars[44] and Mikkelsen had defaulted on his obligations to the young ethnologist by issuing him numerous worthless drafts as payment.[45] The whole situation caused Stefansson much personal and financial embarrassment and he could consider himself lucky to get out when he did.

So Stefansson returned to New York penniless. It was impossible for him to live and to meet all his debts, including those the expedition had placed upon him. In desperation he turned to the American Geographical Society under the impression that it was partly responsible for any financial obligations that Mikkelsen incurred. But the Society refused to honour the unauthorized drafts. Their role was entirely auxiliary and supplementary to the English promoters of the expedition, who, if anybody, were the responsible parties.[46] Stefansson had been misled. The American Geographical Society was sympathetic but could not help him financially; all they could do was to provide him with a desk and encourage him to write scientific articles as a prelude to launching a campaign for his own expedition to Victoria Land.[47] He had to write three "popular" accounts of his exploits, including a summary of the work of the Anglo-American Polar Expedition, for *Harper's* "to get money to live during the winter."[48]

The fate of the Anglo-American Polar Expedition and its personal consequences for Stefansson were a bitter and stinging lesson. He was determined henceforth to be his own master, in command of the situation and responsible for his own fate to the best of his ability. Moreover, as leader of his own expedition, he would see that his enterprise was as well and securely financed as possible. Nevertheless, the northern trip had its positive aspects. Living with the Eskimos, observing their culture, and achieving an increasing ability to speak their language—all this provided him with an opportunity to contribute something, which he believed would be stimulating and provocative. His writings on the north and his concept of the

Eskimo were to help him secure the recognition he sought. The mysterious Minto Inlet people would also provide him with a major purpose for his next expedition.

The definitive record of this particular journey, however, was not written immediately upon his return south, as later became his custom. Rather, *Hunters of the Great North* appeared belatedly in 1922. This was a pity, because by that time the book was obviously influenced by his later arctic experiences and lacked originality. In reality, the book was an over-worked version of his popular writing. The author himself realized the work's deficiencies and regarded it as his "worst book."[49] *Hunters* followed the approach that had become his trademark: full, vividly detailed ac-counts. One could almost discern an obsession, perhaps bred by deprivation, with the simple subject of food. This in itself, one could argue, was a faithful representation of the Eskimo mentality. Stefansson's iconoclastic nature inclined him to reject the tried-and-true methods of describing arctic travels, with their accounts of great suffering and misery that made "ap-petizing" reading for the morbid few: "Accounts of such sufferings as these are appetizing reading for those who revel in the contemplation of misery; they are also amusing to those who know how easily most of these difficulties could have been avoided; they may even some time come to take high rank as works of humour, should the reading public ever become intelligently familiar with the facts and conditions of the north."[50] His own writings, he believed, would explode such myths. He once said that most arctic hard-ships were of two types—those caused chiefly by the ignorance of the trapper in selecting his outfit and refusing to conduct himself like the Eskimo, and those created by the imaginative power of the man who writes an exaggerated account to make his manuscript readable and saleable.[51]

Yet, because he saw it as his duty to familiarize people with the north, and because he underplayed the sensational or morbid, he too employed "imaginative power" to turn mundane, everyday occurrences into bright, appealing subjects. Stefansson was aware of the process which produced "imaginative" writing. He acknowledged that he was prone to exaggeration, and perhaps even misrepresentation, although he did not consider himself "really a liar."

> I . . . have often found on belated reference to my diary that I have told to many men on many occasions . . . facts and feelings which seem to have been absent at the time of an "adventure" but which have by some mental process attached themselves to it later and have

become vivid as the real facts, or have now overshadowed them and even obliterated the facts. Where my contemporaneous record of an event is meagre, these adventitious elements are bound to remain undetected and become for me and anyone who believes me, as if they had happened.[52]

Nevertheless, Stefansson's flair for style produced well-written and lucid prose and that, in itself, made for fascinating and enjoyable leisure reading. The chapters of most of his books, however, manage to convey a self-indulgent, a paternalistic impression, vividly emphasizing the bizarre for his comfortable Canadian, American, and British audience, while at the same time portraying it as something very common, very ordinary, very "humdrum." There was always an unspoken, but carefully underlined pride in his being able to adapt to the Eskimo way and to the northern environment, to become popular with, and respected by, the natives—itself a singular honour—who more often than not scoffed at outsiders. The accounts of all his later expeditions contained episodes which were turned into flashes of high adventure, tales of physical endurance and daring, something that his articles, written at an early, more immediate date for *Harper's Magazine* for instance, underplayed. Yet even in them, the emphasis on the ease and simplicity of living in the Canadian north was evident:

> I was gradually being broken in to native ways; by the middle of October, I had thrown away my nearly outworn woollen suit and was fur clad from head to heel, an Eskimo to the skin. I never regretted the lack of a single item of such arctic clothing as money can buy in America or Europe, and in this my experiences agreed completely with those of the officers and crew who (unknown to me) were wintering some three hundred miles to the westward. A reasonably healthy body is all the equipment a white man needs for a comfortable winter among the arctic Eskimos.[53]

Just as important were his efforts to acquaint Canadians and others with the character of the Eskimo. Again, it was his straitened circumstances during the Anglo-American Polar Expedition that gave him an excellent opportunity to observe their habits at unusually close quarters. Not only had the Eskimo families provided him with folk-lore and cranial measurements, they had fed and kept him during the brutal winter of 1906–7. As he admitted, he was their "guest," and they, perfect hosts. To Stefansson, the Eskimo were a fine, clean, strong people, honest, energetic, and reliable

—"a great contrast to the Indian who is too lazy to work when you want him and too unreliable if you don't watch [him]."[54] On one trip in a whaleboat from Fort McPherson to Herschel Island, he was dismayed by the actions of the Indians on board. Although receiving the same pay, the Indian always shirked his duties, whined, and complained even of light work he had to do. Besides, he was frivolous—something the budding explorer could not tolerate. Yet, despite his obvious inadequacies, the Indian remained haughty and aloof when he had no right to be so. The Loucheux Indians (Athapaskans) he felt were the parasites of the north, making no attempt to hunt and exist like the proud Eskimos.[55]

The self-sufficient, honest Eskimo, on the other hand, seemed to express a childlike joy, with no pretense of sombreness, reserve, or formality.[56] The noble Eskimo became Stefansson's ideal person: "Evolution through centuries has ground these northerners into well-nigh perfect adaptation to their surroundings, so that they live in well-being and a general high degree of creative comfort in one of the least fruitful sections of the world."[57] They were far from being uncivilized or savage; they had been able to adapt to their relatively hostile environment and to Stefansson "adaptability" along with industry and inventiveness, which the Eskimo displayed, were important hallmarks of progress and civilization. The Eskimos were the pathfinders who would show the white man how to survive in the north—if the white man had the patience to learn from his Eskimo teachers.[58] The Eskimo had met the challenge, and the northland was theirs.

Stefansson marvelled at their courtesy and gentleness, thinking at first it was due to the missionary work emanating from Herschel Island[59] until he learned from his "unsophisticated" hosts that such traits had not been implanted by the missionaries: "the kindness of these people is such that I cannot see how anyone who knows them can wish more for anything than that he was rich and could repay their kindness fully. The manner of it is even more felt than the matter—they do everything so natural and delicately that the best 'breeding' could not improve upon it."[60]

In an Eskimo home I have never heard an unpleasant word between a man and his wife, never seen a child punished nor an old person treated inconsiderately. Yet the household affairs are carried on in an orderly way, and the good behavior of the children is remarked by practically every traveller. These charming qualities of the Eskimo home may be due largely to their equable disposition and the general fitness of their character for the communal relations, but it seems reasonable to give a portion of the credit to their remarkable social organization, for they live under conditions for which some of our best men are striving, conditions that with our idealists are as yet merely dreams.[61]

Using techniques superior to those of a southern tailor or furrier, the Eskimo could make better garments against the cold with the materials at hand. He had proved he could thrive on the "barren wastes," secure sufficient food through his prowess as a hunter, and create ingenious accommodation out of animal hides or blocks of snow, whereas in such an environment a New Englander would surely die. At the same time, his moral superiority was quite impressive when matched against the white man's standard of conduct and behaviour. In contrast to the outsider, the Eskimo held an advanced concept of individual equality, was less selfish, more helpful to his fellow man, and more reticent about the faults of his neighbour than any but the "rarest and best of our race."[62] With such remarks, if anything, Stefansson was reviving and updating the concept of the "noble savage."

The Eskimo's communal way of life was very practical, a necessary adaptation to his circumstances. That this modified form of communism would produce parasites seemed to have little effect on the Eskimo, observed Stefansson. Some, it was true, were more energetic, but each tried to do something, and all had been brought up in the tradition of pulling together. They did not seem to be preoccupied with those who did or did not work, because such a concept was foreign to them.[63] Active co-operation was an essential condition for survival in a land of uncertainties. Keeping this in mind, Stefansson realized that it would be wiser and more profitable for an ethnologist wishing to study them at close quarters to co-operate rather than to create a master-servant relationship. Thus Stefansson's relationship with them would be conducted on this friend-to-friend basis.

Stefansson's iconoclastic nature, as well as the evidence before his own eyes, compelled him to try to dispel the myths surrounding the Eskimo and the northern environment. Like a number of anthropologists at that time, he had been influenced by the postulates of Franz Boas who did not hold to the unilinear theory of human social evolution but criticized the notion that western European civilization was "higher" and all other races were to be considered as belonging to some lower order.[64] Thirteen or fourteen years after Boas had made these observations, this became Stefansson's full-time crusade. His aim, he insisted, was to combine scientific writing with straightforward narrative in order to make known the facts which justified his affection and admiration for these remarkable people. He hoped his audience would read between the lines and see "the truth that in even savage bosoms every heart is human. That is a fact which, if understood, contributes to one's general satisfaction in life."[65]

3

The Gold Mines of
Victoria Land

The first expedition, albeit short, was a reconnaissance trip, a time to scout the situation and to acclimatize himself. Stefansson came away from this experience with a better grasp of the Eskimo language, their folklore, and their secrets of how to survive. It was a period in which Stefansson came to realize that for him the north was not so bad and not so inhospitable. This was a new idea to popularize, an idea which should appeal to the imaginations of professional and layman alike. A fresh, provocative approach might just turn established theories on their heads. Moreover, he now regained his self-confidence which had been shaken somewhat during his first two or three months above the Arctic Circle, when he had not felt in command of the situation, but at the mercy of the elements, the natives, and circumstances. To be in such a situation for any lengthy period was intolerable to a man who regarded himself as superior to fate and captain of his destiny. True to his principles of self-sufficiency and living by his wits, Stefansson had managed to meet most obstacles successfully, and later to take advantage of whatever the north had to offer. The Anglo-American Polar Expedition was behind him and he would not look back to it except to learn from its organizational failures. Stefansson's arctic initiation was over. He now set out to organize another expedition that would be fully his own—to claim his "gold mine" on Victoria Land and to make a name for himself.

The fall and winter of 1907 was a period of incubation while plans for his expedition were being crystallized. It was also a time for establishing valuable personal contacts amongst prospective backers and influential individuals in scientific organizations in New York City.

Stefansson's ideas were clarified by his articles in *Harper's* and particularly by such scientific articles as "The Suitability of Eskimo Methods of Winter Travel in Scientific Exploration," published in the *Bulletin of the*

American Geographical Society in February 1908. It was this essay that caught the attention of the American Museum of Natural History. The article presented a cogent plan for furthering scientific investigation of the north without undergoing the usual high costs, for, as the title suggested, adopting Eskimo travel methods—doing in Rome as the Romans did—would be the most efficient method of conducting scientific investigation:

> The writer has no thought of saying that such undertakings are practicable or even safe for the average traveller; but among our millions there should be at least a few who, by undertaking smaller things at first and gradually practising the technique of travel, could come to equal the best achievements of the past and even set new standards. It goes without saying that the "man with one blanket" travels faster and more cheaply than one cumbered with baggage and obsessed with the idea that this luxury and that convenience cannot be left behind.[1]

Thus Stefansson would replace "approved Arctic clothing" with Eskimo clothes, "especially designed sleds" with Eskimo sleds, tents with the snow house, and civilized food with an Eskimo diet. His last expedition "was such as to make [Stefansson] not at all reluctant to return to the same country and same mode of life for another year . . . his conclusion from the experience of thirteen months was that there is much opportunity in the Arctic for good scientific work in new fields with less than half the discomfort and less than a tenth of the expense that one usually wasted on such undertakings."[2]

Such arguments were directed not only at the general public but at the affluent American Museum of Natural History. The American Geographical Society, it appears, did not have the financial means to sustain an Arctic expedition. Nor did it wish to become involved in another expedition which might suffer the same fate as the Anglo-American one. But the American Geographical and Cyrus Adams, its secretary, introduced Stefansson to several influential members of the Museum, including Clark Wissler, the curator of anthropology, Herman C. Bumpus, the director, and Henry Fairfield Osborn, the president of the institution.[3] Informal talks took place over the winter months, and by late February, Stefansson, probably assured by them of the Museum's support, put forward a formal plan of exploration and scientific study.

According to the plan, Stefansson was to spend the winter of 1908–9 on or near Victoria Land collecting ethnological information pertaining to the fabled Eskimo tribe that Klengenberg and his crew had described.

The one-man expedition would leave Athabaska Landing in May of 1908, reaching Fort McPherson by 20 July and Herschel Island by the first week in August. The next stop would be Baillie Island, east of Herschel Island. From there, Stefansson hoped to work his way eastward in a small boat and establish the main winter camp somewhere between Cape Parry and the Coppermine River. Victoria Land would be reached by sailing or sledging across Dolphin and Union Straits. Stefansson would then swoop down upon the unsuspecting inhabitants, if they were still there, gather as much information and specimens as he could, and be back in New York by the autumn of 1909.[4]

The plan was extremely vague and assumed that the details of planning, organization, and direction were to be left to him. Nevertheless, in its particulars relating to Stefansson himself, the scheme demonstrated a very well-developed ability and self-confidence. The ethnologist appeared optimistic about bringing back sufficient information about this unknown tribe within a year, but this seems to have reflected some previous intimation that the American Museum would not sponsor a longer expedition, whose object was based more on rumour and hearsay than on fact. Only tangible evidence that a fruitful field of endeavour existed might result in additional and continued support.

Besides requesting financial assistance from the American Museum, Stefansson asked that "the nature of the Museum's demands and expectations shall be clearly set forth in writing so that I will be definitely informed of them."[5] Naturally, after the Mikkelsen-Leffingwell fiasco, he did not wish to take unnecessary chances with a haphazard arrangement which could only repeat that unhappy experience.

The Museum would be assured of a fair return for its investment, but the extra conditions that he asked for were designed to protect and further his own interests. Stefansson proposed that he should be free to lecture about the proposed trip and to sell in advance, or after his return, his popular account of the expedition in the form of a book or periodical. He was to have freedom to dispose of duplicate specimens, the Museum being sole judge of whether any specimen was a duplicate, and to use prints of photographs taken during the adventure. Finally, he wanted it understood that he would be "free to do or not to do anything not provided for or clearly implied in my agreement with the museum" and "to give out, either before going north or after my return, any statement concerning my purposes, plans or results, and that the museum shall have no special right to criticize such utterances unless they misrepresent, or unduly minimize, the museum's share in the undertaking in question."[6] With the acceptance of these conditions, Stefansson would be his own master, and the Museum would have little control over the entire affair. Three days after he advanced his proposals, the Museum responded. With minor exceptions, his conditions were fully met. True, the Museum insisted on retaining "a general supervision of the scientific work,"[7] but this was a rather weak, indefinite check on the unknown Vilhjalmur Stefansson.

The Museum appropriated only $1,250 for the expedition—$250 to purchase a boat, and $1,000 to be expended in collecting anthropological data and specimens. The institution tried to be as generous as it could and assuming that Stefansson came back with *something*, regardless of the quality, it would likely be satisfied. The Museum did not have a northern collection to speak of, so *anything* that Stefansson could add, whether from Victoria Land or elsewhere in the Canadian Arctic, would enhance their holdings. The institution was entering virgin territory, and did not insist that Stefansson visit any particular region between Alaska and Hudson Bay, but gave him a completely free hand: "Good work in any part of the region will be acceptable to us," it said.[8]

Officially, the expedition was to be known as the Stefansson Expedition. Stefansson himself was to receive no salary. His refusal of a salary had enhanced the project in the eyes of the Museum, since this seemed to promise a very economical operation. By declining to accept a salary from a scientific institution, or later from government bodies, Stefansson was effectively left a free agent. He was always to prefer a grant to a salary, "for a grant leaves me my own master and a salary makes me dependent."[9]

The route was to be much as outlined in Stefansson's proposal: to proceed down the Mackenzie River, and from there either east toward Coronation Gulf or west in the direction of the Colville River district, as he himself might elect. The first objective of the expedition was a scientific study of the Eskimo; the second, the securing of a collection for the American Museum of Natural History, "which will illustrate as exclusively as possible the material cultures of the uncivilized tribes of the country," any surplus going to the Peabody Museum. Finally, the commander was at liberty to enter private agreements with other institutions as he saw fit, provided they did not interfere with the prime objects of the expedition.[10]

This last concession encouraged Stefansson to undertake some work for two Canadian government agencies, which was to pave the way for more ambitious Canadian enterprises in the years to come. Work for the Meteorological Service of Canada and the Geological Survey of Canada would enhance considerably the prestige of his tiny expedition and also help finance the operation.

The Meteorological Service of Canada, under the direction of R. F. Stupart, was anxious to establish six observation stations along the Mackenzie River. This plan had been initiated in Washington by the Carnegie Institute's department of terrestrial magnetism and Stupart's department was to implement the project in northwestern Canada.[11] Among other things, this extra duty would help Stefansson defray his travel expenses down the Mackenzie, for he could claim reduced rates from the Hudson's Bay Company on grounds of being an agent of the Canadian government.[12] In addition, the small financial support and patronage of the Geological Survey was to prove fruitful. The financial support was most welcome, while the association would reinforce the professional respectability of the expedition. Moreover, the backing of the Geological Survey was to give Stefansson an insight into the mind and motivations of the Canadian bureaucracy and establish a valuable entrée that led to the 1913–18 expedition. The Geological Survey was most eager to learn more about Stefansson's planned expedition to the Canadian northlands, and urged him to come to Ottawa before going north.[13] On 21 April 1908, accordingly, Stefansson conferred with a number of Canadian officials. The interview with the Geological Survey was highly successful. R. W. Brock, director of the Survey, anxious to build up the prestige of his branch and expand its anthropological activities in connection with the new National Museum, invited the young man to place the expedition under the auspices of the Survey as well as of the American Museum.[14] Brock wanted both geological specimens and part of the ethnological results, "for he wants this expedition as an entering wedge for ethnology into his department."[15]

Stefansson exaggerated the complete novelty of his role, for certainly this was no "entering wedge," though it was true that the Survey had never before done any serious study of the Western Arctic Eskimo. As far back as the 1880s, the Geological Survey had been interested in the scientific investigation of the native peoples of Canada and this was part of its function by legislation. The Survey's interest up to this point had been "spasmodic and entirely secondary," carried on by the geological staff. Men like G. M. Dawson, Robert Bell, A. P. Low, Charles Camsell, and others had collected Eskimo materials for the Museum in the course of explorations in Eskimo country between 1882 and 1906. Ethnographers before the twentieth century were usually involved in some non-anthropological profession— geology, law, the military, government administration, or missionary activity. They may not have been ethnographers in our modern understanding of the term, but they were often dedicated individuals who believed it their duty to record information regarding native people.[16]

In 1908, Brock was embarking on a long-range program to recruit a specialized staff expressly to work in Canadian ethnology and archaeology for the Survey.[17] The building of the Victoria Memorial Museum encouraged such enterprises. As Brock expressed his concern:

> In the new Museum, one of the most popular sections is likely to be the ethnological exhibit. Very little investigation has been made in Canada of the native races, and what has been done has mostly been under the auspices of foreign institutions. The opportunities for such studies are fast disappearing. Under advancing settlement and rapid development of the country, the native is disappearing or coming under the influence of the white man's civilizations. The older people who are familiar with the folk lore or traditions of the tribe are dying off, and the rising generation under the changed conditions is acquiring a totally different education.
>
> If the information concerning the native races is ever to be secured and preserved, action must be taken very soon, or it will be too late. It is a duty we owe to the Canada of the future to see that such material is saved.[18]

Stefansson's work on behalf of the Survey was to be a continuation of a crusade begun almost three decades before.

As Stefansson understood it, Brock assured him that there would be no problem in advancing funds as long as the work was kept in the public's eye. Publish any results as quickly as possible, said Brock, and then he would approach the government to argue that "we [the Geological Survey] have begun the work; now we need the money to continue it. He says he can get $10 to continue the thing more easily than $1 to begin a new work."[19] Given the times and the nature of parliamentary government, such strategy on the part of an ambitious and experienced bureaucrat was sound —and the lesson was not lost upon Stefansson. Bumpus, the American Museum's director, considered the offer of co-operation attractive,[20] and gave the arrangement his approval. The expedition was to receive five hundred dollars from the Survey, two hundred immediately and three hundred upon the submission of the final report to Brock.[21] Anxious to receive the balance of three hundred dollars, Stefansson quickly submitted a preliminary report based largely on the findings of his earlier expedition.

Within a month or so of the accepted agreement, however, Stefansson was in the process of changing the plans for the expedition. He had now grown certain that his aims could not be accomplished in a single year. Rather than return to civilization in the autumn of 1909, Stefansson con-

cluded that it would be best to extend the expedition into 1910. Furthermore, as much as he wanted to study the Eskimo of far-off Victoria Land,
he realized that his present means were insufficient, and would be better
spent in the study of the "ethnologically and zoologically little-known
Colville District" to the west.[22] Since he needed the cash to purchase supplies for a second year in the north, the commander wondered whether the
Museum would support and provision the endeavour for a second year,
and furnish an additional $1,000.[23] The Museum, naturally, was very
reluctant to commit itself further to an individual who had not yet stirred
from southern Canada. The reply was cautious, pointing out that the
Museum could not pledge itself so far in advance, but would give the
request "careful consideration" on the basis of favourable progress reports
in the future.[24] Stefansson took this response as a positive endorsement to
proceed with his revised scheme and devote the first year entirely to the
Colville area. In fact, he may have been given private assurances to that
effect. In any case, this conformed with the original plan in which the
Colville district had been stipulated as one of the primary areas for investigation. Victoria Land would have to wait its turn. That excursion
would depend on the Museum's assessment of Stefansson's work.

A third object for the original one-man expedition had been to make
an extensive collection of zoological material: mammals, birds, and reptiles.
It was for this purpose that Rudolph Martin Anderson, a former fellow
student at Iowa, was eventually appointed by the American Museum. He
and Stefansson had been contemporaries at the University of Iowa, but
only apparently casual acquaintances. Nevertheless, Stefansson considered
him "an old Iowa State classmate."[25] Anderson had been an assistant in
zoology at the University of Iowa, receiving his B.Ph. in 1903, and his Ph.D.
for his dissertation, "Birds of Iowa," in 1906. From 1906 to 1908, this
veteran of the Spanish-American war and member of the Missouri National
Guard became assistant commandant at Blees Military Academy, Macon,
Missouri. But Anderson was not happy with his position at Blees for he
could devote little time to teaching and none to field work in zoology. He
was increasingly dissatisfied with military life and he longed to resume
research in mammology and ornithology.[26] The opportunity came to change
his status and assume an inspiring and challenging career when he read of
Stefansson's plans. Anderson contacted his former acquaintance, inquiring
into the possibilities of accompanying him north.[27]

Initially, Stefansson was skeptical about being joined by another person. "In the work of an ethnologist, a companion (tho' a pleasure) is a
hindrance in these ways—[an Eskimo] family that can house one man will

not be able to house two," and, Stefansson continued, "(most important) there is a temptation to talk English when one of my chief aims is the mastering of Eskimo."[28] Yet he could see many advantages in having someone like Anderson coming along. Anderson's presence, among other things, would add an aura of professionalism to the zoological side of the expedition.[29] Having such a well qualified man as Anderson as his associate, Stefansson hoped, would produce a "conspicuously successful trip."[30] Minor doubts were pushed aside. He wrote to Anderson that the Museum might be persuaded to include him if his presence would not mean additional expense. Anderson should not be too upset at forgoing a salary; Stefansson was in the same situation. In the long run, the trip might turn out to be of "money value" to both men and, besides, "[t]he whole experience will be a bully one. The trip . . . is not dangerous nor filled with remarkable hardships. As you may know, I spent last winter along with the Eskimos and know what I'm talking about. I'll go back to it as one might return to Germany for a winter at Heidelberg."[31] Stefansson began preparing the groundwork to secure Anderson's appointment as his travelling companion by contacting Frank M. Chapman, the Museum's curator of birds. The time was opportune. The American Museum happened to be considering the possibility of adding a field agent to its staff.[32] Unfortunately, Chapman wanted to use the new slot to man an expedition to South America, but Stefansson used his influence with the Museum's executive to have the position allocated to his expedition. He convinced the Museum that sending Anderson on a northern venture would be cheaper than appointing someone to the South American project, and that Anderson's addition to the arctic expedition would result in the Museum securing one of the world's first and finest arctic collections. In view of the already large South American collection, the Museum agreed to give priority to the northlands.[33] Bumpus, the director of the Museum, already on exceptionally good terms with his newly found ethnographer, made the final decision in favour of the change.

For a moment, matters became complicated; Anderson suddenly became intrigued by the idea of a South American venture and joining the staff of the American Museum of Natural History. He told his future wife, Mae Belle Allstrand, that the "[Arctic expedition] does not exactly appeal to me."[34] But he was quickly brought back by Stefansson, who implied that Anderson's only hope of joining the American Museum was to go to the Arctic and prove his worth there:

> The Museum has for sometime contemplated adding to its staff a "field representative" or "field agent" in zoology, but they have in-

tended choosing for that position only a man who seemed to them likely to be a suitable man not only to do field work but to superintend the doing of such work by others—in other words, they intend that this field agent shall become, as soon as they are clear on the question of his personal fitness, a superintendent of exploration, or the head of a sub-department. Your recommendations are such that they are led to consider you the most promising candidate in view for this position; if you elect to go north, they will not only consider your working towards that position but you will be (I understand) the only candidate working for it and it is not a question of competing for it, merely one of "making good"—in other words, of keeping from being fired—in other words still, you have as good as got the job as soon as you decide to try for it.[35]

Reminding Anderson that the northern expedition was not without its attractions, Stefansson pointed out "you would have to go many times to South America before your work would command the public attention that the north trip would."[36]

Anderson soon forgot about the South American trip. Confiding to his future wife, he echoed Stefansson's assertion that "one good Arctic trip will give a scientific man more standing than four or five trips to South America."[37] Anderson may have been quite an unassuming individual, but he was just as eager as Stefansson to "make good" and a name for himself— even if it meant using Stefansson to do it. The simple act of returning would belie all the myths and erroneous assumptions about the north which had been conjured up by imaginative reporters. He assured his apprehensive fiancée, much as Stefansson had assured him, that the trip would present no hazards. In the long run, he might even have greater success in the field than his commander: "Although we may not succeed in reaching the grounds we wish to, I do not think the trip can be a failure altogether, as I feel certain that the zoological results of my part of the work can not help but bring something, as the north coast has been practically unworked in that line. I have that advantage over a man who is simply exploring and travelling. Then, if we have to do some spectacular 'stunts' we shall have that much more to talk about."[38]

Clearly this was the greatest chance of his career: "All this territory has been practically untouched in my line, and very little by anybody and a 'scoop' counts for as much in scientific as in newspaper work—for the first writer or first authority on a subject has a great advantage in the way of publication."[39] The expedition was receiving good coverage in the papers, mainly because of the free rein given to reporters' imaginations.[40]

Like Stefansson, Anderson was not going to allow any opportunity to become famous slip through his hands. Anderson also hoped to realize something from the publication of magazine stories when he returned. Stefansson had first rights of publication by the agreement with the American Museum, but Anderson could publish anything he wanted, anywhere, and at will, after that. All he had to do, he told his fiancée, was simply take good pictures of musk-oxen, caribou, or polar bears, and write a short narrative for "anything with 'the lure of the magnetic north' about it finds a ready sale nowadays."[41]

The strong similarity between the aspirations of both men helps to explain why they got along so well on their first expedition. Anderson's diffidence was the perfect foil for Stefansson's ego. On a number of occasions, Anderson received verbal dressings down by his commander, but he always managed to shrug them off. For example, when Anderson refused to agree that the Eskimo were the "chosen people," he was told by Stefansson that he "[did] not properly appreciate the beauties of the communistic life"; that "after all he [Stefansson] has told me, I have adopted the point of view taken by missionaries, travellers and *other* illiterate people."[42] Anderson admitted he might have been provoked by such scathing remarks had he been carrying a chip on his shoulders,[43] but he was able to cope with such a nature by holding his tongue and temper—no doubt with the American Museum's position always before his eyes. That he already was cynical about his associate appears in a letter to his sister just after they had arrived in the Arctic: "One point of disagreement is that he considers any attention to cleanliness, hygiene and camp sanitation as 'military fads.' If you have read his articles in Harpers, you may have noticed that there is only one really great Arctic and Eskimo authority—who has learned more in one year than all previous explorers combined. But I understand the situation and don't worry much about it."[44] Still, the relationship remained relatively smooth for four years. Any other attitude on Anderson's part might well have torn the two-man expedition apart.

Only six months after his return from the Anglo-American Polar Expedition, Stefansson was ready to go north again. Anderson met the commander in Toronto in April 1908, where he was told about the expedition's newest function and was made responsible for learning the fine points of setting up meteorological stations. Then the two embarked on their trip, travelling to Winnipeg, Edmonton, and Athabaska Landing, reaching Fort McPherson by early July using rail, sternwheeler, scow, and whaleboat. According to Stefansson, their equipment was as simple as possible: two identical cameras and film supply; two special rifles and 1,000 rounds of

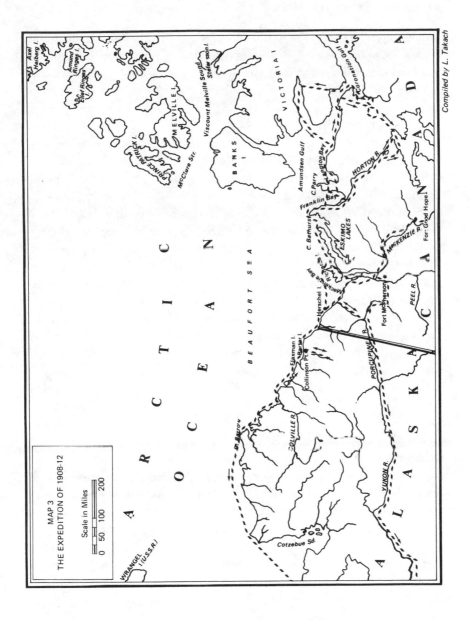

MAP 3
THE EXPEDITION OF 1908-12

Scale in Miles
0 50 100 200

Compiled by L. Takach

WRANGEL I. (U.S.S.R.)

A R C T I C   O C E A N

Axel
Heiberg I.
Amund
Ringnes I.
Ellef Ringnes I.
PRINCE
PATRICK I.
MELVILLE I.
McClure Str.
Viscount Melville Sound
Stefansson I.
VICTORIA I.

BANKS I.

BEAUFORT SEA

Pt. Barrow
COLVILLE R.
Collinson Pt.
Barter I.
Flaxman I.
Herschel I.
Mackenzie Bay
PORCUPINE R.
YUKON R.
Cotzebue Sd.

A L A S K A

Amundsen Gulf
C. Parry
Dolphin & Union Str.
Franklin Bay
C. Bathurst
HORTON R.
ESKIMO LAKES
MACKENZIE R.
Mackenzie R. Delta
Fort McPherson
PEEL R.
Fort Good Hope
Coronation Gulf

C A N A D A

ammunition; half a dozen "ordinary" rifles and shotguns and ammunition, for the use of the Eskimos; two sets of field glasses; pens, pencils, paper, and notebooks; two silk tents; tobacco for their Eskimo employees; aluminum cooking utensils; "and very little else." The outfit weighed less than a ton. As for food, he considered that carrying food to the Arctic was "carrying coal to Newcastle."[45]

En route, they had set up the meteorological stations in accordance with their agreement with Stupart's Metereological Service of Canada and discharged that commitment. As soon as the expedition was safely north, Stefansson told the Museum that he was going to stay two years "and shall from now on [9 July 1908] go ahead with that purpose in view";[46] earlier he had hinted such a possibility might arise if he, as the man on the spot, found such a move were necessary. Obviously he had made up his mind long before they left Toronto. Though aware that the Museum could not officially pledge itself so far in advance, he felt he had Bumpus's "personal opinion the Museum would probably continue to support for another year if I decided when on the ground that a second year's work would be advisable."[47] With little fuss, support for a second year was indeed granted, and the ease of his victory gave the commander a false sense of security, a feeling he could fall back on his benefactors again and again if he so wished. It was easier to obtain ten dollars to continue an enterprise than one dollar to begin one.

In retrospect, the decision to remain another year was wise. In view of the wide scope of the expedition, very little could be accomplished thoroughly and satisfactorily within the one year time limit. Besides, from the outset, Stefansson was plagued by a host of minor, irksome problems which demanded much time and energy and eventually necessitated a third year in the north.

These problems ranged from an immediate shortage of cash owing to the unexpected increase of freight rates since his last trip,[48] to a refusal on the part of the Royal Northwest Mounted Police to co-operate in his schemes. The police, custodians of the order, good government, and well-being of the northland's inhabitants, were annoyed that such a flimsy expedition as Stefansson's had been allowed to enter the country in the first place. Staff Sgt. Fitzgerald of the Herschel Island detachment would not have allowed anyone into the country unless he had one year's supply of provisions, a procedure followed during the Yukon gold rush. "Such men as Stefansson claim that they can live on the country. They can[,] by some-one else supplying the food. All these people are a drain on our supplies[.] I[t] is impossible to refuse a white man if he is short of food."[49]

Fitzgerald, in all sincerity, had refused Stefansson's party matches to discourage him from continuing, hoping thus to avoid a possible tragedy, but the explorer, after securing the matches from other sources, turned the incident around to his advantage: "we had not come north to study the habits of the police at Herschel Island."[50] The match incident was blown out of all proportion, mainly to make good copy and intriguing reading. Stefansson later admitted that it was necessary, from a "commercial" standpoint, "to prod a missionary now and then when things get too quiet." Taking missionaries and others to task was necessary for professional reasons. It was desirable from a monetary standpoint as well, if a publisher "can hoodwink the public," the "man who buys the book because he thinks I am 'great'." Even though such an image of greatness was, in Stefansson's words, "rot," it was in his financial interest, as well as other explorers', to let the publisher take liberties in publicity matters, and for himself to remain "mum and not give the game away. . . . Amundsen is the most unblushed advertiser of the lot. He has press agents and deliberately laid plans that out Herod Herod."[51] In the match incident, it was the police who were being prodded, even though Fitzgerald was merely carrying out his duty and thinking of the safety of the newcomers, Stefansson and Anderson. Stefansson had managed to raise some dust out of a rather mundane incident. The police (and the missionaries) would only have been human if they had not taken too kindly to the author of such opinions.

However, Stefansson was not wholly dependent on the police for food since he had adopted Eskimo eating habits and customs of storing food. Whenever his party cooked, the Eskimos flocked to his tent and ate heartily. The thing to do when out of food, he told Anderson, was to reciprocate; Eskimo hospitality would suffice: "Stefansson says one must do the same as they do—when one is hungry, go to some native's tent, squat down, and wait until he gives you a 'hand-out'."[52] Stefansson could never, according to Anderson, live off the country as he had detailed it in published accounts:

> Mr. Stefansson himself started off in the fall of 1908 (about 20th of October), to try to winter with the Colville River Eskimos, having two supposedly good Eskimo hunters working for him, but got starved out of the country before Christmas and had to retreat to Point Barrow, where he spent most of the winter as the guest of the whaling station, government school teacher, and missionary, finding the study of Eskimo linguistics more easy and practicable than "living on the country."[53]

This is how Anderson "perceived" the situation. Although Anderson's statement is harsh, it is valid and accurate to some extent. Even Stefansson conceded this point, stating that he had to withdraw from the region in question "on account of the insufficiency of the food supply," to use

Stefansson's words, and did spend the winter with whites.[54] Stefansson made no additional comments on this particular episode. However, Anderson, sharing a different scientific perspective, was unjust in his comment on Stefansson's invaluable study of Eskimo linguistics and appeared unable to appreciate this worthwhile endeavour. Yet Stefansson's dependence on the natives and whites and his pre-occupation with hand-to-mouth existence, against which he himself complained incessantly,[55] meant that he was not able to do as much scientific investigation as he would have liked. In actual fact, though, he was gaining more and more experience with the northland and its people, collecting artifacts for his principals, recording native folklore and pursuing linguistic studies. One gets the impression that either Stefansson may have been oblivious of these achievements—although this is unlikely—or that he may not have considered them important in themselves. Stefansson, in search of something which would distinguish him, may have despaired at his inability to reach the fabled people of Victoria Land because of the food problem. He confessed in his diary:

> The continual nervous strain of a hand-to-mouth existence, where there is not even the shelter of a poorhouse in case of failure, has a telling and cumulative effect. Without in the least relinquishing my hopes of many more years of arctic work, I continually feel more strongly the desire to be so well equipt in future that I shall have at least a year's supply of food somewhere awaiting me to tide me over a season of failure. Just *knowing* of such a reserve if one never had the comfort of a mouthful of it to vary one's diet, would lessen by half the strain of the winter. This is a hard country for a hungry man.[56]

The most important, though never well-publicized, "obstacle" in Stefansson's path was the Museum's refusal to extend its support beyond the first two years. Although the Museum had given him a wide rein, by the winter of 1909–10 they were growing disturbed at what they considered the poor results of the first two years. The time spent with the local Eskimos had proved invaluable, but Stefensson had not achieved one of his main goals: the investigation of the Victoria Land Eskimos. The Museum either anticipated or surmised that he would soon approach them for a third year's additional support, and they were correct.

Stefansson was confident that the Museum would finance the expedition for another year. He felt certain that "even our small achievements to date come well above the limits set as a possible . . . minimum," and that only a general change of policy could prevent the Museum from providing the necessary credit. If, however, the Museum did not lend them additional financial assistance, both Stefansson and Anderson would, in all likelihood, continue in the field, "as they have no power to recall us or direct our movements." In the meantime, Stefansson would continue using the credit of the American Museum to pay additional bills "in the hope that they approve our plans, having merely a verbal understanding with the [whaling] captains that a refusal to honor drafts is possible and that I shall endeavour to make them good personally."[57] Stefansson felt certain that matters would work out to his satisfaction.

However, by April 1910, the Museum decided to withdraw before it was too late and recall Stefansson and Anderson "as they had been in the field now for about three years, at a cost of more than $4000, and with practically no results."[58] As early as the previous November, based on reports and results to date, Clark Wissler expressed serious doubts to his superior about Stefansson and the expedition. He was certain that little would come of it, save the collections. Having talked with other ethnologists, he had come away with "a poor opinion of [Stefansson's] ethnological results." Wissler was not willing for the Museum to become obligated to Stefansson "any more than can be helped, at least until we have some tangible evidence of his worth." Stefansson's reports were vague and inconclusive and Wissler criticized the adventurer for being superficial, "satisfied to stop with the general impression, just the point where our real field work should begin."[59] This was a criticism that would be levelled again and again at Stefansson over the years. However, it should be noted that at the time no one could be sure of the value of Stefansson's work. The field reports were considered unsatisfactory and they had not received any artifacts. The Museum's opinions may have been premature, but they were also sorely pressed for funds. D. M. Le Bourdais, in his book on Stefansson, later stated that the Museum gained more than 20,000 specimens from Stefansson and Anderson's endeavours, with a market value of more than $40,000, not to mention the obvious ethnological and zoological information.[60]

The ultimate decision to discontinue support was taken by the Museum after it received a discouraging note from Anderson, indicating he would prefer to quit the north as soon as it was convenient. He pointed to a fundamental conflict of scholarly interest:

> From a personal standpoint, I must admit that the results of the past two years have been unsatisfactory to me. My relations with Mr. Stefansson have been cordial at all times, and he has aided my work in every manner possible under the circumstances, but our method of exploration is, at the best, unfavourable to zoological work, although

it may be fairly satisfactory for anthropology. Practically two years have been spent in getting ready—a great part of the time at hard labor for bare living. Two winters have been endured in the hope of making up for lost time in the short summer harvest season, and the previous summer months sacrificed in the continual rush of moving. Collecting work on the move is difficult and usually unfruitful, and, at best, only skims the ground superficially. While this method of exploration may demonstrate that a white man can live where an Indian or Eskimo can and perhaps endure as much, the corollary seems to be that they are aborigines not able to accomplish much more than a bare living, and a white man cannot be expected to do much scientific work under similar conditions.[61]

Anderson's memo did much to persuade the American Museum to drop the project. Anderson was right in his assessment as far as it went. While most kinds of scientific work—like his own—require a man to remain relatively stationary and to devote himself wholly to one activity, a field ethnologist, like Stefansson, was best served by living with, moving with, and sharing the experiences of the people he studied.

The Museum fully understood the difficulties that had been encountered, but they could not in good conscience spend more money on an endeavour that had not provided fruitful results.[62] The money was needed elsewhere, particularly for South America and Africa[63] and the Museum was obliged to withdraw its support, although both men were perfectly free to stay in the Arctic at their own expense.[64] Not until May of the following year (1910) were the formal instructions sent out to the expedition. Anderson, who was working independently of Stefansson in the Baillie Islands, received his notice three months later, almost to the day,[65] but Stefansson apparently did not hear of the decision until early December 1910,[66] too late to do anything.

Stefansson was shaken upon receipt of the Museum's decision, but he would not have returned south even if he had received the notice earlier.[67] The news came in the first week of December. Four months earlier, after two years of frustration and delay getting together the supplies to carry out his investigations,[68] Stefansson had discovered his "gold mine," the natives of Victoria Land. With the prospects for success now looking so bright, Stefansson would have stayed in the Arctic as a "cabin boy" rather than leave: "It was more than I could stand for, to hang around in destitution and inability to move for two years and then come home when at last I had all the tools [the natives of Victoria Land] in my hands and fair weather for the work we came to do."[69] Nor would Anderson leave his commander in the lurch without knowing his whereabouts. He informed Bumpus that he was duty-bound to stay, even against his better judgement.[70] In fact, Stefansson attributed the Museum's eventual re-instatement of the project and the expedition's chance to "make good" to Anderson's stand.[71] The prolongation enabled the party to bring to the world some astonishing and intriguing news.

"AMERICAN EXPLORER DISCOVERS LOST TRIBE OF WHITES, DESCENDANTS OF LEIF ERIKSSEN." So ran the headline of the *Seattle Daily Times* for 9 September 1912. In essence, the world was told that Stefansson had discovered a "tribe of white people" who were "purely of Norwegian origin," remnants of the Norse Greenland colony which had disappeared in the fifteenth century.

Between May and August 1910, Stefansson had encountered a new and intriguing group of Eskimos who appeared to have the physical characteristics of Europeans "especially in the manner of beards, which are uniformly blonde, some even red. I have seen none with blonde hair, but Captain Mogg and others who have wintered north of the Kan-hirg-mi-ut report hair dark brown and blue eyes." This "European appearance," according to Stefansson, might be due to climate "or other physical cause than mixture of white blood," but he toyed with the idea that some survivors of Franklin's expedition might have assimilated with the Eskimo. Perhaps the characteristics of the Victoria Land people could be traced back to the colony of Greenlanders that had disappeared in the fifteenth or sixteenth century.[72] This possibility held real appeal for their discoverer. Stefansson later denied he had put forth any such exclusive explanation for the physical characteristics of these Eskimos. He did suggest that while "there is no reason for insisting now or ever that the 'Blonde Eskimos' of Victoria Land are descended from the Scandinavian colonists of Greenland, but looking at it historically or geographically, there is no reason why they might not be."[73] To this view, he adhered until his death.

In fact, in public he disclaimed any connection with the "Blonde Eskimo" stories, calling them "half-truths, non-malicious fiction, and sheer nonsense,"[74] the product of over-imaginative writing on the part of J. J. Underwood of the *Seattle Daily Times*. In private, however, the ethnologist was somewhat gleeful that the whole affair had aroused academic circles around the world. In Sweden and Germany "our work has caused more *popular* interest than the discovery of the North Pole—which is by no means true of America, however."[75] In any case, the attention finally being paid the expedition was well deserved. "It is well to be modest in public, but privately we needn't be so diffident. If we had been as much behind the scene in other exploits as we have been in our own, we might think that what credit we are getting is [as] well earned as it is in a good half of the other cases."[76] Stefansson merely warned Anderson to refuse any newspaper interviews which might violate his agreement with *Harper's*; otherwise the only limit in talking to reporters should be the adventurers' own ideas of "good taste."[77] Later he suggested that, although Anderson "did not see the two blondest groups—those of Prince Albert Sound and near Pt. Williams"—as long as each adhered to the facts, as determined by Stefansson, there would be no fear of contradicting one another.[78] Anderson could only follow his commander's directives.

Stefansson later was extremely disturbed by the criticism levelled at him by two of the most respected polar explorers, Fridtjof Nansen and Roald Amundsen. Nansen considered Stefansson another Dr. Cook, a trickster, while Amundsen was violent in his characterization of Stefansson, calling his alleged conclusions "palpable nonsense" and an "amusing figment of the imagination."[79] It was at about this time that two camps appeared, one supporting Stefansson as an honest and dedicated scientist, the other condemning him as a mere popularizer and part-time charlatan.

To some degree, Stefansson had no one but himself to credit or blame for this publicity and notoriety. Some of his findings and hypotheses in connection with the Victoria Land Eskimos were published in the *New York Times* in the fall of 1911, well before the Underwood sensationalisms. Moreover, he wrote a lengthy letter to Professor James Mavor on 12 December 1910,[80] parts of which eventually appeared in the widely read London *Times* of 13 August 1912, which did much to place Stefansson in an unfavourable light. Stefansson admitted to Mavor that his finds might lay him open to the charge of sensationalism. Nevertheless, the only historical event that could possibly explain the high admixture of white and Eskimo blood that Stefansson believed to be present amongst the Copper Eskimos was the disappearance of the Greenland colony in the late Middle Ages. In similar correspondence with Bumpus and Wissler, he firmly expressed his belief in their Norse (white) origin.[81] Soon, however, common sense and experience told him that perhaps he had been too rash and foolhardy, that he should modify his beliefs and couch his assertions in more carefully chosen words. No doubt he took Mavor's advice to "avoid sensational conclusions. I am afraid that they do not do very much good."[82] Stefansson's mentor, Mavor, like others, was apprehensive because of Stefansson's limited training in the subject.[83]

It is interesting to note that the school which had trained him and in a way sent him on this work was cool, at times hostile, toward its pupil. Harvard was never very impressed with his professional abilities. In 1912, a senior member of the Department of Anthropology, Dr. W. C. Farrabee, who knew Stefansson well in his Harvard days, stated categorically that Stefansson "does not enjoy the full confidence of any member of our anthropological faculty."[84] The tone of Farrabee's curt response, which was never expanded upon, seems to indicate that this attitude had existed for some considerable time, and was not related solely to the question of the "Blonde Eskimos." Despite this professional suspicion, which was to follow him into Canada, Stefansson remained undaunted by his detractors.

Why Stefansson portrayed his newly found Eskimos in such a dramatic and sensational fashion is unclear. Perhaps he was over-dramatic or only feeling sorry for himself when, on his thirtieth birthday, a crucial one in any life, he lamented that in the year just ended (1909) "there lie too few and too small accomplishments, too many miscarried plans and imperfectly accomplished purposes."[85] Always gnawing at his conscience was the feeling he had accomplished nothing to show for himself, that people would not notice him, or recognize the fruits of his work, or support his research.[86] The news that the Museum would discontinue its support had been a keen disappointment. He may have concluded that he had to sell himself and his work to succeed as well as survive in his profession.[87]

Stefansson made the best of his "scoop." He knew that he was breaking ground in Eskimo studies and while he may not have been the best-trained ethnologist he was undeterred. He believed that by being the first to do something of note he would establish a reputation.[88] He was correct. Not only did he receive publicity from the controversies generated over his hypothesis, but he won back the support of the American Museum. Clark Wissler, who had not been impressed with the early results of the expedition, was responsible for placing the expedition back on the Museum's good books.[89] Soon after the account of Stefansson's discoveries had received full coverage in the Sunday edition of the *New York Times*,[90] the Museum, under Henry Fairfield Osborn, decided to appropriate another $1,000 "for the continuation of their work . . . in addition, to this appropriation . . . the Museum stands ready to pay the cost of transportation of any collections which either Mr. Stefansson or Dr. Anderson may send to the Museum, and we further stand ready to pay the travelling expense of both . . . when they return to the States."[91] However, notwithstanding their decision to support Stefansson's efforts, F. A. Lucas, the director of the Museum, wanted to terminate the expedition as quickly as possible. He was of the opinion that "the information and material gained would not be at all commensurate with the labor and the cost of the expedition . . . I feel that it is much better to do a few things well, than to do many indifferently." Lucas was certain that the Museum had spread itself too thinly in connection with this arctic exploit.[92] Osborn, though impressed by Stefansson, replied that the expedition was "somewhat beyond our field and it would have been wiser not to have undertaken it. It has, however, brought the museum a great deal of publicity and promises to bring it some fine collections. I once wrote Mr. Stefansson, but hearing from him that they had decided to go on without pay at their own expense, it seemed the least we could do was continue to provide them for another year."[93] Stefansson and Brock had been right: it would be difficult to stop an enterprise once it had received formal sanction. In the end, the Museum spent almost $13,600[94] for an expedition that was supposed to cost, at the most, $2,300. This experience, with its reversal of fortunes, may have given Stefansson the notion that publicity was the key to success, be it scientific or popular.

The question of the so-called "Blonde Eskimos" has been frequently raised to challenge Stefansson's scholarly competence. Consequently, since his encounter with the people of Victoria Land in 1910, a number of investigators have tried to solve the puzzle of how far and for what reasons the appearance and the culture of the Copper Eskimo differed considerably from the Alaskan and Eastern Eskimo.

A number of theories have been put forward concerning the origin of the Copper Eskimo. Some studies placed the original centre of Eskimo development in the central Canadian Arctic, between the Mackenzie River and Hudson Bay. There, supposedly, had dwelt inland tribes of "Proto-Eskimos," in some way related biologically and culturally to the northern American Indian. These inland tribes eventually spread to the central Arctic coast and then east and west along it.[95] Another school of thought, which included Diamond Jenness, one of Canada's foremost anthropologists, suggests that much of the Eskimo cultural development took place in the western Arctic and recognizes, quite correctly, the existence of an Asiatic or Alaska-derived Thule culture dating from prehistoric times. This second group[96] saw the distinctiveness of the Copper Eskimo as resulting from a recent advance of inland "Eschato Eskimo" groups to the Coronation Gulf which either supplemented or amalgamated with an older coast culture. Both schools based their positions primarily on cultural and linguistic traits and neither really concerned itself with physical differences.

Stefansson himself paid very little attention to cultural and linguistic affiliations between Eskimo groups. In 1910, no one knew much about the subject, and although Stefansson wished to follow it up, he never had the opportunity. He was only guessing when he tried to account for "whiter" physical traits among Victoria Land Eskimos by suggesting that it might be linked to the disappearance of the Greenland Colony, which had re-appeared, he believed, in assimilated form on the banks of Coronation Gulf. Diamond Jenness seems to have one of the most plausible explanations for the physical characteristics of the "Blonde Eskimo." From his studies amongst them for the Canadian Arctic Expedition (1913–18), he con-cluded that any European-like features in this particular group of Eskimos were due to natural causes, such as bleaching that caused the lightness in the hair, and repeated attacks of snow-blindness that led to the occasional light, bluish colour of the eyes.[97] Yet the anomaly is almost impossible to explain.

Stefansson's suggestions implied that there had been an intimate contact, in one fashion or another, between the Eskimos of Greenland and those of Victoria Land, at some point in history. More particularly, he claimed that a large group of Greenland Eskimos, including Icelanders, had migrated to the vicinity of Coronation Gulf. If this was the case, then later investigations might be able to find connections between the Copper Eskimos and those of Greenland. While by 1910–11 Stefansson knew some-thing about the Alaskan and Copper Eskimos, he knew virtually nothing about eastern Eskimos, since he had never studied them at close range.

A modern study does not support Stefansson's hypothesis. Robert J. McGhee, in his "Copper Eskimo Prehistory," demonstrates that there was a closer relationship between Alaskan and Greenland Eskimos, but very little connection between Copper and Greenland or eastern Eskimos. Mc-Ghee contends that Copper Eskimo culture was a derivative of Thule culture, and that the local variations from the Thule culture do not repre-sent an infusion of a non-Thule culture. Rather, the variations are a response to geological, ecological, and climatic factors.[98]

Yet even against the general level and trends of nineteenth and early twentieth century ethnology, Stefansson, perhaps, was not the best qualified person to study these Eskimo groups. In many important respects he had been influenced by the work and professed methodology of Franz Boas, who had done ethnographic work for the American Museum in the 1890s.[99] Boas adopted a three-step plan in his approach to the subject. First, a field investigator must examine in minutest detail the mores, traits, and everyday activities of one particular tribe. To do this, he should learn the language of the group he is examining and, ideally, keep his notes and records in that language to prevent distortion. In addition, the investigator should use archaeological techniques and become totally familiar with the physical environment and the subject's relationship to it.[100] Stefansson followed this first step by very thoroughly recording the daily life and folkways, learning the native language, and gaining an understanding of his environment. The next step was to investigate a number of nearby tribes within a geographically small area to trace the history of the growth of ideas and transmission of customs. This meant collecting museum specimens and folktales, and investigating native languages within a small area.[101] Stefansson did little of this among neighbouring Eskimo tribes in the Coronation Gulf-Victoria Land region. He would have liked to study comparative linguistics and mythology, but this was beyond the scope and resources of his 1908–12 expedition since the Museum had decided to withdraw support.[102]

These first two steps were necessary for the final stage to which most ethnologists of the day subscribed: a careful search for universal laws of cultural development, the discovery of "psychic" laws governing the growth and transmission of ideas of all mankind.[103] This was one of Stefansson's goals, but he realized in 1912 that he was not in a position to achieve this unless certain conditions were met:

> I have no ambition to make all knowledge my province—except so far as to allow any intelligent interest in all progress; I do not want even to make all ethnology my province, but the archeology and ethnology of all America is probably thoroughly woven into one whole, and it would be a fine thing to have the money that would enable one to give the necessary time to the study of the results others gain in every part of our continent—then I might be able to see the bearing of my own work, the meaning in relation to the whole phenomena which now stand isolated. Not only could I then profit by the work of others, but others would be more likely to profit by my work.[104]

Stefansson was more ethnographer than ethnologist at this stage, and he knew that he had just scratched the surface. He was forsaking his ethnological pursuits in favour of playing the anthropologist. His collection of word lists, folktales, descriptions of Eskimo life, and the like—incomplete as it may have been—was impressive and reflected his early training. But it is likely that physical anthropology and ethnogeny, into which he was now venturing, were another matter. Even by contemporary standards, much more work was required. It was for these reasons that in 1912 Stefansson wanted adequate backing and recognition to carry on further work in the north. Yet, ironically, by the start of the 1913 expedition, his ethnological desires were to become secondary.

With a view to following up and rounding out his investigation, and to capitalize on the publicity given his work, Stefansson felt he must return south. Not only must he take advantage of his personal success, but the American Museum's recent hesitancy meant that he would have to re-establish old contacts and create new ones with the scientific world. Besides, after four years in Canada's northland, "I want Broadway by archlight and the Strand at five o'clock; after iglu I want the Century Club and the Criterion; after *Kajigi* monologues on the forefathers' wisdom I want scientific conventions where we learn things. . . . To take the place of the sailor's drunk I want an intellectual orgy . . . till my next journey—like the sailor's next voyage—calls me to the stagnant country where precedent is king."[105] Being behind the times and out of touch was unendurable for such a restless spirit. He also wanted to solve his money problems and secure the backing of some institution to pay for his expenses while he continued work in the Arctic. Now was the time to take advantage of a situation.

The uncertainty that the game will be considered worth even a small cheap candle by those who know of the game at all—the small circle of scientific men who are not always sympathetic or generous—who are not even always scientific. Peary was "a man of one idea" and the best thing about him was that it always seemed to me that he was satisfied with that idea—if he got to the Pole he would have something worthwhile—he could say to himself (as the world would say to him) : "You have a right to be satisfied" . . . and he would answer truthfully: "I am satisfied". . . . I have the education that colleges and books give. . . . I have the education that experiences give, I know the land[,] I am learning the language of the people—and that learning is my work, together with telling what I have learned. For twenty years yet I am likely to have strength to fight the cold climate and to find food for myself and my companions as I have found it the past years. If I am to follow Peary (as I started out to do a few months ago), what I want to confide to any reader of my journal is that the one thing I want is the interest (shown by the giving of money and the lending of willing ears) that shall keep me at work here twenty years. When one gets old, it is said, one begins to long for simple rest, and to find in the hope of rest a satisfactory goal . . . I want to have free time now and then, between spells of work up here to be with men who are not asleep. I am hoping that, if scientific bodies can be found to pay my expenses while I work, my own "popular" writing can pay for my play time. Wherever, in Europe or America, there are men shaping the thot of our time, there I want to be (if they will tolerate me, for the share I am trying to do) to spend my play hours with them.[106]

4

The Building of the
Canadian Arctic Expedition

Like the Anglo-American Polar Expedition, conception and execution of the 1908–12 expedition was another vital stage, an upward step, in Stefansson's career. He had improved his technique as an explorer by learning first hand the mechanics of launching an expedition, and improving his skill in negotiating to keep the enterprise alive when its sponsors seemed skeptical. Moreover, he had gained such success so as to widen immeasurably his base of support, bringing him immediate fame, as well as controversy. His find of primitive Eskimos in Victoria Land, the methods he applied to their investigation, and the controversies generated by his theories had catapulted him into world headlines and put his northern pursuits on an altered course. The four years of this expedition had enhanced his influence with American scientific institutions, and with important forces within the Canadian government. Once he had learned how to handle them, he had created an expedition on his own merits, combining his force of argument with a friendly assertiveness that could not be denied. Stefansson admitted that he could "talk a man into anything if he didn't know me . . . I have at least meant well at times."[1] In the long run, perhaps one of the most questionable conclusions he came to was that an enterprise should be kept going even in the face of a threatened loss of official support, until he secured results that would redeem it and return him to the good graces of its sponsors. Yet, in the "Stefansson–Anderson Expedition," as the foray of 1908–12 was officially called, the aspect that brought such recognition and influence was not so much his discoveries and investigations, as the publicity attached to his finding of the so-called "Blonde Eskimo." This association of success with publicity was to lead Stefansson astray, and would deflect his scientific pursuits for a dozen years or so. His pioneering and promising work amongst the Copper Eskimos was never completed. Unfortunately for Stefansson's scientific career, he tried to apply these assumptions regarding the attainment of success to his next expedition, sponsored by the government of Canada.

In 1911, Stefansson knew that his work was incomplete. Far more comparative research was necessary, at least fifteen years he felt—"enough time at my work between Victoria Land and Smith Sound to become 'one of the family,' in at least a dozen places."[2] Stefansson's new expedition—as he envisioned it in the fall and winter of 1912—was to be far more ambitious than that of 1908–12, involving six scientists, a ship, and supplies to last until mid–1916. Although the American Museum of Natural History had been impressed with Stefansson's and Anderson's achievements,[3] it was quite hesitant about granting full and unqualified support to the new project. Initially, the Museum refused to take an active part in organizing the expedition and would only express its approval and vouch for the enterprise as being worthwhile. Museum officials, accepting the worthiness of Stefansson's project, had concluded that the American Museum should not spread itself too thinly by supporting projects which had little direct bearing on the Museum's current planning and policy.[4] Besides, they had just underwritten an extensive northern expedition under the direction of Donald B. MacMillan to search for Peary's legendary Crocker Land, said to exist north and west of Ellesmere Island.[5] MacMillan had accompanied Robert E. Peary on his unsuccessful 1906 quest for the north pole. While attempting to reach 90° north latitude in 1906, Peary was certain that he had seen snowclad mountains to the west of him, roughly in the direction north and west of Axel Heiberg and Ellesmere Islands. It appeared as though Peary had come close to substantiating Dr. R. A. Harris's theory, but in all probability this incident was merely another sighting of an ice-island. Nevertheless, such observations set off another wave of exploration. The Museum claimed it could not spare a penny for a second arctic expedition.

Stefansson was not allowed to solicit funds from the trustees of the Museum or from any person who had been a patron. The city of New York had been thoroughly canvassed for the Crocker Land expedition, leaving only a few crumbs for Stefansson.[6] Not only was the Museum afraid Stefansson might duplicate and encroach on work done by the Crocker Land expedition, but it was still apprehensive about his temperament and suitability to carry out Museum work. At one point it entertained the idea that Stefansson should be MacMillan's companion. There was immediate and strong adverse reaction to this suggestion by people like W. C. Farrabee of Harvard's Department of Anthropology and E. O. Hovey, the doctor for the Anglo-American Expedition. The frequent calling into question of Stefansson's trustworthiness, reliability, and personality no doubt surprised the Museum authorities and added to their uneasiness about supporting Stefansson on a large project of his own.[7]

Osborn may have sympathized with Stefansson's cause, but there was little he could do. Stefansson's only full supporter was Clark Wissler, who received permission to take an active part in the organization of the expedition, entirely independent of the Museum.[8] Wissler's pressure, and his hint that the expedition could receive outside financial aid on the condition that the American Museum withdraw its support,[9] forced the Museum to take an active part in the proposed scheme. Much to the Museum's dismay, during the winter Stefansson had hammered out a scheme with the National Geographic Society of Washington. Admiral Pilsbury, one of the Society's directors, announced that the main purpose of the National Geographic's expedition would be "geographical[,] for the ethno graphic investigations fall within the province of geography. The time to be covered by the expedition will be three winters and four summers, beginning with the summer of 1913. The field of operations will be Victoria Island, Banks' Land and Prince Patrick's Island, all situated north of the mainland of North America and forming, with Melville Island, the western most of the group of the American Polar Lands."[10] The goal of the proposed expedition was to discover and delineate any new land or, if no land was found, to determine by soundings the limit of the Continental Shelf.[11] This aspect in particular upset the American Museum of Natural History, which had already underwritten a related search for Crocker Land under the leadership of Donald MacMillan; the Museum, naturally, feared that Stefansson's plan encroached upon its own northern program.

Prior to his seeking help from the National Geographic, Stefansson had, in the fall, concluded a verbal agreement with the Museum regarding the Crocker Land expedition. He was asked "not to make any attempt to reach any part of the archipelago of which Crocker Land forms a part, until after Mr. MacMillan had had a chance to reach it." Stefansson maintained he had every right to explore the Beaufort Sea by ship, but agreed not to make any sledge journey toward the hypothetical continent until after 1914.[12] With the National Geographic, Stefansson was under no such restrictions, and apparently the Museum was afraid that he might not abide by prior arrangement.[13] Faced with this possible threat and to protect its investment in MacMillan, the Museum had no alternative but to buy into Stefansson's expedition to the tune of $22,500. The Museum had come to terms. It was now willing to co-operate actively with the National

Geographic Society. The basis of its proposal was that all geographic results and publications should lie with the National Geographic, while the ethnological and zoological material and results—with which the Museum was chiefly concerned—were to lie with the New York institution.[14] The Museum recognized that, to ensure that Stefansson's and MacMillan's interests did not collide, a division of territory was necessary. By supporting Stefansson, it hoped to control the situation and not allow an angry scientific rivalry to develop.

It can be assumed that the National Geographic would have liked to be the exclusive sponsor of the expedition, but its president, Gilbert Grosvenor, was attracted by Stefansson's idea that a special ship would facilitate the exploration.[15] But a ship would be very expensive, and the National Geographic needed the co-operation with another body, namely the American Museum, to secure such funds. An agreement was drawn up between the 24th and 25th of January 1913, at Grosvenor's home in Washington, among Stefansson, the American Museum of Natural History, and the National Geographic Society. It was understood that the polar region would be divided, "that Prince Patrick's Land will be Mr. Stefansson's base, and that, while in a general way the territory will be divided for geographic exploration, either partners striking this supposed coastline may proceed in the direction of the other party without infringement,"[16] but only after the hypothetical continent had been reached.

The title of the expedition was to be "The Stefansson–Anderson Expedition of 1913, 14, 15, 16," the leader being Stefansson and the second-in-command, R. M. Anderson. Its purpose "shall be the thorough scientific exploration of the unknown Polar region to the north and west of Banks Land and Prince Patrick's Island." The National Geographic Society was responsible for the planning of the geographic, meteorological, tidal, and physical observations, while the American Museum was to be in charge of anthropology, biology, and zoology.[17]

In consideration of the joint financing, all material results, collections, and data—including photographs (except motion pictures)—were the sole property of the National Geographic Society and the American Museum of Natural History, "including exclusive rights of publication."

> Mr. Vilhjalmur Stefansson . . . agrees to prepare and have his assistants prepare immediately upon their return from the Arctic regions such popular and scientific reports of the expedition's work as may be called for by [the sponsors], in whom exclusive rights of publication will lie. The leader, Mr. Stefansson [,] also binds himself to prevent any mem-

ber of the expedition publishing material unless said material has been released by the Editor of the National Geographic Magazine. It is also agreed that the leader shall have the use of any or all photographs or pictures for the purpose of making lantern slides to illustrate any lectures he may wish to make upon the expedition's return.[18]

This innocent-looking stipulation was to provoke considerable disharmony. Nevertheless, it appeared as though the sponsors were to maintain stricter control than had been evident in the 1908–12 expedition.

This new arctic foray was not, in reality, an extension of the 1908–12 expedition, for the simple fact was that the emphasis and direction of the venture had now shifted to geographic exploration. Archaeological and ethnological study of the Eskimo in and around Coronation Gulf—the purpose for which Stefansson had started organizing the expedition—had slipped to a secondary place. To obtain the support of the National Geographic, Stefansson had reluctantly accepted this order of priorities. Compromising his objectives was the price to be paid for his eagerness to return north.

> Of course geography is science, but it is chiefly anthropo-geography that attracts me. It is a sense of my pledges and what is expected of me that keeps me at sea exploration. After all, the geographic side of this expedition was originally 'played up' by me to get money for the archeological and ethnological work planned by Dr. Wissler and me. It did not seem to us possible to get the money for anthropological work purely from sensationalism—we were Jesuists in the means chosen to the end desired.[19]

Priority was given to completion of the map of the coast lines of Victoria Island and Prince Patrick Island, then to three off-shore journeys to discover new land, or at least the edge of the continental shelf, and to systematic tidal observations. Stefansson's original priorities were given lesser importance, and were to be found only in the fourth and fifth clauses of the January 1913 agreement:

> (d) By summer exploration of Banks Island, Victoria Island, Prince Patrick Island and of any new land that may be discovered, an attempt will be made to determine the former range of human occupation of the Arctic Islands as well as the character of the culture of the people involved. Further archaeological work will be done in the districts investigated by the American Museum of National History and the Geological Survey of Canada Arctic Expedition of 1908–12.

(e) The biological and historical problems connected with the already ascertained physical differences of the Victoria Island Eskimo from the typical characters of their race make it seem important that more full investigations shall be undertaken to determine by exact mechanical means[,] such as color photography, the degrees of their divergence from type. All other ordinary investigations of an ethnological nature will also be pursued, including a detailed study of phonetics by mechanical and other means.[20]

Stefansson had to face another problem. Added to this shift in emphasis, was the fact that the National Geographic and American Museum could not decide on how their respective financial allocations should be administered. The National Geographic was to contribute $22,500, of which $8,000 was to be payable in 1913, $5,000 in 1914, $5,000 in 1915, and $4,500 in 1916. Their funds were to be deposited in a bank selected by Stefansson. The bank was to act as his financial agent.[21] The American Museum was also to contribute $22,500 but, unlike the National Geographic, it felt that past experience had shown "that it was absolutely necessary to have a committee in charge of the business management and to conduct the expedition on business principles, not giving out any orders (i.e. honour drafts) unless funds were available to defray the expenses."[22] The American Museum did not wish to have Stefansson in charge of expenditures. The National Geographic, even after the American Museum representation, preferred not to assume business responsibilities. Yet both institutions were aware that some sort of common arrangement had to be worked out. These were small points to the societies, but to Stefansson, who was also called upon to provide an indemnity bond as a guarantee,[23] such arrangements meant he would lose personal control. Yet there was little he could do, for there was no clause this time giving him the freedom of action and decision he had had in 1908.

Besides, according to Stefansson, $45,000 would not be enough to carry out the project.[24] More help would be required. Once again, with the blessing of Osborn,[25] he turned to the Canadian government, particularly to R. W. Brock of the Geological Survey, who would naturally have an interest in the expedition. After Stefansson had obtained the full backing of the Geological Survey, he secured an interview with Robert L. Borden and asked the prime minister to provide an additional $25,000 on behalf of Canada.[26] Borden remained non-committal and Stefansson relied on Brock to carry on the fight.[27] Within the week, the expedition had been entirely removed from the hands of the National Geographic and the

American Mueum of Natural History. The Dominion government, after some consideration, took it over entirely as a national enterprise. Such an arrangement would simplify matters for Stefansson, who could count on the backing of a powerful institution and perhaps obtain a freer hand in the expedition. It would also make life easier for the Canadian government. With the ending in 1911 of Bernier's expeditions, undertaken during the Laurier years, the Conservatives were anxious to have a northern program of their own. Moreover, the government expressed some anxiety that any discoveries of new land by aliens might complicate the vexing question of territorial sovereignty in the Arctic.

The Canadian government, although tardy and sometimes muddled in its actions, was never complacent about the question of arctic sovereignty. The activities of the Royal Northwest Mounted Police after 1903, W. F. King's *Report* on Canada's title to the northern islands (1905), and the subsequent voyages of Captain Joseph E. Bernier, were testimony to Canadian apprehension over the future of the arctic archipelago. It may have been Bernier's persistent campaign, and the polar exploits of Cook and Peary for instance, which led a worried Senator P. Poirier to invent the "sector theory" and attempt to apply it to the northern islands. In 1907 Poirier was quite forceful in demanding that Canada make a formal declaration of possession or face the prospect of forfeiting her rights in that region. The Senator suggested that the Arctic be divided like a pie, with the North Pole as the centre. Norway, Sweden, Russia, the United States, and, of course, Canada would each be given a portion. The Dominion's slice would lie between 141° west longitude to roughly 60° west longitude, thereby encompassing a triangle stretching from Canada's arctic coast to the north pole. "This partition of the polar regions seems to be the most natural, because it is simply a geographical one. By that means, difficulties would be avoided, and there would be no cause for trouble between interested countries. Every country bordering on the Arctic would simply extend its possession up to the North Pole."[28] The issue was sidetracked by Sir Richard Cartwright, minister of Trade and Commerce in the Laurier cabinet, and the senate leader, who assured Poirier that due attention would be paid to the matter, since "negotiations," never specified, were in progress. To the Liberals, it might not "be part of the policy to formally proclaim any special limitations."[29] Yet Poirier's proposal was not forgotten, for two and a half years later Bernier, commanding an official Canadian government expedition and armed with a royal commission to annex specific lands, placed a copper tablet on Melville Island, claiming the entire sector for Canada.[30] Bernier's actions were not only a fulfilment of a dream, but also, in large measure, recognition of the annexation of islands by 1904. Cartwright's assurances probably did little to comfort those Canadians who wanted a forthright position. American institutions, such as the American Museum of Natural History and the National Geographic Society, continued to finance northern expeditions. The spectre of foreign institutions, carrying a foreign flag, making discoveries in areas which Canada considered her own was hard to swallow. Canada could not help but be fearful.

The same was also true of the Canadian reaction to the Stefansson–Anderson Expedition of 1913, under joint sponsorship of two American institutions. Unlike the 1908–12 expedition, this one was primarily geared to the discovery of new land in the Arctic. Whose land would it be? No doubt the Canadian government was perturbed by the manner in which these two American institutions had arbitrarily carved up the northern reaches of the Canadian "sector" for exploration and discovery by the Crocker Land and the Stefansson–Anderson expeditions. A subcommittee of the cabinet after interviewing Stefansson on 7 February 1913

> decided that if it could be arranged we thought it advisable for the Dominion to pay the whole cost of the proposed expedition, on condition that Mr. Stefansson would become a naturalized British subject before leaving and that the expedition would fly the British flag. In this way we would get the entire benefit of the expedition and Canada would have any land that might be discovered. . . . The subcommittee . . . feels strongly that the Dominion Government should have a hand in this expedition and if possible control and pay for it.[31]

Canadian authorities would try their best to wrest it from the Americans. Yet the tone of the cabinet's decision suggests that, if either Stefansson or his backers refused to co-operate with the Canadian authorities, the Dominion was prepared to do little, aside from token official scrutiny, to discourage private explorations.

The responsibility for providing an easy transfer of the expedition to Canadian auspices devolved upon Stefansson. According to Anderson, Stefansson accepted the Canadian offer without consulting the American Museum, the National Geographic Society, or himself.[32] This was not entirely true—Anderson was merely the last party Stefansson conferred with before taking any action. Then, at the very last moment, the name of the expedition was changed to the "Canadian Arctic Expedition of Vilhjalmur Stefansson" to distinguish it from the former Stefansson–Anderson expedition and to emphasize its "Canadian character."[33] This did nothing to enhance the future relationship between the two men. As for the American backers, the Borden government hoped that Stefansson would be able to persuade them to relinquish control:

> Mr. Stefansson would not say definitely whether he would agree to this arrangement or not but stated that he thought it would be very satisfactory to have the whole cost paid from one source. He did not seem to have any particular objection to taking the oath of naturalization, although he did not say definitely he would do so. It seems he is under a good many obligations to the National Geographic Society who promise to pay $22,500 towards the expenses of the expedition. Mr. Stefansson did not feel at liberty to agree to do the work entirely under the auspices of the Dominion without first obtaining the consent of that Society. He thought, however, that he will have no difficulty in getting such consent, as scientific work which the Society is anxious to have done would be in that case paid for by the Dominion government and the funds of the Society could be used in other directions.[34]

No mention was made of the American Museum, whose quick acquiescence could be predicted; it had never wanted to be actively engaged in the scheme and had only given in reluctantly to Stefansson's manoeuvrings. When Stefansson broached the question to the New York institution, Osborn, on behalf of the Museum, readily wished Stefansson well,[35] undoubtedly thankful that the Museum was not being forced now to support two costly northern exploratory schemes. Anderson assented to the transfer, for he had little influence in the matter. Besides, the American Museum now could only offer him a position for one year. After a conference with Brock, the Geological Survey offered him a more permanent position in the Victoria Museum (now part of the National Museum of Man) at a salary equal to that of the American Museum of Natural History.[36]

The National Geographic was a different matter. It had more than a passing interest in the project. The Society had spent much time and effort in an endeavour which would further their own scientific program "to have that portion of the map cleared which you [Stefansson] propose to explore, and it was our faith in you as the best-equipped and most experienced man to do the work that inspired the Society to make our appropriation . . . to assist in your expedition." Realizing that they could not match the Canadian government in terms of funds, the National Geographic relinquished its claim upon the expedition gracefully "providing you can make arrangements with the Canadian government that will permit your expedition to depart in May or June, 1913." The Society was so intent on seeing "their" expedition succeed that they stipulated that "[i]f the Canadian Government cannot assist you this year, the Society reserves its claims upon your expedition and is prepared to send you North in May or June next."[37] It became doubly important then for the Canadian government to push ahead as soon as possible with its newly acquired expedition or forfeit it to the National Geographic. The ensuing haste, however, led to an ill-organized and two-chambered expedition which did much to impair its efficiency. The take-over and resulting alterations by the Canadian authorities also put Stefansson in a slightly different position. The Dominion's plans and priorities were overlaid on his own, and would produce inconsistencies between groups of individuals and their purposes. The personal controversies generated—admittedly, common to most expeditions—were also heightened by the rush to get the enterprise in the field by mid–1913.

From late February to June 1913, Stefansson, Anderson, and the Canadian government were caught up in a wild round of activities designed to send the expedition north before the season became too late. On 23 February 1913, the committee of the privy council established the critical guidelines under which the expedition would operate. Specific and final instructions were hammered out late in May, on the eve of the expedition's departure. In addition to the discovery of the new lands "[t]he expedition should bring back information as to the minerals which exist in these regions, as to the food fisheries which live in the sea, and as to the meteorological . . . conditions which prevail in these northern latitudes . . . The expedition will also have occasion to examine . . . the operation of the American whalers which frequent the northern waters of Canada, and of putting into force the customs and fisheries regulations which these whalers should observe."[38] Government departments involved in the enterprise were to be the departments of the Naval Service, which was entrusted with "the general direction of the expedition," Marine and Fisheries, Interior, Customs, and the Geological Survey, a branch of the department of Mines. Detailed instructions were issued at a later date and, by their very nature, would contribute to the general confusion and disharmony:

> The scientific work of the Canadian Arctic expedition under V. Stefansson relating to geology, geography, anthropology and biology (exclusive of marine biology) shall be under the direction of the Geological Survey, and the scientific staff engaged in the above work shall report to the Geological Survey.
>
> Summary reports of the progress of individual lines of investiga-

tion shall be made by each of these officers yearly, if possible, and the final report as soon after the return of the official as is practicable.

All scientific data related to the above lines of investigation, including manuscript notes, specimens, and photographic material resulting from the expedition, are to be the property of the Geological Survey and are to be turned in to the Survey as early as possible and not later than the acceptance of the manuscript report. Prints and photographs selected by him may be given to the leader of the expedition for his own use.

In planning the scientific work in the field and affording the necessary facilities for its execution, precedence is to be given by the leaders to the various branches of the work in the order of relative importance herein specified.

In the northern party the relative importance of the investigations are as follows:—exploration—1. geographical 2. oceanographical and biological (marine) 3. geological 4. magnetical 5. anthropological 6. biological (terrestrial) (meteorological is not specified as that can always be carried on without interference in the other investigations.) In the southern party the relative importance of the investigations are:—1. geological 2. geographical 3. anthropological 4. biological 5. photographical.

The officer appointed to the expedition to take charge of the depot shall make meteorological observations, and attend to the chronometers, tide gauge and recording instruments, except when relieved by one of the other officers who is temporarily detained at the depot.

The work for the northern party cannot be definitely specified in detail, as it will depend upon circumstances and must be left entirely to the judgement of the leader. The discovery of new land and its exploration are the prime objects of this exploration: the oceanography of the unknown sea and exploration of Banks and Prince Patrick's Island are also important, though secondary.

The work of the southern party shall be primarily the investigation and aerial mapping of the copper bearing and associated rocks of the mainland between Cape Parry and Kent Peninsula, and for approximately 100 miles inland, and on southern and eastern Victoria Land.

The work undertaken by these parties should be of a high order for this class of exploration and should mark a distinct advance over previous work. To secure such results the geographical and topographical subparties should follow closely the regular scheme for field parties engaged on reconnaissance work adopted by the Geological Survey. In working from the base depot these parties should be practically complete, distinct and independent units. This does not imply that a biologist or ethnologist could not accompany such a party, but merely that the programme of work and freedom of movement should not be interfered with or hampered by biological or ethnological considerations.

The chief of the southern party, as executive head, must afford every reasonable facility as circumstances permit to enable these sub-parties to carry out the above most important work. Mr. J. J. O'Neill shall have charge of the geological work and Mr. Chipman of the geographical work with Mr. Cox as his assistant.

The anthropological work shall consist of ethnological work and archeological research. So far as practicable, the work shall be divided between the two anthropologists (equally), one being given the eastern and one a western territory. When circumstances force them to work in the same area, Dr. Beuchat shall study religion, festivals, folklore, social organization, text and linguistics, and Dr. Jenness shall study physical characteristics, hunting, fishing and technology in general.

The biological work will consist of marine and terrestrial biology. Dr. Anderson will have charge of the mammology and ornithology, and Mr. Johansen, if with the southern party, of the marine biology, entomology, botany, etc.

In all branches of scientific work full and representative collections are to be made, so far as possible, for the scientific collections and museum of the survey.[39]

The estimated cost for the four-year expedition would be between $75,000 and $85,000, roughly two-thirds of which would be required in the spring of 1913 to buy a vessel and outfit the party. Supplementary estimates for the "patrol of the northern waters of Canada" were to provide money for the expedition of 1912–13 and 1913–14. Scientific material, other results, and collections belonged to the government. "Mr. Stefansson would, however, be free to deliver public lectures, write magazine articles, and make general use of the information he had acquired, provided the first use of this information is given to the Canadian Government." Stefansson's services were to be free, and he was to have "full responsibility, and to have the choice of the men going on the expedition, and of the ships, provisions, and outfit needed for the trip."[40] He was answerable only to G. J. Desbarats, deputy minister of the Naval Service.

At the same time, the government cleared up a constitutional problem involving itself and the mother country within the context of Empire; this would give added authority and weight to the annexation of lands in the Arctic not transferred by the order-in-council of 1880:

> So far as the lands on which the flag is so planted are already, in virtue of the Order-in-Council [1880] part of Canadian territory no question can arise as to the authority of your Government to deal with the matter, but as it is an established part of the law of the Empire that no Governor has a general delegation of authority to effect annexation of territory, His Majesty's Government are advised that in order to remove any doubt as to the validity of the proceedings of the Canadian Government—with the aim of which they are in full sympathy—it is desirable that formal authority should be given for the annexation of any lands to the north of Canada not already belonging to any foreign power which may not yet be British territory. I have accordingly received His Majesty's commands to convey to the Governor-General authority, with the advice of the Privy Council of the Dominion, to take possession of and annex to, His Majesty's Dominions any lands lying to the north of Canadian territory as defined in the Order[-]in[-] Council of 1880 which are not within the jurisdiction of any civilized power.
>
> . . . As it is not desirable that any stress should be laid on the fact that a portion of the territory may not already be British, I do not consider it advisable that this despatch should be published, but it should be permanently recorded as giving authority for annexation to the Governor-General in Council.
>
> . . . I have to add that if your Ministers consider it desirable His Majesty's Government will be prepared when the result of the expedition and the extent of the lands in question are known, to issue a fresh Order[-]in[-]Council supplementing that of July 31, 1880.[41]

Thus armed, Stefansson set about to acquire the men, material, and ship necessary for the extensive voyage. In reality, most of the organization, selection of men, and general administrative work was relegated to Anderson who, because of the May deadline, was forced to work under extreme pressure.[42] Yet within three months, Anderson was able to put together a very respectable organization, including fifteen scientists or specialists. Stefansson was to have had exclusive control over this. His trip to Europe, however, to attend a scientific conference and purchase delicate scientific equipment meant that someone he knew and trusted would be left with this responsibility. The only stipulation for selection of personnel that Stefansson required was a rather formidable one. "No one will be taken anywhere except to the base from which he is to work. From that base there will be no question of being taken to other places—every man is expected to *get* to wherever he wants to be within 400 miles of a base. We will provide Eskimo companions but the white man will have to walk as many steps as they and to depend on themselves."[43] This was a rather tall order for scientific men who, for the most part, would be going north for the first time: Stefansson, it is obvious, wanted recruits in his own image. And this was to spell trouble for his future relations with members of the scientific staff. Personally, he was reluctant to take any man who refused to adapt— even at the price of lowering the scientific status of the expedition: ". . . if they will insist on having hardships [to face] dismiss them in favor of men less qualified technically and physically, for the right temperament is more important than health or strength."[44] Stefansson may have been correct, but during the expedition he would become scornful and paternalistic because even these handpicked individuals did not aspire to his demands.

Anderson, already swamped with applications, attempted to comply with Stefansson's desires regarding the personnel, but had to turn his attention to the provisioning of the venture. With little or no experience, he accomplished the task admirably, following the suggestions of Captain Pederson who Stefansson had hoped would command the expedition's vessel. Complications were to arise when it was decided that, because of the expanded scope of the expedition and the division into northern and southern parties, a second ship would be required. But the resulting confusion and chaos attendant upon proper provisioning could in no way be a reflection on Anderson's or Stefansson's initial efforts.

Perhaps the touchiest aspect of readying the expedition and the best example of the folly of haste was the choice of the *Karluk* as the ship. On his return from the north in 1912, Stefansson made plans to secure a vessel suitable for his new exploits. He engaged Theodore Pederson, a respected whaling captain, and three firms of shipping inspectors to scout out suitable vessels for sale on the Pacific coast. Three vessels were found: the *Jeannette*, the *Elvira*, and the *Karluk*. The last was the preference of Stefansson's scouts. Despite the fact that she had been a whaling ship since 1889—a long time for any wooden barquentine—she was considered suitable for ice work. Since the whaling industry was in an absolute decline, she was rather inexpensive as whaling vessels went, according to Stefansson. In 1909 she was sold for $15,000; in 1913 she was for sale "at $10,000 although her condition is better than it was four years ago on acount of certain important repairs which have been completed since." The government would have to look no further, for Stefansson, seeing a bargain, had placed a $500 deposit on the *Karluk* in full expectation that his sponsors would pay the balance.[45] And this the government did,[46] anxious to proceed at full steam as soon as possible, without so much as looking into the question. Stefansson always maintained that the *Karluk* was the only vessel capable of withstanding the strains of the arctic ice, and that charges of her being unsound were unwarranted.[47] Yet the condition—real or imagined—of the *Karluk* is crucial to the understanding of later relations between members of the expedition.

Almost as soon as the government had purchased the *Karluk*, and had her transferred to Esquimault Dock, the engineer commander, having higher technical standards than Stefansson or even an American whaling captain, advised Ottawa that substantial repairs were still required. Despite Stefansson's contention that important repairs had been completed before his purchase, the *Karluk* needed initially $4,400 of repairs;[48] less than a month later a further examination revealed "additional defects" to the tune of another $1,500.[49] This meant that roughly $6,000 was being spent to repair a $10,000 ship that had, according to Stefansson, undergone important repairs prior to sale. The lists submitted by both the engineer commander and Captain R. A. Bartlett, who was to command the ship, indicate that the *Karluk* had to be overhauled from stem to stern.[50] To top this off, on the eve of the *Karluk's* departure from Esquimault, Desbarats received a coded message revealing Bartlett's honest appraisal of the ship's fitness even after all the repairs: "Captain Bartlett has made careful examination of Karluk, he states he considers ship absolutely unsuitable to remain in winter ice. Karluk could take expedition and leave them, ship returning south for winter. Her lines and build are unsuited for being jammed in the ice, besides not having sufficient beams and sheathing."[51] Such a judgement was, no doubt, partly based on Bartlett's association with Peary in the Eastern Arctic, for the vessel used there, the *Roosevelt*, was built to Peary's demanding specifications.[52] Bartlett's standards were not only demanding, but based on experience as well.

Such a revelation so late in the game could prove embarrassing to Desbarats and Stefansson. All Stefansson could do was reply rather weakly that the "Karluk has wintered in the Arctic a dozen times and is as good as any whaler in Western Arctic. We have to use [the] only ship we have."[53] She may have been a good tough whaling ship capable of wintering in the Arctic in a properly prepared winter haven, but to deliberately put her into the ice—or even entertain such an idea as Stefansson did at one point[54]—

would not be the wisest course of action. What was serious was that the Dominion government concurred with Stefansson, even though it was evident that the *Karluk* had been a bad buy. Under normal circumstances, it probably would have paid more attention to the safety factor, but the pressure of time made it take a tremendous risk with the lives of the men who would sail on the *Karluk*. But there was no turning back; the expedition had to proceed as best it could with the available men, resources, and equipment. All it awaited was Stefansson to take command.

As preparations for the expedition went ahead in early 1913, Stefansson was in Europe and the United States. While abroad, he made advance arrangements for a lecture tour of North America. The lectures would be based on the exploits and findings of the forthcoming Canadian Arctic Expedition.[55] Anderson acknowledged that Stefansson's reason for the trip, to obtain equipment, was legitimate but charged that his major preoccupations were to attend the International Geographic Congress in Rome, and to "sell all the prospective results of the expedition" to magazines, papers, and newsreel companies.[56] This was largely true: publicity was arranged and story rights were sold. The government had given the commander this privilege, and Stefansson went on to ensure his control by persuading the Canadian government on the eve of the expedition's departure that "every member [of the Canadian Arctic Expedition] should promise to take every precaution in his power to prevent news of the expedition getting into circulation prior to the issuing of the official announcement of the expedition and every man should agree neither to publish any written article nor to give lectures within two years from the return of the expedition, except on special permission given by the leader of the expedition."[57] It was obvious that Stefansson was trying to protect his exclusive contracts with the news media. It should have been apparent that, even with official government sanction, he could not but arouse disappointment and outright hostility from aspiring scientists. The latter depended on publication to establish or enhance their own professional status. They did not discover Stefansson's "arrangement" until after the expedition was heading towards the Arctic.

With Stefansson away spending the "play time" he had thought of in 1912[58] with fellow scientists on both sides of the Atlantic, and with time running so short, the Canadian government was anxious that he return and assume the helm. Small details concerning final arangements and personnel had to be completed; otherwise, warned an anxious Desbarats, "[the] expedition will be delayed if you are unable to attend these."[59] Stefansson was able to spare only a few days at a time in Ottawa. On 3 May 1913, for instance, he swooped into Ottawa, attended to aspects of the expedition and took the oath of allegiance to the king, thereby becoming a British subject.[60] Then he departed.

And yet his excuses for being away were often purely personal: "Had I been able to stay in Ottawa, instead of New York, things no doubt would have gone somewhat smoothly with regard to the Expedition but I simply had to get my book ready for the press in order to have something to live on, for, as you know, I have no salary from anybody; and the details of the Expedition down here take so much of my time that I have been able to put only an hour or two a day on the matter of getting the copy of my book ready."[61] Only in the last week of May did Stefansson arrive to spend time in Ottawa and then he was rushed. The entire expedition was waiting for him on the west coast. Brock, Desbarats, and Stefansson devoted the last days of May to arranging the final instructions to be issued,[62] much to the chagrin of Anderson and other members of the southern section, who had not received at any time any written orders or instructions while in Ottawa.[63]

Because the expedition was to be expanded and divided into two sections, Brock accepted Stefansson's suggestion that a second ship, the *Alaska*, be purchased.[64] Stefansson himself was not happy with the prospect of a split command which, it appears, was instigated by the upper echelons of the Geological Survey. The latter were concerned about the possible neglect of their work for the sake of exploration. The Geological Survey really wanted something entirely different from Stefansson—a scientific investigation of the stretch of seacoast around Coronation Gulf. The only connection with Stefansson's exploring plan was that his ship was to be used to get these scientists to their base of operations. Stefansson did not look forward to the creation of a divided command in any shape or form:

Because it has been suggested that the expedition recruit among its members certain representatives of government departments who shall not be fully under the command of the man at the time in charge of this section to which they are detailed, I would suggest that you might make some inquiries from Mr. Murray in regard to the Shackleton Antarctic expedition, where a similar situation existed.

Serious difficulties which have never gotten into the public press occurred on Shackleton's expedition on account of just such arrangements as are now proposed with regard to our expedition: in one case because the captain of the ship refused to follow the instructions of the commander of the expedition; and in several cases because scientific men had special agreements with the expedition or because they had been allowed to carry scientific apparatus which was either their own personal property or the property of some person or organization other than the expedition.[65]

His warning went unheeded for, although the final instructions did give Stefansson overall command, the expedition was divided into sub-groupings with scientific work relating to geology, geography, anthropology, and biology under the direction of the Geological Survey. The scientific staff would report to the Geological Survey. The sub-parties were to use orthodox methods in their investigations following closely the usual procedures adopted by the Geological Survey.[66] They were to stick to their particular projects and carry them out in no unusual fashion. According to Anderson, Stefansson was not pleased:

> [Stefansson] stated that it was desirable for the expedition to accomplish work of value, and that if the opportunity offered [appeared] to do such work, that the leaders of the parties should not hesitate to go forward for the reason that such activities were not explicitly covered by instructions in advance. Instances were cited where former expeditions had failed to accomplish adequate results when opportunities had occurred on their voyages, through lack of initiative of commanders, and their relying too closely upon detailed orders from Ottawa, which in the nature of things would not cover all possible contingencies or possibilities.[67]

Despite these drawbacks, Stefansson was confident, telling the press that he could "wipe off the face of the earth a million miles of unexplored territory."[68] Asked as to the possible commercial value of any new lands, he pointed out that "two hundred years ago Canada was considered to be nothing better than a trapper's waste and a land of ice and snow. Sixty years ago Alaska was sold for a song and no one thought it was worth developing. Six years ago the nations refused to be bothered with Spitzbergen, and now its coal fields have made it coveted by all. It is not beyond possibility that the new lands to the north, if there are any, will be of value some day."[69] This argument from analogy was a Stefansson trademark, appealing on the surface but dangerous if applied to any and all situations. Here was a theme that he would extend to embrace all northern territories in Canada, one that can be properly identified with the name Stefansson. The year was 1913; all Stefansson had to do was prove himself.

5

Breakdown

Stefansson had built his second expedition into an imposing edifice, apparently succeeding beyond all his imagination; he appeared to have the backing of an agency, the Canadian government, with unlimited resources. He had freed himself of the tight financial controls of the American organizations with their limited funds. He sensed he was on the threshold of acquiring unlimited influence with those men—particularly in Canada —who made policy and controlled the public purse strings.

Yet in Stefansson's striving for security and adequate backing for his new expedition, something of his own goals were lost. By force of circumstances—the struggle to acquire backers—he compromised his desire to continue and refine his ethnological pursuits in exchange for a grandiose expedition geared mainly to geographical exploration. Even before the expedition, which was Stefansson's own creation, was under the Dominion's control, Stefansson's position and function were subtly altered. Stefansson found that, by yielding to the goals first of the American institutions and eventually to the blandishments of the Canadian government, his original purpose had been blunted. He had had to sacrifice his original intentions regarding the people of Victoria Land. In a sense, he was being used by the Canadian government for its purposes, not his own. The enterprise had grown beyond his control. Throughout the expedition, Stefansson's position as its head was to be challenged. He reacted by trying to build up his freedom of initiative to offset this predicament.

For its part, the Canadian government was somewhat derelict in leaving the planning and organization of so complex an enterprise to Stefansson and Anderson, whose experience in the field was limited to equipping and operating a two-man expedition, not one with more than two dozen individuals, and disposing of funds that were less than one one-hundredth of those the new expedition was to entail. Stefansson, in particular, was not the sort of man who could devote concentrated attention to minute and petty details. In the spring of 1913, he appeared too busy with publishers and conventions to attend to his proper duties. So eager was the Canadian government to have its own expedition that it acted somewhat imprudently and rashly in taking over Stefansson's project virtually intact. The expedition was further expanded, but there was no attempt to think out a new integrated program. The Geological Survey was merely attached to Stefansson's enterprise with little thought being given to details of command or logistic support. The ensuing haste and flurry and internal contradictions of the structure and objectives of the organization would leave their mark. Assembling the Canadian Arctic Expedition was one thing; getting it to work properly was another. There were storm warnings on the northern horizon. Even before the Canadian Arctic Expedition reached the Arctic, it began to crumble.

Dissatisfaction began in Ottawa itself, especially in the Geological Survey. R. W. Brock, along with his lieutenant, O. E. LeRoy, were understandably intent on protecting the interests of the Geological Survey, despite the fact that the formal instructions gave overall authority to the Naval Service. Brock, of course, had been chiefly responsible for the government's initial involvement with the expedition; the Geological Survey's affairs included natural and human history as well as geological investigations, and Brock did not want to see sole priority given to exploration. The Geological Survey staff were anxious that they and their department be given as much latitude as possible. Many must have shared the sentiments of K. G. Chipman, the southern section's topographer, which were penned in the preface to his diary:

> This book is the diary of K. G. Chipman while geographer with the Canadian Arctic Expedition. He has been attached from the Geological Survey of Canada and has in no way severed his connection with that institution. His instructions for work are signed by R. W. Brock . . . and on his return from the expedition [he] returns to the Survey. His salary is paid by the Survey and the regulations of that institution together with some few regulations in his instructions, apply to his work while with the expedition. He is not bound, unless it is of his own free will, by any expedition or any other regulations pertaining to his work.[1]

In other words, Chipman regarded himself as being directly responsible to one part of the expedition, that outfitted by the Geological Survey; in no way, he implied, could he be made to answer to the Naval Service or to the commander of the expedition.

This, moreover, was the position of more than one member of the Geological Survey. As later events were to underline, the government scientists were acting as a group. And they had been encouraged to take this position by their superiors in the Geological Survey, particularly W. H. Boyd and O. E. LeRoy.[2] These two gentlemen, having the ear of the Survey's director, R. W. Brock, were instrumental in formulating the Survey's policy within the Canadian Arctic Expedition. To Boyd and LeRoy's way of thinking—and later to some indeterminate extent that of R. G. McConnell, Brock's successor—the Naval Service had committed a grave error in allowing the expedition to fall to Stefansson.

> In our opinion, the Naval Service showed great weakness and should instead have taken a strong hand and appointed one man of un-doubted executive ability and well experienced too in outfitting Arctic Expeditions.
>
> A comparison of the method of outfitting the Canadian Arctic Expedition with the methods used by Shackleton, Scott, or even Captain Bernier serves to show the entire lack of practical supervision by the Naval Service, and the lack of an efficient and qualified leader. The expedition actually started from Canada not knowing what they had on board the ship but yet knowing that they were incompletely equipped.
>
> We considered the condition of affairs so serious before the men left Ottawa, that we then approached Mr. Brock and recommended that he withdraw Messrs. O'Neill, Chipman and Cox from the ex-pedition pointing out the improbability of these men being able to reach their base without waste of valuable time. We offered, if given the opportunity, to place these men in their field of work independent of Stefansson's expedition by August 1st, 1913. This proposal was not entertained. . . .
>
> Messrs. Chipman and Cox were made aware of our views regard-ing the apparent lack of the necessary qualifications of the leader. They continually sought our advice which was freely given and it was to our regret that we were not in a position to take the necessary measures to withdraw them from the expedition.[3]

LeRoy went further and questioned the scope and validity of Stefans-son's authority, as well as his administrative talents. He argued that

Stefansson "only assumed 'full responsibility' theoretically and showed himself lacking in executive ability and irresponsible."[4] Boyd and LeRoy were so intransigent that later in 1914, when it was feared that Stefansson was lost and Desbarats suggested that the government should send out a search expedition, both stated categorically that enough Survey lives had already been lost on the *Karluk*. This made it "imperative that the Survey shall not allow other of its members to take any risks out of the ordinary to rescue Stefansson, whose life, to put it quite pointedly, is not worth it."[5]

It is not difficult to see that the Geological Survey was very upset about the expedition as conceived and enlarged and, on top of that, having to answer to the Naval Service and to Stefansson. The Survey, like "interested members of the Naval Service,"[6] could not change the nature of the decisions taken by the government. The agency had tried to manoeuvre itself out of the predicament by getting Brock and Desbarats to agree that Survey members were to employ standard Survey procedures in their work and answer directly to their department on matters of research. This at least might help smooth the waters.

On the west coast, most of the Geological Survey men, about to head off to the Arctic from Victoria, became despondent. Their enthusiasm for the adventure waned each time they turned their eyes toward the *Karluk* which symbolized to them the pre-history of the Canadian Arctic Expedition and its probable fate. Chipman, whose disposition and views were to mirror the Survey's pessimistic convictions, was perhaps the most eloquent in damning the vessel. The *Karluk* possessed a grimy appearance: "There she was piled high with fresh meat, vegetables, snowshoes, skins, alcohol drums, canoes, and many and varied boxes and cases"[7] and the entrances to the cabins were blocked with bales of nets, boxes, and wire rope.[8] But she was no great prize for "engineers, mates, the cook, and everybody condemned her."[9] The new steering gear and re-fitted engine were in the habit of breaking down.[10] "Time has simply increased Captain Bartlett's condemnation of the Karluk. She is supposed to do seven knots and we perhaps average five for the trip."[11] The chief engineer, Munroe, pointed out that the *Karluk* was a brigantine whaler, with an auxiliary "coffee pot of an engine. . . . never entended to run more than two days at a time."[12] Her engines were virtually useless. Once, when she ran into a piece of driftwood, the ship, being unable to push it out of the way, was forced to stop, then go astern.[13] She fared no better in her first encounters with ice.[14] It was even hinted that, prior to purchase by the government, a naval expert engaged by the Hudson's Bay Company "did not consider the Karluk as a safe ship for freight cartage."[15] Apparently, both Captain Pederson, who had recommended her to Stefansson, and Captain Mogg told expedition members that the *Karluk* was not built for arctic work, but solely for North Pacific sealing.[16] According to Chipman at least, the *Karluk* inspired little confidence amongst her crew and passengers.

After the purchase of a second ship, the *Alaska*, for the Southern Party's use, most of the men's time on the voyage from Victoria to Nome "was spent as longshoremen, opening cases and dividing the contents into two parts which were then repacked into boxes and labelled N or S."[17] Yet it was impossible to locate material that would be destined for the Southern Party; no one knew where anything was because no system had been devised for numbering and stowage of the *Karluk*.[18] Chipman wrote in his diary, "the responsibility for systemizing things has never been given to any one man, and with so many doing a little and doing it differently, there has been no system or responsibility whatsoever. I guarantee that many omissions and duplications will reveal themselves in the next year or two. I was thoroughly mad today and once more said that if I had known three months ago all I know now, I'd never had been here, however, I *am* here and it is all experience."[19] Stefansson, too, corroborated Chipman. Somehow, for example, fifteen kegs of vinegar found their way to the *Karluk*'s hold. Stefansson was dismayed:

> I never looked at the provision list to see whether we have more in other parts of the ship, but even 15 kegs are, in my opinion enough for 15 years . . . [o]wing, no doubt, to the hurry in which the work was done, a good many of the boxes repacked by our men at Esquimault when the division [of goods] was made between the northern and southern parties, were either poorly packed or, in some cases, half empty . . . we have had a good deal of trouble and difficulty in finding certain articles that got shoved underneath the other cargo.[20]

While in Victoria, Chipman failed to detect any enthusiasm in other members of the expedition, "all the experienced and responsible members [were] thoroughly disgusted" having no confidence in Stefansson and little assurances of getting good work done.[21]

Disillusionment with the *Karluk* was matched by the Geological Survey staff's evaluation of their commander, Stefansson. At Nome, aside from suffering criticism from Anderson's wife, who had accompanied her husband, Stefansson was confronted by disgruntled and soured men. He was to make light of the whole affair later, claiming that it was a simple case of scientific men worrying about petty matters, such as having enough water to take a bath, or their refusal to believe that fresh water could be obtained from the top of old salt water ice.[22] Never once did he mention the seriousness of the confrontation or issues at stake.

Yet, at a general meeting in Nome, the spokesman for the men, James Murray for the Northern Party, and K. G. Chipman for the Southern, corralled Stefansson, posing fundamental questions about the expedition: "questions très graves, sur lesquelles nous n'étions nullement fixés, et auxquelles il était indispensable qu'il répondit."[23] The questions were practical ones, which the men felt had to be answered: food supplies for the Southern Party, clothing, sleeping bags; headquarters for the Southern Party huts, travelling equipment (sledges, dogs, sledging provisions), fuel, communication between bases, mail, co-ordination of the work of the Southern Party; authority to trade and purchase locally articles necessary for the ethnologists, Beuchat and Jenness. They were questions which Chipman, in particular, had raised in Ottawa where Stefansson's answers "are the same now as then."[24] Stefansson "could not tell us where the southern base would be . . . his idea is still that it should be where there is fuel and game —efficiency of work is entirely secondary," Chipman recorded in his diary.[25] It must be admitted that Stefansson failed to expand his ideas to adapt to the new circumstances of the expedition. Apparently, Stefansson was taken aback by this confrontation. He not only considered Chipman a "kicker," but he informed his inquisitors that they were "impertinent,"[26] that they had no business to ask such questions, and that they should have confidence in him.[27] As Beuchat reported "[d]e plus Stefansson a pris un air très blessé et nous a fait clairement comprendre qu'il considérait cet interrogatoire comme attentatoire à son autorité."[28]

Those most upset by Stefansson's position were certain members of the Northern Party, particularly Murray, the oceanographer. Stefansson intimated quite forcefully that he intended to put the Northern Party's ship, *Karluk*, into the ice.[29] The general feeling was that she would never come out and would be crushed by the relentless, unforgiving pressure.[30] Murray was certain that, if this were done, all his work would be ruined, and he might lose his life.[31] He was therefore anxious that the Northern Party should establish a base on shore as well as on board the *Karluk*. Stefansson's response shocked all concerned, for he ignored Murray's pleas and stated that lives were secondary to the attainment of the objectives of the expedition.[32] In 1921, Stefansson would write that he "was one of those who think the fighting of the Great War worth while not so much to attain what was attained as to prevent what has been prevented. But I could never see how any one can extol the sacrifice of a million lives for political progress who condemns the sacrifice of a dozen lives for scientific progress. For the advance of science is but the advance of truth, and 'The truth shall make you free'."[33] He tried unsuccessfully to dump Murray in favour of Johansen, but the latter also refused to accompany the Northern Party because of Stefansson's lack of concern.[34] Stefansson pointed out he could order Johansen to accompany the Northern Section but would not use compulsion;[35] instead he implied he could enlarge Johansen's work role since "he did not feel bound by his instructions and . . . would reverse them if he chose."[36] Johansen, although anxious to do more important work, refused the carrot. To appease Murray, on 17 July Stefansson promised to place another vessel, the *Mary Sachs*, at his disposal for oceanographic work. On the very next day, however, Stefansson told Chipman that the *Sachs* would be used primarily to establish a base at the "upper end" of Prince Albert Sound.[37]

Stefansson's ambiguous position and manner generated considerable tension between the rest of the expedition and himself. It should have been obvious to Stefansson—as it was to become later when the expedition went from crisis to crisis—that, as far as arctic expeditions were concerned, he was a one-man operator, an improvisor, lacking the requisite administrative ability to run such a large, highly structured venture. His apparent non-concern for the overall operation may have stemmed from a lack of interest in its all-embracing scope. After all, not only had a Southern Section been tacked on by the Canadian government, but Stefansson had previously compromised his anthropological expedition to gain financial support from geographically oriented institutions. In the light of the unsatisfactory results of the "confrontation" at Nome and the failure of the scientific staff to secure the assurances they desired, the expedition members decided to make the best of the situation. Members of the Southern Party moved goods from the *Karluk* to the *Alaska*, and struck out for Collinson Point. After the Southern Section had established its own base camp at Collinson Point, many members had the nagging feeling that Stefansson would interfere with their work. They felt that once the Northern Section was established, Stefansson would come to the Southern Party and take charge.[38] The Southern Section had eight individuals involved in full-time scientific investigation, and no assistants. The organization of Stefansson's section, they maintained, made the commander redundant—unless new Eskimo peoples were discovered on whom Stefansson could apply his talents. Jenness, not Stefansson, was to make the ethnological investigations around Coronation Gulf. It was assumed by members of the Southern Party that if no new natives were discovered—or if the *Karluk* were lost—Stefansson would become merely a general assistant and make his way back to Anderson's headquarters. This was totally unacceptable to the men of the Geological Survey, because of what they considered to be his unsatisfactory attitude and their own immediate responsibilities to their Ottawa principals.[39] As early as July 1913, the members of the Geological Survey had forecast the turn of events and they had made up their minds on this issue long before the expedition headed north. Their determination to oppose such an intervention to the point of resigning and returning south, if it occurred, worked to their advantage.

But return he did. Captain Bartlett, contrary to Stefansson's instructions and contrary to the experience of whalers in the waters north of Alaska,[40] had not kept the *Karluk* close to shore. On 13 August 1913, the vessel became caught in the ice and grounded. There was a general feeling on board that the *Karluk* would remain frozen in for the duration of winter,[41] and the crew made preparations accordingly. On 20 September 1913, Stefansson, never content with inactivity, together with a number of companions—Diamond Jenness, George Wilkins, and a few Eskimos—left the *Karluk* in the hope of finding game to provision the ship; the excursion was to take approximately ten days. The evidence suggests that this was a normal hunting trip.[42] With the passage of time, Stefansson's detractors accused him of abandoning his ship because he knew full well that it was in great danger. Mrs. Anderson wrote to her husband about a conversation that she had had with Frederick W. Maurer, a member of the *Karluk*. According to Maurer, Stefansson was visibly upset by the *Karluk*'s situation: he would not eat, appeared intimidated by Bartlett, and wandered aimlessly about the ship. Maurer claimed he had overheard a conversation between the commander and Jack Hadley, a passenger, in which Stefansson definitely expressed his fear for the loss of the ship, the end of the expedition, and an adverse world reaction.[43] Yet such testimony was given after the fact, and perhaps influenced by the subsequent course of the expedition. Nor can more credence be placed in a report of the Royal Northwest Mounted Police, which implied that Stefansson's actions had been suspicious. The report, which finally filtered down to Ottawa, recorded that "Stefansson appears to have left the 'Karluk' just in time, as you will see she had disappeared the next morning."[44] In fact, Stefansson indulged in some grievous soul-searching over the *Karluk*'s disappearance and there is strong evidence to suggest that he wished he had never left her.[45]

Nevertheless, it was Stefansson's misfortune to be away when the weather turned for the worse and a violent storm carried the *Karluk* away on its ill-fated drift. In August 1913 the *Karluk* was trapped in the ice off Alaska and caught in a northwesterly drift. On 11 January 1914, she was crushed by the ice pressure and abandoned. Some of the crew reached nearby Wrangel Island, while others struck out on their own to find safety. In all, however, eleven men died in one fashion or another, including five of the scientific party.[46] It was and is the greatest arctic disaster since the disappearance of the Franklin expedition. Subsequently a charge was made that these events had "resulted from the Karluk's being 'unsound'."[47]

The *Karluk*'s disappearance left Stefansson without a crew and, in reality, without his Northern Section. Things might have worked out had he been in a region rich in ethnographic material and was thus able to use his anthropological talents. But the north shore of Alaska could never offer him anything like the relatively untouched Eskimos of Coronation Gulf. In the meantime, Stefansson began working on another plan to salvage something out of a venture which he now considered on the brink of failure, both for his prestige and self-esteem and for the sake of the whole expedition. He would do almost anything, he said, to this end.[48] In this effort, he was to encounter further hostility from the Southern Section who, quite understandably, feared undue interference. The main work of the party on board the *Karluk* was to have been the exploration of the region west of the Parry Islands, particularly west and northwest of Prince Patrick Island. Without the *Karluk* and its support, this was impossible, but by late October 1913, Stefansson had formulated a new plan:

> Now that we find ourselves situated as we are, we shall try to do as much scientific work as there is opportunity for. The two main features of my plans for the winter are a sledge journey north from Barter Island and the exploration of the Mackenzie Delta. It seems to me that a sledge journey north from Barter Island may possibly prove of considerable geographic interest. . . .
>
> If we were to attain a point only 100 miles from shore, we might, by doing so, determine the edge of the continental shelf at least, while if we find ice conditions favorable, 300 miles does not seem too much to hope for. So far as I know, no vessel has been over 50 miles from shore in the longitude of Barter Island.
>
> The Mackenzie is the largest river in Canada, and it is likely to attain sometime a commercial importance second only to that of the St. Lawrence . . . It seems likely that a careful survey of the more important of [the Mackenzie Delta's] channels will bring to light a route which will be safe for a steamer drawing 6½ feet which it could

carry all the way, that is, 1500 miles south to Smith's Rapids. As it is impossible to tell when the Mackenzie may spring into an importance comparable to that of the Yukon, it seems that the charting of its delta and the soundings of its channels, is a work of great practical value, for freight can be brought much more cheaply from such specific ports as Victoria or Vancouver to the lower portion of the Mackenzie Valley than it can to the south down the River, so long as a canal is not dug past the Smith's Rapids. If rich mineral discoveries do not bring the Mackenzie into sudden prominence, there is bound to be a steady, but slow, growth brought about by the non-mineral resources of the country.[49]

With this in mind, Stefansson set about to prepare for his new scheme and wrote to the Naval Service in full confidence they would assent; although the original plans were altered, they did tally with the wide scope given in the original instructions.[50] In mid-December, his appearance at Collinson Point threw members of the Southern Party into a turmoil— "What we had always expected *might* happen, *had* happened."[51] The day following his arrival, Stefansson held a three hour conference on board the *Mary Sachs* with Chipman, Cox, O'Neill, and Johansen, but they were suspicious of his reassurances that he would not interfere in the affairs of their party. They were unimpressed with his Mackenzie Delta surveying scheme, which Chipman—the man Stefansson wanted for the task— privately scoffed at as being "work of a lifetime."[52] It was ironical, and an indication of Stefansson's inability to judge character, that he was totally unaware of Chipman's disposition, for he concluded that, initially at least, he commanded the topographer's confidence and enthusiasm for the work.[53] Chipman, whose strong views seem to reflect best the feelings of the Southern Party in general, was certain that Stefansson could not help but interfere:

> He is [the] leader of the whole expedition, the men look on him as the man who hired them, and Anderson has been accustomed to giving in to him. Aside from the question of which is the stronger character[,] I am very certain that if Stefansson comes in here, he will become the real boss of this party. He may not have any intentions of assuming control or interfering in any way but the men *will* go to him and even if he refers most of the cases to Anderson he is sure (it is his nature) in many of them to give an opinion not a decision. To the men there is something of a glamour about him and they will go to him whether he wants it or not. Even in this one day here men have gone to him

and he has not only given them the decisions but he has criticized several things and has taken steps to see that they are different. . . . He is perhaps right in these things but he is plainly taking authority out of Anderson's hands. . . . if Anderson has any backbone he will either make Stefansson assume full control or absolutely none. No compromise can be satisfactory situated as we are.[54]

Chipman and other members of the Southern Party never wavered from this position and when a similar situation arose in February and March of 1914 they were to impress it upon Anderson, demanding that he take a bold stand. The members of the Geological Survey assured him of their support in any confrontation.[55] Stefansson's presence, they felt, would be "insidious" and lower their efficiency and quality of work. After having read over Stefansson's instructions and the personal instructions from Brock to his men, Chipman became convinced that "Command of the Southern Party is distinctly given to Dr. Anderson. In our personal instructions, there is nothing to indicate that we are in any way responsible to anyone except to our department and the leader of the Southern party."[56] This view was consistent with that of other members of the Southern Party and with that of their superiors in the Geological Survey in Ottawa. Their views, like Stefansson's, may not have been impartial or objective; for each side responded in subjective fashion to the issues at hand. This was to be the root of much discord.

Chipman was to remain quite unhappy about Stefansson's position and his presence. He and others were alarmed over the prospect that the *Mary Sachs*—bought by Stefansson for the use of the Southern Party—would now be diverted for Stefansson's exploration of the Beaufort Sea.[57] Chipman sympathized with Anderson, his chief, who was also very disappointed with Stefansson's arrival. "He [Anderson] says it was on the condition that he had entire control of this party that he came up here."[58] Both Anderson and Chipman were amazed that Stefansson had considered the safety of ships and crew secondary to pursuing the objectives of the expedition.[59] Now Stefansson appeared anxious to include Anderson's men in his own expeditions. Anderson, for one, could not concur in Stefansson's view that the end justified the means; "[Anderson] did not think it necessary to sacrifice his self-respect to attain ends."[60]

From Anderson's and Chipman's point of view, Stefansson lacked something every gentleman should have, integrity and dignity. Anderson saw Stefansson as unscrupulous. Chipman—and perhaps others—saw him as not only unscrupulous but debauched. When he approached Stefansson to protest about the vice and prostitution around them, and members of the expedition having relations with the Eskimo women, he was upset that Stefansson showed little concern. All Chipman could say was that he regretted "that some precaution was not taken to have an expedition of this size sent out by the government composed of men of some moral character,"[61] and he included Stefansson in this group. Moreover, Stefansson "doesn't play the game with his cards on the table and consequently we are suspicious of him."[62]

> He [Stefansson] repeated . . . that Peary had told him that he should never talk things over with the men but should simply give them orders and expect the men to follow them implicitly and unquestionably. He says he prefers to talk things over and to be frank with the men. My [Chipman] estimate of the situation is that for a leader of an expedition there are two types of men—1. a commander who will issue orders as orders and they will be carried out as such. The other is the man who is a leader and whom the men follow and co-operate with because of personal loyalty and confidence. The first type necessitates men who will carry out orders implicitly and applies to small expeditions with a definite object and of the college student type. The personnel of this expedition and its wide advertisement as having the largest scientific staff and men who are specialists in the line precludes its being classed in the first type. Stefansson says he does not wish to be such a commander and it seems to me that he is failing to follow in under the second head . . . there [is] on the part of the men no feeling of confidence or loyalty and consequently we follow only so far as our interests are concerned. What is needed with the staff we have is an efficient business manager and this he is too much of a dreamer to be.[63]

This attitude had been with the scientific staff since Victoria, becoming more determined with each small provocation—real or supposed. Chipman believed that Stefansson had to be put down before his actions, even his mere presence, hurt the Southern expedition irreparably: "I believed that if VS were confronted flatly and definitely he would back down and matters would be adjusted. I said it would have to be a showdown and that it was better to have it now. I was ready to stand behind anything he [Anderson] did."[64] If and when Anderson acted, he would not be acting on his own but with the collective and imposing support of his staff.

Stefansson was well aware of their hardening dispositions but went about his revised plans as though nothing was happening, thereby heightening tensions and suspicions. The Mackenzie Delta project was let slide, only to be revived later with much indecision by Stefansson over who should undertake it.[65] It was natural though that Stefansson should follow through with the second revised scheme, the ice expedition into the unknown Beaufort Sea. Perhaps he sensed that this activity would give the expedition the success and publicity that could not be achieved with just the routine scientific work of the southern expedition. Stefansson seemed convinced that the work of the southern expedition would not be enough to make the enterprise respectable, that the government had to be given something for its money and to ease its concern over the sovereignty question. For instance, in February 1915, the explorer indicated that Anderson's position of the previous year had been damaging to both of them for "by reducing my chances of success [Anderson] has reduced that of all of us. Had luck favored us with 'land' or some other spectacular triumph, we would all have ridden in on a tidal wave of success. Likely, I would, perforce, have received the lion's share, but [Anderson] would have received his also. Even the most ultra-scientists are influenced by the paper they read at breakfast as much as by their technical journals."[66] Only by August 1915, after completing some successful sledging trips, could Stefansson confidently feel that, despite the alleged roadblocks placed in his path and despite the lower priority given the northern work after the *Karluk*'s disappearance, "the expedition is not going to be a failure after all, not even the northern programme."[67] Yet, within three months of this statement, he was in one of his melancholy moods. On another of his birthdays, as was his wont, he lamented "I am 36 today half an ordinary lifetime, and very little accomplished."[68]

But early in 1914, Stefansson was being challenged seriously. By mid-February 1914, matters came to a head and he was faced with a serious confrontation from the rest of the expedition. Over the winter months, Stefansson, with the ice-trip always in the forefront, had been busy trying to scrape together a new Northern Party from the resources that remained after the *Karluk*'s disappearance. To this end, he had been buying up entire stores from local agents whenever possible. In the case of two stores, he spent roughly $20,000. Stefansson realized that this was a large sum of money, "but I felt that the articles secured and the things they would enable us to attempt were worth it to the expedition and to the governmen."[69] Soon after these purchases, Stefansson claiming he was "without supplies" took an additional half ton of rations from the police stores at Herschel Island.[70] There was very little the police could do, for he was armed with a note from the comptroller of the Royal Northwest Mounted

Police, ordering them that "every assistance be given to the members of the Expedition."[71] His actions, apparently, were placing him in a bad light with men like J. W. Phillips, commander of "N" division at Athabaska Landing. Phillips had been alienated by Stefansson's brusque and cavalier attitude toward the police. In the eyes of the police, according to Chipman, Stefansson seemed to care little about the whereabouts of the *Karluk*, spending more of his time bragging about his new book, *My Life With the Eskimo*, published after the expedition had left Victoria. This apparent lack of concern did not improve the police's opinion of him.[72] Chipman's delight in such stories is an example of the sort of feelings that plagued the whole affair:

I learned here that VS completely succeed[ed] in "getting the goat of everybody here" [Herschel Island] and at Fort McPherson. It is strange but no one seems to have a good word for him; seldom have I seen a man for whom there are fewer good words than is the case for VS along this coast. It may be partially due to the climate or the men here but rather most of it must be due to VS himself. Inspector Phillips says he started out when he came here by telling him the incident of Fitzgerald and the matches and of Inspector Bates and the lunatic at Baily Island when VS wanted the RNWMP to send there for a lunatic [Eskimo] and Bates did not do so; and told how he practically had both these men removed. Inspector Phillips is not the *kind* of man to [be] bluffed or threatened by any intimations of such power. Everyone says Phillips is very strict and conscientious in his duty; and he wont let VS run the police force for him. The police were talking of taking butter and jam on their patrol to the fort and VS said "OK don't take any for me, I don't want such luxuries." He ate so much of what the police were taking for themselves that the patrol reached the fort short not only of luxuries but of any grub at all. Several times at the island VS was talking in the barracks to the white men and a native came in and he abruptly broke off without apology and talked with the native. This seems to seriously offend class distinction . . . Everyone here talks of the waste of grub from VS's outfit while on the *road* —this waste going to the natives under his eyes. A 50 lb. box of hard bread was used up in two days. Of the luxuries VS said "Oh the poor natives, they seldom have such things—we must give them some," and the natives proceeded to help themselves. Soon white men are without sugar, butter, rice, etc. VS secured from the fort 200 boxes of flour for our use in the delta work. Of this 50 boxes reached Peterson's place the rest going to the natives. VS talks of how he loves the natives['] grub, yet he secures his full share of white man's food, and of luxuries such as butter and jam he seems to get more than his share. Evidently the grub pile is just about the most serious of all considerations in this country and a man has to be mighty big or else mighty well liked to get away with what VS is doing in that line.[73]

As Cox reported, Stefansson seemed to have "an unfortunate knack of 'getting in the wrong' everywhere he goes."[74]

Chipman and other members of the expedition could gloat over such stories and rumours in comfortable amusement, although they may have had some qualms about the expedition's credibility with the northern population. However, once Stefansson began in February 1914 to request more supplies for his trip from the *Belvedere*, another vessel bought for the use of the Southern Section, they sat up and took notice: "if we let him go on we are doing so at the expense of our own work—to say nothing of our own reasonable comfort."[75] It was at this point that Anderson, with the support of other members of the Geological Survey, finally took a stand against what they believed to be encroachments on the success of their work.

When Stefansson's lieutenant and former member of the Anglo-American expedition, Storker T. Storkerson, arrived to collect goods and material for the ice foray—chisels, chronometers, dogs, sleds, and food—Anderson informed him that nothing could be spared.[76] Stefansson himself had not come since he had seen no need. He was sure his request would be filled. Besides, he had felt it necessary to go to Fort McPherson "to get and send mail."[77] Some of his opponents claimed that such a move was a deliberate Stefansson tactic. In their opinion, Stefansson had never had any intention of coming in person: "It is much easier for him to shove . . . off on someone else such an unsatisfactory and thankless job."[78] The fact that mail took precedence over expedition business made members of the Southern Party question Stefansson's credibility.

Stefansson had known about the mood of the members of the Southern Party since December, despite his statement that he had not expected such a development,[79] and had been careful not to cross swords with them.[80] Anderson, though, would not deal with Storkerson. Stefansson reported later that he was told that he would fail to get supplies unless he came in person, and that the topographic section, namely Chipman, would not perform any Mackenzie Delta survey work "until I came to Collinson Point and they would make it clear to me just what my position on the expedition was and receive assurances that their work would not be in future hampered or interfered with by me."[81] If the expedition on the sea ice was to move at all, Stefanson would have to go to Collinson Point.

News of the impending falling out spread rapidly along the arctic coast, diminishing Stefansson's credibility *vis-à-vis* white men and natives. White men, particularly those who sold their supplies, thought that the government might not honour Stefansson's commitments, that he was too much of a risk, and insisted on "an increased price as compensation."[82] Not only had Storkerson been refused the supplies requested by the commander, but he was finding it difficult to enlist natives to join the expedition. The native problem had really little connection with the 1913 situation, except to aggravate it.[83] Stefansson had apparently incurred the wrath of the Reverend C. E. Whittaker who had befriended the explorer on his previous arctic exploits and had been unfairly treated by Stefansson, who decried the unwholesome influence of missionary activity on the Eskimo in his book, *My Life With the Eskimo*.[84] In any case, Whittaker had sent a letter to the natives of Herschel Island warning that "VS and some of those with him wilfully and maliciously refused to believe in the work of God; they are bad after your women; look out for them; do not have anything to do with them."[85] In addition, Whittaker counter-attacked in public lecture and print in Toronto, denying that the missionary influence had been destructive. He claimed Stefansson had no use for religion and the Ten Commandments and charged that Stefansson had left a wife and child behind in the Arctic.[86] "We know the lives that abandoned men live away from the law and public opinion . . . We should care as much about the Salvation of souls as Stefansson cares about the bodies."[87]

Stefansson arrived at the Collinson Point camp on Sunday, 8 March, ready to do battle. After supper, a delicate "conference was held lasting until 3.00 a.m. the following morning." It is not clear who delivered the opening salvo, but, according to Chipman, Stefansson began "by telling us the history of the expedition and showing us that in conception and organization it was all his. He insisted that, in their arrangements and under the instructions, it was all his and that RMA [Anderson] was entirely the second in command . . . He insists that the plans and organizations are his and his alone and that the scientific instructions were outlined by him."[88] Stefansson had said much the same thing to George Phillips, a naval functionary at Esquimault: "No one realizes that it is all my expedition, that I formulated all this plan . . . long before the government had anything to do with the expedition."[89] Stefansson ignored the argument that the revised, two-tiered organization and scientific instructions were prepared by O. E. LeRoy of the Geological Survey at the request of R. W. Brock.[90] As supreme commander, he could change the program of the expedition to assure its success in any way he saw fit.[91]

Such an attitude upset all the Southern Party. The men simply wished to know where they stood in the overall plans, whatever they were to be, and they wanted it in writing.[92] Neither Anderson nor the other members of the Geological Survey would stand any longer for verbal orders "which often conflict and are too changeable . . . to work under with any degree of satisfaction." If Anderson were to take responsibility for his section, he had to have written guarantees: "I don't care to have the man higher up in a position to shift responsibility when he chooses to change his mind or forget."[93] Otherwise Anderson was willing to step down and let Stefansson run the entire show if he thought this would be more satisfactory. Stefansson refused, knowing that this would cause the bulk of the Southern Section to pick up and return to Ottawa.[94] The conference reached its peak when an exasperated Anderson rebuked Stefansson in an emotional outburst in front of the other members of the Southern Section saying that "on their last expedition he had wasted three years of his life[,] that he vowed that if he ever went with [Stefansson] it would not be further than Coney Island[,] that he had done best work when alone and that if they accomplished anything it had been more by good luck than good management."[95]

Anderson acknowledged that his authority was subordinate to Stefansson in all respects, but he suggested there were occasions when a subordinate might be justified in refusing to obey him.[96] Stefansson's attempt to "raid" the supplies and talent of the Southern Section was such a time. To Anderson, the Canadian Arctic Expedition would not be a scientific endeavour of the highest calibre if Stefansson had his way. "Mr. Stefansson . . . made the remarkable statement that the Expedition was not essentially scientific; that scientific men were inclined to be narrow-minded and engrossed in their own lines; that private individuals or a government would not finance a scientific expedition on its own merit unless it has the spirit of adventure to catch the public interest."[97] In Anderson's eyes, the expedition was a vehicle to promote the image of Stefansson, and to some extent he was right, considering some of Stefansson's aspirations. Anderson felt that he had been entrusted with the command of the Southern Party and that he was responsible to the government. He would see to it that Stefansson did not waste, in useless stunts, supplies and equipment initially intended for scientific research. The members of the Southern Party were men, he added, who had joined the expedition hoping to do some good scientific work, and they disliked being interfered with by someone who was a "bull-con artist" with no appreciation of scientific values. The scientific staff, Anderson reputedly went on, were afraid he would turn this expedition into a farce and a laughing stock as he had done with the previous one, this time by making useles ice journeys over the Beaufort Sea and wasting good supplies for newspaper notoriety.[98]

To Stefansson, however, the ice journey over the Beaufort Sea was not a stunt but a main feature of the original plans negotiated with the National Geographic Society and afterwards accepted by the Canadian government. The *Karluk* might have disappeared, but the ice work would be continued after Stefansson had weighed both sides of the question and had made his decision: "Seeing that I was in command of the expedition . . . it seemed to me that [if] the resources of the expedition were still adequate for this exploration with some prospect of success, I intended to attempt that exploration. I had considered all matters relating to the prospect of the whole expedition in a manner which seemed to me to be careful and I had decided that this ice work could be done without interfering seriously with the other work planned."[99] Without consultation, Stefansson had asserted his position and made the arbitrary decision which upset other members. He would take "volunteers"—even from the Southern Section—who were willing to live on a comparatively simple diet and he would use equipment that the Southern Party could spare without impairing their prospects for successful work. However, Stefansson himself was to decide what the Southern Section could spare and this left him open to charges of undermining the efforts of Anderson's section.

To Stefansson "the whole matter was only talk, and when the talking was over the plans of the expedition were just as they had been before . . . [T]he only matter to become serious was when I said I intended to take the [*Mary*] *Sachs* to Banks Island—as I had told Dr. Anderson in December I intended to do . . ." The *Mary Sachs* had been purchased as a tender for either section, but with the *Karluk* gone, Stefansson "now judged she was more needed by the northern than by the southern section."[100] Such issues caused many members to cry "foul." Stefansson implied that Anderson and company wanted to change the direction of the Northern work and were trying to thwart his program and embarrass him. This was not true. His opponents did not care what he did on his own, as long as his actions did not interfere with their work. The expedition—its ships and supplies—they contended, was not his private property to do with as he wished.

Stefansson considered such opposition a breach of discipline. Taking the initiative, and convinced of the correctness of his stand, he informed Ottawa that no action should be taken against Anderson and others—

implying that he was disposed to be benevolent towards them. However, he suggested that Desbarats should bring the dissidents into line before another incident occurred:

> I should suggest as for the best interests of the expedition, so long as you have confidence in my judgement, it is sufficient if it can be impressed on Dr. Anderson that he will be expected to attempt in good faith to carry out instructions given him by me and that the mere fact that he considers some other course wiser will not be considered an adequate excuse for disobedience unless it can be shown that grave conditions existed of which I had no knowledge when the instructions were issued. I consider it desirable, though less important, that the other members of the scientific staff understand they are under my command though they be on the southern section.[101]

The whole episode boiled down to different points of view as to each man's respective right to carry out his program. Each side felt justified in its own position regarding priorities, but Stefansson considered Anderson's position as mutinous. Strictly speaking, it was. Whether or not Anderson's intransigence was indeed justifiable is another matter, difficult to resolve even from the vantage point of today.

Stefansson had been visibly shaken by the confrontation at Collinson Point, especially by the position of his onetime friend and ally, Rudolph Anderson. It was hard for him to believe such a turn of events, and he offered the following explanation, put in terms of personal antagonism rather than honest differences of opinion between Anderson and himself:

> I believe it to be true that Dr. Anderson believes himself to have been badly treated by me and that out of an expedition 1908–12 where both of us did much hard work, and he not the less of the two, he, the abler man as he believed, got much less credit than I. By brooding, these things have grown, and altho' I believe it to be the opinion of most of those associated with the two of us the winter of 1912–13 that I tried to get for Dr. Anderson all the credit and notice I could, I also believe it to be the opinion of those who know him and not me that I have deliberately deprived him of credit . . . On our first expedition we often differed on matters of policy and I always carried forward my plans . . . It is therefore not difficult to sympathize to a degree at least in his feelings toward me. That they have carried him too far I am sure of and I am sorry for. I cannot see anything but that so far as he has hurt any individual he has hurt himself most of all for it does

not seem likely that any thorough consideration will justify all he did. It is regrettably clear that he lessened by half at least the prospects of success and doubled the danger of the ice work of 1914 without benefitting any individual member of the expedition or any section of it. I have had and still have a high regard for Dr. Anderson's ability along many lines and his character in many ways. It was, however, clearly a mistake, for which I am fully responsible, to take him with me on an expedition such as this. . . . the unfriendliness and lack of confidence which undoubtedly existed among the scientific staff rested on the fact that Dr. Anderson who knew me did not like me and had no confidence in my scientific or practical judgement.[102]

This summation of Anderson's alienation held more than a kernel of truth though it was not the whole story. The scientific members' distrust of Stefansson had developed along a parallel course with Anderson's disillusionment, sometimes in contact with it, sometimes not. Rather than personal jealousy being the sole cause of Anderson's feelings, there appears to have been a change of perspective and a search for different values, which in the end did not mesh with those of Stefansson as they had during the 1908–12 expedition.

In 1918, Anderson poured out his invective to Isaiah Bowman, editor of the *Geographical Review* and secretary of the Explorers' Club of New York, stating that he had lost his respect for Stefansson during the 1908–12 venture:

[Stefansson] was an international Socialist then, not having really started his "bounder" career among the great and nearly-great, and had a very express contempt for anything so provincial as patriotism. Patriotism was an ignoble virtue, rather than a fault[,] comparable to a rooster fight[ing] for his dung hill. He himself was a cosmopolitan superman above country, a Pacifist, disclaiming that he owed anything to a country which brought him out of poverty, allowed him to sponge his education through state universities and three years of Harvard . . . in case of war he would go to Canada or any other country which was neutral and pacifistic. I call[ed] that rot merely twaddle at the time, not recognizing that yellowness is congenital and will out in an emergency.[103]

To Anderson, a veteran of the Spanish American War, and then part of the military establishment at Blees Academy, such a philosophy was cowardly and traitorous and should have been fought at every turn. The

Karluk episode more than anything was proof of Stefansson's treachery for Anderson; he would not believe that Stefansson had had any intention of returning to the ship: "[a] commander first to leave his ship and crew . . . has forfeited the respect of every man who has been in the Arctic and every man who has any instinct of the duty of a seafaring man, and . . . of an explorer."[104] Anderson became convinced that nothing Stefansson had done or would do could surprise him: "A man who has no principles or ethics (or rather a chameleon standard) in some things cannot be depended on in anything. Stefansson always maintained that morals were very relative, the average standards of the people you were with, New York morals were not Iowa or North Dakota morals and N.Y. morals not Arctic morals."[105] He was sorry that he had returned north with Stefansson.

Even while in Ottawa during the spring of 1913, preparing for the expedition, Anderson had had second thoughts and regretted being involved in arctic work, "since it has passed out of the province of the American Museum." Under Canadian auspices, he was certain that the prospects for furthering his own zoological work would not be bright "with so many conflicting interests to reconcile, and so many amateurs to personally conduct."[106] Apparently the American Museum had promised to hire Anderson after the 1908–12 arctic trip on a full-time basis, but they could not afford to keep him beyond 1913. However, by working for the Victoria Memorial Museum in Ottawa Anderson could find the requisite security to pursue his studies. Once again, this museum position was obtained by Stefansson's negotiations and influence. It did mean, however, that Anderson had to accompany the new Canadian Expedition as part of the price. Then, during the spring of 1913, he was given the thankless task of looking after all the details of planning and organization while Stefansson was in the United States and Europe. By the time he reached the west coast of Canada, Anderson knew full well the disposition of other members of the expedition, particularly those of the Geological Survey. At that time he was not, strictly speaking, the spokesman for any "anti-Stefansson" faction; however, he was just as upset as his colleagues with Stefansson's vague statements and manner during the Nome meetings. Moreover, he was taken aback by the additional instructions from Ottawa, which no one had seen before, giving Stefansson the exclusive right to issue news to the media and forbidding other members to write articles for at least a year after the expedition's return. This, the men felt, was an unjust monopoly, and the last-minute nature of the instructions was blatantly unfair. Even R. W. Brock had fought against these privileges, asking Desbarats that "if anything is specified regarding the prohibition of magazine articles for one year by officers of the expedition, it should be so worded as not to exclude a scientific article in a scientific magazine but only popular articles, etc., for gain, as it may happen that some scientific facts should be published in a scientific journal."[107]

The Naval Service did not heed this suggestion from the Geological Survey, but issued instructions solely to favour Stefansson's private interests. Young and ambitious men, whose salaries were nominal, had been attracted to the expedition by the prospect that their individual work would further their careers.[108] Now this opportunity was, they felt, being taken away and there was nothing that could be done because the prohibition was official. Stefansson even went beyond the official orders, suggesting that all literature, diaries, and writings were to be handed over to the government so that every written word could be examined by an ethnologist, presumably himself, for material on the Eskimo.[109] "In other words," argued Anderson, "scientific specialists in other lines were not competent to judge as to what they were willing to put on record officially to publish." The members were unanimous in their disapproval of Stefansson's idea. They agreed to give him scientific information if he asked for it, but would not allow any individual to take all their literary work, or probe their private feelings and opinions. "The feeling spread, particularly on account of the impression that the camouflage was being taken off the formerly supposed great scientific expedition, revealing it as at bottom a newspaper and magazine exploiting scheme" engineered by Stefansson.[110]

The only publication concession Stefansson made was to his onetime partner. By a private agreement concluded on 12 June 1913, Anderson was given authority to send news from the Southern Party, using "all reasonable care . . . to fulfill Stefansson's agreement with the *London Chronicle* for first reports for newspaper publication" of all news of the expedition. Further, Anderson was given the right, by the authority vested in Stefansson, to write or publish popular accounts of the "work and experiences" of the Southern Party after the expedition's return. Anderson agreed to furnish a narrative account of the Southern Party for publication and to submit all magazine articles dealing with the work of the Southern Section to the *London Chronicle* for use "in conjunction with Mr. V. Stefansson's articles on the whole expedition." General articles dealing with arctic life, "embodying experiences of the past" and not related in any way to the present expedition could be published by Anderson at any time. However, all newspaper rights to the story of the expedition belonged to Stefansson, Anderson not being permitted to engage in newspaper correspondence unless authorized by Stefansson.[111]

Whether Anderson demanded this agreement is not clear, nor are Stefansson's motives for conceding it. It may have been that Stefansson was trying to regain Anderson's support, which was essential to the smooth running of the factionalized expedition. Shortly thereafter, Stefansson, wishing above all to have a harmonious expedition, went even further and offered Anderson a share of the newspaper profits if Anderson would issue all the expedition orders under Anderson's name. Anderson was incensed by this and told Stefansson that he "wouldn't have anything to do with his game."[112] He told the commander that he would have to issue his own orders on his own responsibility, otherwise he would become merely a front.

Anderson was under a tremendous strain, challenging Stefansson, protecting what he considered the rights of the Southern Section, and at the same time coping with a number of serious personal problems. These personal affairs involved not only a crisis of conscience, but also the relationship between his wife and himself. For two years Mrs. Anderson had prodded her husband to publish popular articles and thereby make a name and a little money for himself.[113] She even went so far on one occasion as to ask Stefansson to urge her husband on.[114] There does seem to have been some truth to Stefansson's contention that he tried to help Anderson but that the latter did not seem inclined to publish when he had the chance.[115] Stefansson agreed to do his best for her husband even though he was certain that it was Mrs. Anderson who had helped create the rift between the Southern Section and himself, by mounting a whisper campaign against him.[116] On his part, Anderson had come to the realization, after much soul-searching, that he did not have the necessary public relations talents, and moreover did not wish to subscribe to values which he no longer shared:

> Whenever I think of "exploring" I get disgusted with it . . . because I haven't any talent for making it pay. There are a good many things I like to do for the work's sake, but I get sort of panic stricken when I think of having to tell about it afterward. People expect me to talk, and you know I can't lecture "for sour apples," or write anything that interests very many people. As Bartlett says, a returned explorer is like a politician out of office. I think myself exploring new lands ought to be left to navy or army officers—they can do things, and are not expected to make a "spiel" about it afterwards.[117]

Mrs. Anderson understood full well her husband's situation and that subject never recurred in subsequent correspondence. But her initial prodding and Stefansson's subsequent petitions only strengthened Anderson's resolve that publishing and Stefansson's type of livelihood—as Anderson perceived it—were not for him. Moreover, he realized—and it must have been an agonizing realization for so quiet and brooding a man—that he lacked Stefansson's special abilities.

When Anderson had read *My Life With the Eskimo*, which became available only after the expedition was in the north, he commented that Stefansson had done some very good writing in places but that it required editing; Stefansson's sniping at the "poor old missionaries," he felt, was "mostly buncombe."[118] More seriously, however, Anderson thought that *My Life With the Eskimo* was not only full of half truths and misrepresentations—which he never spelled out in detail—but he was convinced by the first chapter that he had been taken undue advantage of.

> So Stefansson finally called his book ["]My Life in the Arctic." That title suits me exactly—there are so many phases of his life which were a continual initiation to me. I don't know what he put into it, as I never read more than the first chapter of proof, which was largely an account of his trip down the Mackenzie substantially as I had it in my journal of field notes. He borrowed the same to refresh his memory on a trip to Ottawa as he said his notes were not connected at that period.[119]

To readers the final result seemed to be Stefansson's own, and his borrowings without proper credit do seem to have exceeded the bounds of good taste. In no way would this have endeared him to Anderson. A comparison of the initial chapter of *My Life With the Eskimo* with Anderson's field journals for the period 15 April 1908–13 August 1908 reveals that Stefansson incorporated much of the colourful material directly from Anderson's descriptions and narrative of the journey and that his account followed Anderson's diary very closely indeed.[120]

Finally, Anderson blamed not only Stefansson for his plight, but also his own foolhardiness in allowing himself to go on another arctic expedition when his pregnant wife, who had returned home, appeared to be in a dangerous emotional state. Although Mrs. Anderson did give her husband moral courage, she seldom let an opportunity pass to remind him of his neglect. Time and time again in sad, heart-rending letters she would write him of her loneliness, insecurity, agitation, and fits of crying.[121] In early November, Mrs. Anderson gave birth, but three days later the baby died. By a touch of fate, it was Stefansson who carried the sad tidings to Collinson Point in early March and had the unpleasant duty of informing Anderson. The pressure of Stefansson's presence, anxiety over his possible requests, combined with the news of the tragedy, conspired to bring about the following unpleasant scene between Stefansson and Anderson:

> I [Anderson] hardly had a peaceful minute for a week, starting with an acrimonious discussion lasting until 3.00 a.m. with the chief trouble-maker. No chance to brood over private grief—VS struck a very unfavourable time to make any compromise with me, when I was thinking of my poor girl in Sioux City, from whom I had just received the sad news. I think I must have given a good imitation of a bear that has lost a cub—hard and bitter towards the Arctic and everything in it—just the proper mood for fighting without losing my head or temper. Poor dear girl, you are the heroine in all conscience. I feel quite guilty when I think of your lonely condition. I had counted on the boy being some company for you. I suppose your kind friends think that I have deserted you since they talk us up and down. I suppose they think marriage kills romance.[122]

At that particular juncture then, there could have been no compromise and, in the months and years to come, Anderson preferred to leave Stefansson to his own devices and, though he was willing to ignore "the chief troublemaker" for short periods, he never forgot.

6

The Politics of the
Canadian Arctic Expedition

By the spring of 1914, it was obvious that the Canadian Arctic Expedition was turning into a nightmare. The expansion of the expedition, the shoddy, hasty preparations, and the fuzzy and contradictory nature of the official instructions, all conspired to bring more fundamental tensions to the breaking point. Differing points of view regarding the expedition's purpose had created two camps, pitting Stefansson against virtually the entire Southern Section. No compromise was possible.

Stefansson was no charlatan; rather, he was an individual intent on achieving success for the expedition and for himself. Public acclaim was to be his vehicle for reaching greatness, and his method of securing government and private support for this and any other expeditions. At this juncture, Stefansson appeared to be more a promoter than a scientist. Publicity-seeking may have obscured his finer points; the explorer impulse may have overridden his professional instincts. Stefansson was convinced that to remain in the public eye and keep the support of the Canadian government, his plans must proceed without hindrance until their inevitable success. However, his constant efforts to impress his view upon the expedition that success must be achieved at all costs convinced his opponents of their own moral superiority. There could be no common ground.

The scope of his authority was being challenged, for his opponents had placed much weight on the specific instructions received from the Geological Survey, as opposed to what they considered the more nebulous and sometimes inconsistent general instructions. In their eyes Stefansson's actions during the first year of the expedition were suspect and the aims of the expedition were sullied by a man whose motives they considered less than scientific. In a sense, one might argue that each side was right; the confrontations became a question of how each faction perceived the

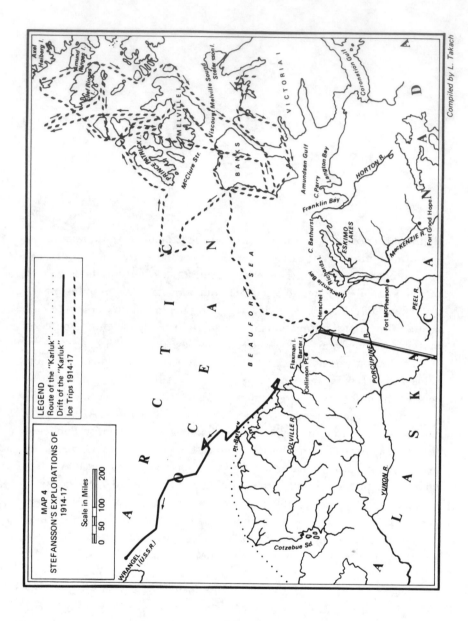

MAP 4
STEFANSSON'S EXPLORATIONS OF
1914-17

Scale in Miles

0 50 100 200

LEGEND

Route of the "Karluk" ....
Drift of the "Karluk"
Ice Trips 1914-17

ARCTIC OCEAN

BEAUFORT SEA

WRANGEL I.(U.S.S.R.)

Pt. Barrow

Cotzebue Sd.

COLVILLE R.

Flaxman I.
Barter I.
Collinson Pt.
Herschel I.
Mackenzie Bay
Richards I.
Fort McPherson
Porcupine R.
Peel R.

ALASKA

YUKON R.

CANADA

McKenzie R.
Fort Good Hope
ESKIMO LAKES
HORTON R.
Franklin Bay
C. Bathurst
C. Parry
Langton Bay
Amundsen Gulf
Coronation Gulf

VICTORIA I.

BANKS

Stefansson I.
Viscount Melville Sound
MELVILLE
PRINCE PATRICK I.
McClure Str.
Ind. Ridges I.
Axel Heiberg I.
Amund Ringnes I.

Compiled by L. Takach

"truth," this perception being sometimes more important in human rela-
tionships than the objectively determined truth itself.

It was not long after the expedition was underway that Ottawa
received a taste of what it had helped to create. The authorities were quite
aware of the initial differences of outlook between the sections of the
venture, particularly between Stefansson and the Geological Survey, and
they could not help but be painfully aware of the goings on. Ottawa did
not receive Stefansson's version of the Collinson Point episode until sometime in early 1915, a year later. Instead, he sent his superiors reports and
copies of correspondence which focussed on less crucial issues which tended
to place Anderson's leadership abilities in an unfavourable light. They
learned, for instance, of the Southern Party's apparent lack of discipline
and the laxity of its chief, from a letter Stefansson wrote to Anderson:

I learned first from outsiders and it was later confirmed by members
of the expedition that the establishment at Collinson Point was run
on a sort of system of volunteers with the result that some men did
more work than others of the same rank and that on occasion certain
important things were neglected or done in a slip-shod way. While
"settle it among yourselves" is an attitude on the part of a commander
which is likely to keep him out of trouble that arises[,] it tends to
create friction among the men and is not likely a policy that leads to
the greatest efficiency. I take it that the business of a commander is,
among other things, to shoulder responsibilities, one of which is an
equitable division of labour among the men according to some system.
This is necessary if anything much is to be done beyond spending the
winter peaceably in the house.

Another point is that while both natives on their own account
and others working for the ships have secured considerable game . . .
we, as favourably situated as any of them, have secured none. There
were numerous men during a considerable portion of the fall and
winter doing no work at Collinson Point . . . Our food resources are
limited; men sent out to hunt would have been physically better off
for it and dog feed and man food would have been saved . . . I don't
think that scientific men should neglect their work to hunt, but at times
when there is no scientific work being done and when no active
preparations are being made for any it would be more enjoyable for
them and in every way conducive to the interests of the expedition to
let them occupy some of their spare time hunting[.][1]

He concluded his remarks by advising Anderson not to mollycoddle the members of the scientific staff, or to wait on them, but to leave non-scientific and administrative matters to others and to pursue his own zoological work. Stefansson, who had never been close to the detailed planning, equipping, and organization of the expedition, did not seem to realize the scope and intensive nature of Anderson's responsibilities. Anderson had more on his mind than keeping the men busy. Stefansson was probably correct in advising his second-in-command "to run a tighter ship," but in view of the very diverse objectives of the Southern Section, Anderson felt that he had to forsake much of his own scientific work for the smooth running of his section. "Every dog, every man hired, and every charge in our outfit [has] so much more responsibility to RMA that with two years ahead of us we must know where we stand."[2]

Anderson's reaction must have been one of exasperation. Far from resolving whether Stefansson could encroach, or was encroaching, on the resources of the Southern Section, Stefansson's memorandum had managed to ignore their real grievances. Chipman was certain that such tactics were deliberate. "He has the prestige which makes anything he says carry weight, and he has an easy assurance in the telling which is not always convincing but very readily conveys an impression that varies with the facts and . . . puts persons or things in an unfavourable light."[3]

In addition to the petty squabbling, there was a growing realization by Ottawa that the expedition would be digging deeper and deeper into the government's pocketbook, far beyond the original $75,000 estimate for the entire venture. Only a fool could have believed that the vast expedition would be operated on such a small sum, and most officials conceded that unforeseen developments had to be provided for. However, the spending of $512,628 over the next five years far exceeded all expectations.[4] Throughout the first summer, Stefansson reported that the expedition needed more money. These early requests were essentially valid:

> The assembling of stores at Esquimault was begun on the basis of a requisition made out by Captain C. P. Pederson and approved [by] Dr. R. M. Anderson. This requisition was on the basis of Captain Pederson's whaling experience, and contains many items which we consider either too luxurious, or too bulky for an arctic expedition (certain can foods, for instance) as well as others which on general principles we considered unsuitable (large quantities of salt meats for example). As the plans for the expedition developed it became evident that we should have more men to take care of than Captain Pederson's original requisition contemplated and it seemed to me advisable that

the quantities of supplies be greatly increased beyond the original recommendation which was done for all the reasons to be inferred from the preceding summary and also because the uncertainties of arctic exploration made it advisable that the only limit placed on the supplies . . . shall be imposed by the carrying capacity of the vessel or vessels to be used.[5]

The *Karluk*, Stefansson's ship, ran the risk of being caught in the ice and would need "as much food and fuel as she could carry."[6] In the Southern Section, only the ethnologists, because of the nature of their work, would not require extensive provisioning:

> The other men have work of a more exacting and confining nature and for that reason abundant provisions must be made for them, as also for the reason that many of them are men who expect and in some cases demand more comforts than ordinarily fall to a Polar explorer. They do this largely on the basis of their experience with scientific work of the government done in more southerly latitudes and they fail to see why they should not on an Arctic expedition be as sumptuously outfitted within the limits of transportation possibilities as they would be working in British Columbia or Ontario.[7]

Not only had past governmental practice bred such complacent attitudes, he implied, but the nature of the expedition had been changed almost beyond recognition by the government—from a scientific staff of six men, backed up by one ship and $75,000, to one of thirteen trained specialists, two or three ships, and still roughly $75,000. It was inevitable, therefore, that the cost of the revamped project would exceed the original figure, but "the increased cost is more than counterbalanced by the increased development of the Expedition along other lines."[8] Stefansson's logic was hard to fault, and the Naval Service realized that the onus was on it to make certain that, throughout the expedition, the requisite funding was there. Few questions would be asked. Desbarats, basing his arguments on those of Stefansson, informed his superior, the minister of the Naval Service, that immediate action had to be taken before the expedition was beyond civilization.[9] A further $135,000 was provided by October 1913.[10] Again it had proved easier to raise ten dollars to continue a venture already in the field than to secure one dollar to begin a new work.

The most serious problem the Ottawa bureaucracy faced in 1914 was how to deal with Stefansson's plans for an ice foray into the Beaufort Sea using a revitalized Northern Section, following the loss of the *Karluk*. Both

Brock and Desbarats were aware of the differences of opinion within the expedition, and both moved quickly—even before the Collinson Point episode. Guidelines aimed at preserving a modicum of harmony were agreed upon. They assumed that, after the disappearance of the *Karluk*, Stefansson now was left with a practically intact Southern Party, two small vessels, a motor launch, and smaller boats, and they made their further plans on this basis. If such were the case, it would be unwise and undesirable for Stefansson to attempt to detach members of the Southern Party to organize a new Northern Party. "The division of forces would probably defeat the object of sending out [the] Southern party by weakening it and the results obtained by . . . [Stefansson's] explorations of Banks and Fitzpatrick Island would not compensate for the sacrifice." It was strongly impressed on Stefansson that the Southern Party must be kept intact in order to carry out, as best it could, its own program of research in the Coronation Gulf area.[11] Desbarats, for his part, confided to Stefansson that, although the Northern Party's ice work would be valuable, "as a greater part of the expenditure for the expedition has been incurred on account of the Southern Party it was essential that this party should show results for the money so spent."[12]

The government's position then, if anything, gave support to Anderson's criticisms of Stefansson's actions. One thing that Desbarats did spell out, though, was that Stefansson was to be the final authority on the division of the ships between the two parties.[13] Anderson was given full authority as second-in-command, to direct the ships and crews, when—and only when—Stefansson was not available.[14] Yet, this specific area of authority would be directly and successfully challenged and even abused. Desbarats's priorities would reinforce Anderson's intransigence.

Stefansson may have resented these orders. By them, his own plans had to take a back seat to those of the Southern Section, but he nevertheless expressed agreement with Desbarats's instructions and comments. They were "most satisfactory, [j]ust what I think they should be."

> They command nothing, because he realized that local conditions must decide, but they advise just the things which I have always had in mind which are comprised in pushing the work of the northern section but be sure the southern section is not handicapped by lack of resources. Both sections being equally my expedition engaged in carrying out my plans it is scarcely likely that I would do anything else.[15]

Stefansson always denied that he had in any way tried to weaken or cripple the Southern Party.

Although he was happy with Desbarats's position, Stefansson was visibly upset by Brock of the Geological Survey. The latter had cautioned the explorer to avoid making the "fatal mistake" of weakening the Southern Party to enhance the Northern work. Brock maintained that aside from what Stefansson himself was doing, the Northern work had been terminated with the disappearance of the *Karluk*.[16] In a personal reply, Stefansson proceeded to upbraid Brock for his presumptions in casting what Stefansson felt were aspersions on his scientific ability and his common sense:

The advice itself would not have made me sore had it not been for the fact that it repeated the advice solemnly impressed on me by my juniors and subordinates on the expedition a few months before. Not that I did not agree with them—the fact that made me sore was that everybody should assume that I alone had no sane ideas in regard to the conduct of the expedition. It was like being told by a young woman you take to dinner just which is the fish fork. If later on you were to show that you knew the fish fork from the others she would never cease believing that it was she who first taught you. Don't you think I knew the fish fork from the others? . . .

I understood clearly in Ottawa that you considered yourself to be a scientific man and in some sense much fuller and more orthodox than you supposed me to be. May I use the Socratic method on you? Then, why did you suppose that? Was it because of your position as head of the scientific department? If that was the reason, do you really and truly believe that it was your scientific orthodoxy that chiefly gave you your government place? That question can with confidence be answered in the negative even with all the degrees of latitude and longitude between us. Then why did you fancy your training was superior? I haven't the time to recite academic history, but the number of years and the recognition won are likely to get flattering consideration from each of us in his own case. Have you found in measuring yourself against others in your field that you stood comparison well? —Then have you any reason to think that the same has not been the case with me?

In other words, what you knew of me and what I know of you is not enough to give either a title to lord it scientifically over the other. Wouldn't it make you a trifle sore if I were to assume on the basis of what this or that man or organization thinks of my work that I stand a head taller than you in certain broad mutual aspects?[17]

Stefansson was obviously quite jealous of his status and prerogatives

within the expedition and was unwilling, in view of the serious situation in
the field, to have his abilities challenged by Brock, Anderson, or others.
And he was determined to have his ice trip in order to fulfil his concept of
the expedition's objectives. Yet the type of trip that actually took place was
unplanned, an improvisation. Initially, his exploration and ice work north
of the mainland had entailed using the heavily-provisioned *Karluk* as a
floating and drifting base from which to make sledge forays into the unknown. When that became impossible, he revised his plans to explore over
the ice with a well-provisioned sledge party. The lack of co-operation and
hostility on the part of Anderson forced him to strike out from Martin
Point without the requisite logistical support. Moreover, there were
numerous times during the first ice expedition in 1914 and those of 1915–
17, when he and his companions were short on rations. It became apparent
that much of what was accomplished had been due not to the working out
of any preconceived notions of the resources that lay waiting for his party,
but to good luck. Stefansson was in this operation a man alone; he set out
to prove to the government, his critics and antagonists, and above all, to
the public, that he could contend with hostile nature in dramatic fashion
and survive.

On the first ice expedition, which began on 22 March 1914, the party,
although high in optimism, soon began running low on food.[18] They were
living essentially on the supplies they had carried from Collinson Point.
Added to this was the uncomfortable feeling that the lateness of the season
and the softness of the ice might turn the expedition into a "dangerous
enterprise."[19] Stefansson always maintained that the falling out at Collinson
Point had taken up too much time, robbing him of the benefit of an early
and, hence, safe travelling season. He blamed Anderson for placing roadblocks in the way of the ice party, reducing the possibility of doing more
work. The only actual help he received from members of the Southern
Party was from J. J. O'Neill, the geologist, who gave Stefansson his pocket
chronometer "for Stefansson was short of reliable chronometers."[20] However, another reason for the delay appears to have been that Stefansson
was suffering from a severe case of hemorrhoids at the time. As he confessed in his diary, he fabricated excuses for the good of the enterprise, to
conceal what he considered a humiliating malady.[21]

On 7 April, the members of the logistical support party—Crawford,
Johansen, and McConnell—turned back, leaving only Stefansson,
Storkerson, and Ole Andreason. On 1 May, Stefansson began to worry
about the shortage of dog food, because the dog team was unable to pull
as much and as far as it had previously. To give the dogs strength, food

originally designated for human consumption had to be used; the party then was left with twenty days' rations, "and when that is done the Lord help us all if we don't get game."[22] This certainly does not support Stefansson's certainty that food would be forthcoming; if anything, it indicated that Stefansson was going on faith, on the stubborn hope that something would turn up. Then on 8 May 1914 their fortunes changed: "Saw two seals together abreast of our camp, but they were beyond 400 yds. of unsafe young ice and the light struck them badly. I fired one shot but did not hit. They came up on the same spot five times which we watched. This is promising for us—the presence of seals—as well as interesting *in view of our former belief that seals kept within a few fathoms depth from shore.*"[23] Stefansson was elated by the prospect that game might be secured so far from land. Within the next few weeks they killed three bears and a number of seals, more meat and blubber than was essential for their immediate needs. But they did have to think of the future, and were not prepared to trust that other areas might be so bountiful: "We now [31 May 1914] had on hand over 1400 lbs. of bear meat and 2 seals. This may seem a wanton waste of game and bad but *Our Plans* depend so on providence that I look upon this much as insurance against want should we need to spend the summer on the sea ice."[24]

To his reading public in 1922, Stefansson maintained that everyone else had been wrong about animal resources which he knew were there beforehand:

> I admitted freely at the start that my plan of travelling away from land on indefinite distance over moving sea ice, relying for food and fuel on animals to be secured by hunting was considered unsound by every popular explorer and every critical authority on polar exploration . . .
>
> In rebuttal I appealed to the science of oceanography which . . . is as well established as most of the biological sciences. Thousands of observations taken by careful men had established this principle clearly laid down, for instance, by Sir John Murray in "The Ocean" and in his larger work "The Depths of the Ocean," that the amount of animal life per cubic unit of Ocean water is least in the tropics and increases gradually as you proceed toward either pole. This is really a fact of common observation, although the ordinary observer neglects to make the proper deduction.
>
> . . . [T]hat animal life in the ocean is extraordinarily abundant on the edges of the ice-covered area . . . is well-known. It is equally well-

known that there are great currents that sweep into the Arctic and under the ice . . . It is asserted that fish do not take kindly to the ice covering over the sea at high latitudes. The polar ocean is generally several miles in depth, and what difference should it make to a fish though there be numerous pieces of ice floating on top? . . .

But even if all the fishes were to turn tail and swim south when they came to the edge of the ice, there would still remain the tremendous quantity of plankton or floating life which without volition of its own is carried north under the ice . . .

Why is it logical to assume that these will all have died and disappeared before a particular cubic unit of water in question gets into even the center of the inaccessible area? Even were it to die and disappear when the center of the inaccessible area is reached, it would have by then lasted long enough to serve all our purposes. We were going to start from that edge of the ice from which the drift is assumed by Nansen and others to be northwestward or northerly; we should assuredly have with us as fellow travellers all these docile animals that allow the currents to carry them where they please. It was thus I reasoned that the animals upon which seals live will be found everywhere under the ice of the polar sea. And if the feed is there, the seals will follow the feed. We can travel along with confidence, killing seals as we need them[,] using the bear and part of the fat for food and the rest of the fat for fuel.[25]

Stefansson tempered his statement by acknowledging that on the ice, just as on land, there would be certain barren areas in relation to seal life.[26] But this would not perturb an undaunted and experienced explorer for he could travel confidently if he adhered to the following doctrine: "Do not let worry over to-morrow's breakfast interfere with your appetite at dinner. The 'friendly Arctic' will provide."[27]

In all the subsequent ice work, however, food remained a chronic problem, characterized by few periods of feast and more of famine.[28] When it came down to it, luck more than planning or reliance on a particular theory carried the day. Luck and Stefansson's dogged determination to carry on, not sure what lay ahead. The "paramount" nature of the ice work[29] in his scheme of things kept up his spirits. Stubbornly, grudgingly, the "Friendly Arctic" from time to time did come to his rescue. But it was never as well thought out as he suggested. Despite this, Stefansson—really the last *great* explorer of the old school—considered his method was the perfection of arctic exploration. He was certain he had ably demonstrated it through the mere fact of his party's survival. Travelling with an almost empty sled and living off the country was "no work for a pessimist," though he considered his method easier than the traditional pemmican method "where the eating of dogs and [the explorer's] starvation follow the emptying of the last meat tin."[30] Perhaps it was, but technological change was passing his method by.

For the most part, Stefansson was fortunate in having men who were, he considered, optimists; men who, although new to the fare, became accustomed to it. According to Stefansson, harmony in the Northern Section was the order of the day.[31] Throughout the entire span of the expedition, however, there were to be a host of difficulties within his Northern Party. Most of these differences were related to the tensions of living together at close quarters and to the idiosyncrasies of the commander. Despite Stefansson's assurances that his method of exploration would see his men safely through the expedition, there were a number of occasions when his men were either dissatisfied or balked at continuing their efforts. This reluctance was particularly true of the 1917 trip, the last for Stefansson, just when his method had—in a limited way—proved its viability in the trips of 1914– 16.[32]

There were several reasons for the discontent. Some men were dissatisfied with the nature of the work. E. L. Knight, one of Stefansson's ice companions, complained to his diary that little concrete work was being achieved, most of the time being spent waiting for animals in order to secure enough food.[33] If anything, this was one of the main charges levelled at Stefansson's methods; time and effort spent on actual provisioning meant little headway—other than pure exploration—with scientific observations. Stefansson's method was fine for anthropological pursuits when one moved with the natives, but such was not the case with these explorations. To apply Stefansson's method to all forms of arctic investigation was highly unrealistic. There may have been much truth to Anderson's observation:

> Their method of rushing blindly from one seal to the next seal they can kill does not allow the stops that must be made to get suitable weather observations, and anything such parties can add to the maps (if [Stefansson] can persuade Geographic Societies with sufficient eloquence to hoodwink them) will be as misleading as the old charts . . . I can give VS credit of marked ability when he sticks to his trade, but when he decided he could be a geographer and oceanographer with absolutely no training except as a dog-musher and pedestrian with literary leanings, he got beyond his depths.[34]

The only satisfaction the 1917 trip had brought Stefansson was the conviction that at least one man, Storker T. Storkerson, was "the best man I ever had." "His only fault is his proneness to fail to keep contracts, and to 'change his mind'. So long as you keep him in humor he is energetic, resourceful and fruitful enough, and at any rate is no coward."[35] Storkerson, was the one person who was essential to Stefansson, for the simple reason that he had requisite experience, having served on the Leffingwell-Mikkelsen Anglo-American Polar Expedition. In many ways, in fact, Stefansson was utilizing Storkerson's exploration techniques. It appears that Storkerson, more than Stefansson, was responsible for many of the critical decisions made while they were on the ice, for Stefansson would not move until he had sought Storkerson's advice.[36] From 1914, Stefansson handled Storkerson with kid gloves, usually giving into his whims and moods, because of his special talents. These concessions reached the farcical, but Stefansson felt them necessary to secure harmony with his trusted and essential fellow traveller. On 20 May 1915, for example, Stefansson "[a]greed with Storker Storkerson this day that if Storker Storkerson's 'back is sore' when we reach Prince Patrick Island, or if he thinks his wife needs him in Banks Island, V. Stefansson is to try to land Storker Storkerson in Banks Island and get him to Cape Kellett by June 15 if possible."[37] Stefansson may have trusted his lieutenant, but Storkerson certainly had reservations about his commander. He was certain that since he had set out from Martin Point, he had been given little support by Stefansson who "has an idea that no one except himself knows how to handle [a] stove."[38] Neither was he keen to live on a straight meat diet as Stefansson insisted. Storkerson agreed that they could subsist on such a regimen, but he contended the party would be incapable of doing any hard work, as were Eskimos before the introduction of beans, flour, and potatoes.[39] Apparently even Stefansson agreed with this assessment, for he did write in his diary that eating cereals made him "feel more active and energetic."[40] On top of this, Storkerson criticized his commander for not exerting enough authority. "There has been no attempt to discipline the men doing almost what they like and if he wants anything to be done he has to beg or coax them to do it[;] in some cases they have been telling him what to do[.] [I]t is his own fault he has been treating them like equals consequently they think they are just as good as he is, and that he cannot get along without them."[41] Storkerson should have been the last person to talk.

Stefansson, never the best judge of character, would eventually find out his lieutenant's sentiments,[42] but he always had the ability to forgive, and the two eventually became close associates. In the Arctic, with so much free time and very little to talk about, personal frictions and gossip-mongering were bound to flourish. Back-biting and back-stabbing were rampant; *all* were involved and no one could escape indulging in so trite a pastime. "Tales Out of School," Stefansson observed, were being circulated and embellished about one another, and particularly about himself:

> It seems strange so many should be anxious to co-operate in scuttling the ship when they have to gain by it only the harm they work the commander. But seeing the like is known from most exploring expeditions from Columbus and Hudson on, it is, perhaps more than any-thing[,] to be looked upon as a further proof that human nature has not altered materially. Tennyson is in a small minority when he says that men may rise on stepping stones of other dead selves to higher things; it is far more commonly accepted that the way to rise is on stepping stones of dead or discredited fellows.[43]

Although all sorts of stories were circulating, some true and some not, Stefansson grew almost paranoid about their effects, certain they were deliberately designed to undermine not only the actual work, but his prestige as well. That was the way he felt concerning the Collinson Point incident in 1914, and he continued to be so inclined throughout the remainder of the expedition. The continuing "struggle" for the *North Star* is a good case in point.

On the 1914 expedition, shortly after Stefansson had left Martin Point, he had ordered the *North Star* to meet his party at Banks Island, requesting that Wilkins should take charge of the *Star* and proceed as early as possible to the west coast of Banks Island. This would provide insurance for the ice party and cover the possibility of the *Karluk*'s crew coming there. Similarly, the other vessel, the *Mary Sachs*, was first to carry ten tons of supplies to a point in Dolphin and Union Straits for the use of the Southern Party, then proceed west and north to winter in Banks Island.[44] Anderson refused to abide by Stefansson's written orders, arguing that if the *Sachs* had to place a cache, she would never have the time to reach Banks Island. Particularly "as there would be no one who has much knowledge of navigation or who is directly enough responsible to the Canadian government to be depended on to take proper care of Government property or to make sufficient energetic efforts to get the vessel to some point where she could communicate with Mr. Stefansson and to make the resources of the vessel of use to the expedition and to the Government during the winter."[45] If that were the case, Anderson speculated, then the *Sachs* "with her good equipment for winter exploratory work" would finish by being of no use to either section, and the Southern Party would be penalized by having to send badly needed men to look after supplies which might be deposited "at some unknown or unsuitable place." Anderson decided, therefore, to transfer Wilkins from the *North Star* to the *Sachs*, feeling he was more reliable and could take charge of a larger vessel that could carry more equipment and more supplies, thus providing more resources for Stefansson's party. At the same time, to ensure this action did not handicap the activities of his Southern Party to any great degree, the *North Star* would stay with Anderson.[46]

Wilkins did not like the idea, but finally gave in to Anderson's pressure, thus infuriating Stefansson as the commanding officer: "he [Wilkins] should have obeyed [my orders] irrespective of countermanding orders from any officer of inferior rank."[47] But Wilkins had little choice. There was not much he could do but obey Anderson, who was second-in-command and the authority on the spot. To Stefansson, Wilkins's backing down was a tragic mistake. In the commander's estimation, the *Mary Sachs* was not properly or adequately equipped, as Anderson had assured. Anderson's questioning the validity of Stefansson's project and creating difficulties was unnecessary "imagination."[48]

> On the basis of this characteristic I formed on my second expedition (his first) the opinion that in spite of many excellent qualities Anderson was unsuited to command an Arctic expedition—an explorer must not be a pessimist, he must believe that things can be done. As Caesar said of his soldiers: "they conquered because they thought they could." But he gave me many proofs in four years of his ability to carry to success instructions which he thought would fail.[49]

On this basis, Stefansson claimed, he had selected Anderson for his present position, but he now had serious reservations about his choice. Stefansson disliked especially the transfer of Wilkins from the *North Star*, and he had grounds to be suspicious. Wilkins, Anderson claimed, was trustworthy enough to look after government property because the *Mary Sachs*'s present crew were not directly responsible to the government. Yet the commander, Captain Bernard, was a salaried employee of the Canadian government, while Wilkins worked independently for the Gaumont Company—a moving picture outfit—and "never received a salary from the government and whose connection with the government is the most indirect of any member of the expedition whatsoever."[50]

Moreover, did Anderson have such authority to act? He knew by

August 1914 that Ottawa did not want the Southern Section to be dis-
banded and this, he argued, justified his earlier stand at Collinson Point;
he was also given authority to allocate the ships in his commander's absence. But the sailing orders of the *North Star* were a direct order from
Stefansson, who had full authority, confirmed in Desbarats's latest statement, to do with the vessels as he saw fit. One must conclude that Anderson's actions, even by the loosest interpretation, were insubordinate. And
Anderson's defence, that he was acting in the best interests of the expedition
in overruling Stefansson, was bound to come under attack if, in fact, his
change did not work out for the best—as it did not. The *Mary Sachs*,
suffering from mechanical and caulking problems,[51] had to be beached at
Cape Kellett. Stefansson did not press the issue then, but was convinced
that much more would have been accomplished if he had had the right
ship to do the job.[52]

The following year, Stefansson took no chances about acquiring the
North Star for his 1915 exploration program. Stefansson planned a trip
over the ice north and west from Prince Patrick Island into the unknown.
Because of delays, however, it became necessary to begin the trip from
Cape Alfred. Again he had to trust others. Stefansson had wanted to secure
the *North Star* himself, for as he confided to his diary it was "with regret
and intense physical pain that I now give the command of the ice work to
Storkerson and go to fetch the *North Star*." All the members of his party
were agreed that if anyone else went the orders would be ignored by
Anderson.[53] He eventually felt Wilkins, who returned on 6 April, was
competent and trustworthy enough to carry out his orders. Stefansson had
found it impossible to leave. The commander appeared to be the only
moderating influence to keep in check the drunkenness that was now
prevalent in his party—particularly one member's affection for mash and
"denatured alcohol" which made him a "maniac and murderer" dangerous
unless controlled.[54] The situation was controlling Stefansson. With Wilkins
on the scene, Stefansson would not have to give up the ice work which he
felt was his main duty. However, Wilkins's appearance in the Southern
camp was to Chipman only further evidence that Stefansson was afraid
to come himself.[55]

The *North Star* was requested; Wilkins was to bring her as far north
as possible that summer, for support. To make certain his orders were
followed, Stefansson armed Wilkins with enough authority to prevent his
being cowed by Anderson. Wilkins was given power of attorney to act for
Stefansson in acquiring not only the *North Star*, men, and supplies, but to
charter another ship if need be. As well, Wilkins was to carry out any other

business that he deemed necessary and expedient for the good of the expedition.[56]

When Wilkins turned up at Anderson's camp, on the coast of Coronation Gulf in late May 1915, Anderson was furious with Stefansson's direct and explicit orders for the *North Star*, dogs, and men. He would give no quarter. "Wilkins an even-tempered individual put the case for Stefansson as well as anyone could possibly have put it but Anderson's mind was made up."[57] Anderson condemned Stefansson's orders as being "unreasonable." With the *Alaska* wintering at Baillie Island, the *North Star* remained the only vessel his party had for summer work. Any other use of the *North Star*, he contended, would cripple the Southern Party's work.[58] Anderson claimed that Stefansson had no authority over Wilkins and nothing in the original orders enabled Stefansson to exercise or share such power.[59] He ventured to upbraid Stefansson on these grounds. "It appears from the tone of your communication and from the information brought me by the men of your party, that you have assumed an exaggerated, and in my opinion, erroneous, idea of the authorities, powers, and limitations of your position."[60]

Anderson bolstered his stand by quoting from the Naval Service directive of 30 April 1914, which forbade the dispersal of the Southern Party:

> So far as you [Stefansson] personally are concerned I suppose you have the privilege of outlawing yourself, and being as irresponsible as you please, but please take notice that all the members of the Southern Party as at present constituted are in government employ at present in what they have heretofore considered as being a government expedition, are trying to operate a government vessel, and consider themselves bound by loyalty as well as professional ethics to abide by government service. So far as I know at present, no one here is willing to take up privateering at the present time.[61]

Strong words, but a weak argument because the circumstances were somewhat different now, and it was entirely open to question whether or not the Southern Section would be weakened. Wilkins, Anderson argued, had no power of attorney because his "power" was limited to the authority that Stefansson himself possessed in that particular situation—none.[62]

Unlike Anderson, Chipman, who was probably the strongest member in the Southern Section next to Anderson, considered that Stefansson's request was entirely reasonable and legitimate.[63] To Chipman, "orders is orders" and he appeared hesitant about opposing Stefansson at this juncture. "It seems to me . . . that since we were under the Naval Service and since the Government had said definitely that authority and final responsibility had to be in the hands of one man, we were bound to carry out the orders." Seemingly, Chipman had become more cautious since the events at Collinson Point, for he was not willing to back Anderson on this occasion as he had previously. His position now was that "the responsibility of the decision must fall on RMA so I have refrained from saying much." When Chipman enquired as to the legality of Anderson's position, Anderson told him that "every commissioned officer was under the same oath to obey the *legal* orders of his superior officer." Stefansson's orders were, in his opinion, illegal. Chipman felt that Anderson was justified in his position and that the government would uphold him but, in such a tenuous situation, he reminded Anderson, "the responsibility for decisions must rest with him." Anderson may have used the question of the legality of the request as a pretext to further his personal vendetta with Stefansson. In any case, he seemed willing to chance it. But Anderson was influenced by other considerations. Chipman, as spokesman for the men of the Geological Survey, pointed out that if the *North Star* left he would head south, for without the vessel not enough would be accomplished to warrant their staying. "[W]hen RMA asked if I had done all the work I wanted to do I replied—if the Star went—Yes!"[64]

Anderson was in an unenviable position. If he gave in to Stefansson, the work of his section was finished; if he refused the commander, the responsibility for an action that was of dubious legality would be Anderson's alone. It was a risky gamble and the stakes were high, for the case for denying Stefansson's order boiled down to a difference of opinion as to priorities, with no hard facts or evidence to substantiate Anderson's contentions. Stefansson was right in his observation that the root of the matter was that "we were seldom able to agree on the line that divides the merely difficult from the impossible or impracticable."[65]

Wilkins was about to carry out an alternative plan but, rather than alienate Anderson further and break up the Southern Party, he agreed to haul a small engine to Darnley Bay, buy the *Argo*, a schooner similar to the *North Star*, fit her with the engine, and substitute her for the *North Star*. Then, if by the time he returned the *North Star* had sailed, he could use the *Argo* for the Northern work. Having this additional engine seemed to satisfy Anderson.[66] Still, the second-in-command had to carry the heavy burden of disobeying the direct orders of his superior with little reason. Anderson was saved from carrying through this rather expensive and dangerous plan by a compromise that Cox and Chipman engineered on 4

June 1915. It appears that neither man was altogether happy at the turn of events. Under the circumstances, they were prepared to back down from their insistence that the *North Star* was vital to their work in order that it could be made available for Stefansson, thus ending the impasse. The change of heart meant a delay, but under the circumstances Wilkins was agreeable. The Geological Survey men decided that they would use a skin boat fitted with an outboard motor to reach Tree River where they would work until the *North Star* had made a trip to Cape Barrow to pick up a power launch, fuel, and food, and cache them close to the Coppermine. The power launch that the *North Star* would bring back would be sufficient for their exploratory work.[67] Thus Stefansson finally secured the use of the *North Star* for his own work through a series of compromises hammered out by Anderson and Wilkins, with the aid of Cox and Chipman.

Stefansson's "victory," however, left a bitter feeling in the minds of Anderson and the other members of the Southern Section. They interpreted Stefansson's delegation of authority to Wilkins as cowardly and unjust. Once more the cry was that "the whole thing was an advertising scheme pure and simple."[68] Chipman was confirmed in his opinion of Stefansson's scheming and lack of integrity. "It must keep him awake nights to think of ways of avoiding issues, being prepared for whichever way the cat may jump and explaining things after they happen."[69] This criticism of Chipman's may have been justified, for, before long, Stefansson forwarded to Ottawa a long report on the events of early June 1915, written by Wilkins.[70] Wilkins had been hesitant to do so, thinking that it would only make matters worse. As well, he was suspicious of what he termed Stefansson's "habit of misremembering on which he prides himself . . . a mighty convenient thing." Finally, he agreed to prepare the statement after Stefansson had given his word "not to use it unless action is taken by the southern party."[71] Within three days, however, Stefansson sent a copy to Desbarats, along with his own comments. As far as can be determined, the Southern Party had done nothing in the interim to justify Stefansson's use of Wilkins's private letter. Stefansson wanted the record—as he saw it—to pass before Desbarats's eyes where it would point out Anderson's errors and could be used against the second-in-command only as a "defensive" measure.[72] Stefansson had laid the ground well for his own defence should it become necessary. He, in fact, needed to cover his position. Detained by Anderson's stubbornness, Wilkins had not shown up at the pre-arranged time with the *North Star*. In the interim, Stefansson had reacted hastily and bought an additional ship, the *Polar Bear*. He may have acted too hastily. In mid-August 1915, Stefansson chartered the ship at the exorbitant fee of $1,000 a day to take him to Herschel Island for more supplies and news. Once at Herschel Island, there were the inevitable delays which kept him there. The charter fees mounted at an alarming rate,[73] until eventually Stefansson decided to buy the ship outright to save money. The owner, Louis Lane, an unscrupulous individual, was willing to sell: $20,000 for the *Polar Bear*; $10,000 for her cargo, plus $14,000 for chartering fees—a staggering $44,000 for the Canadian government and public to bear. Moreover, the *North Star*, which would now be superfluous, was to be transferred to Lane as additional payment. Lane boasted how he "worked Stefansson for what he could and he was sorry afterwards that he did not ask for more. He would undoubtedly have got it."[74] This seems to have been the case, for ten years later when Mrs. Anderson was entertaining Louis Lane, who prided himself on being "crooked," Lane explained why he was a friend of Stefansson's. "Sure I am a friend of his. Why shouldn't I be? I got $52,000 out of him in 1915 up at Herschel Island, and so I like him $52,000 worth, but he is a liar just the same, a d - - - liar!"[75]

Now that Stefansson had his own ship for the Northern Expedition, he "decided to render his independence doubly secure by the purchase for $6,000 of the auxiliary schooner Gladiator,"[76] which he promptly turned over to Lane as part of the bargain, so that the old captain could get his furs out.[77] Wilkins was quite alarmed at this turn of events. There was a chance that a charge of misappropriation of government funds might be levied against Stefansson for spending huge sums without authorization for more ships "and engaging 21 people half of them more or less unfit for service, and finally left with a cargo of useless supplies so small as to leave us short in some things even for one year."[78] He feared that, since Stefansson had not done the best thing from the Canadian government's standpoint, he (Wilkins) would somehow be drawn into the ensuing row "to justify the expenses . . ."[79]

Wilkins's first reaction to Stefansson's transactions was mixed:

> I had half a mind to tell him what I thought of his actions and congratulate him on his tenacious memory and precisive deductions instead of following the ordinary custom [as I did] and congratulate him on his success. This may seem to be hypocrisy and not my idea of good behaviour but as the saying is 'When in Rome do as the Romans do' or in other words when forced to deal with the unscrupulous our minds must [know] their methods or be overcome.[80]

To Wilkins, the money and effort expended by Stefansson were not commensurate with the results, for the discovery of islands did not carry much weight with him, but "publically of course it is a great thing and reflects some credit at least on myself for being in command of the party that prepared the outfit at his disposal."[81] By the summer of 1915, Wilkins appeared anxious to get out and head back to civilization. He could not bring himself to do it at this time for "[i]n V.S. phrase . . . I should play the game for all that it is worth[.] It is his [Stefansson's] only chance to make a name for himself."[82] Wilkins, however, had little respect for Stefansson beyond catching some glory for his own personal ambitions.[83] In fact, they did not get along together at this juncture even though Stefansson admired Wilkins. For his part, Wilkins was amused by Stefansson's methods in his quest for greatness, but resented being used "as a go between." Besides, Wilkins intimated that Stefansson had delusions of grandeur and likened himself to Napoleon, whom he considered to have been a great and sensitive man. He fancied a particular resemblance with the French leader in another way, the slowness of their pulses: "[Stefansson] claims that the slowness of Napoleon's pulse accounts for his exceptional coolness and clear headedness. One need not extemporize the influence."[84]

Wilkins may have worried about the repercussions, but Stefansson did not, even though his horsetrading would cost the government an additional $85,000 for the year 1915–16.[85] The Naval Service was able to secure the funds from the privy council with no questions asked. No doubt they applied the same criteria as they had with the purchase of the *Gladiator*: "The technical officers of the Department of Naval Service report that the price appears reasonable and that circumstances evidently justified this purchase."[86] The privy council approved Stefansson's purchase of the *Polar Bear* not only because the charges were "reasonable," but because Stefansson argued that the loss of the *Karluk* had made it "essential to the continuance of the work" that the vessel be purchased.[87] He had convinced the Canadian government of his position. No doubt, with the department's deep involvement in the Great War, there was no time to worry about such civilian trifles.

In fact, aside from the Naval Service and the Geological Survey, very little attention was now being paid by the government to the Canadian Arctic Expedition. True, concern was expressed in the House of Commons on several occasions over the fate of the *Karluk*,[88] but Stefansson, after all, was acquiring new territory for the Dominion. Canada was too busy, naturally enough, with the war effort at home and abroad, with problems of corruption in the Shell Committee, and with worries about the growing internal crisis in French-English relations. The controversies over command of the expedition and its spending never once came before Parliament. The

Liberal opposition had its chance, but compared to other affairs of crisis proportions, the Canadian Arctic Expedition's finances were trivial.

The only open attack on Stefansson came in the newspapers in November 1916 after the Southern Section had returned south. The author of the article was not named, but he may have been a member of the Southern Party, for he was identified by the *Ottawa Citizen* as "a government official holding an important office and has spent years in the Northwest Territories." The informant claimed that his information came from the members of the Southern Party and allegedly from Inspector Phillips, of the Royal Northwest Mounted Police, who criticized Stefansson for his extravagance and misuse of public money. The *Citizen*'s source accused the explorer of selling out "body and soul to the American newspapers and magazines for whom he has written, or plans writing, accounts of his explorations. As for discoveries or any scientific research work, this is of secondary importance. The main proposition from Stefansson's point of view is that the expedition should be a money-making venture."[89]

None of Ottawa's politicians took up the question, however. The politics of the Canadian Arctic Expedition, for the most part, remained behind-the-scenes. Such publicity as there was, however, strengthened the resolve of the Naval Service to stop pampering Stefansson and bring him home before the situation was totally beyond control. Their explorer, though, had other ideas.

Stefansson was determined to stay north as long as possible, to prove his own worth and the validity of the Northern Section of the expedition. Besides, he now viewed the region as his private preserve. In the summer of 1915, Stefansson—from a newly discovered island—wrote to Robert Borden, prime minister of Canada, urging him to allow exploration to continue "between the mainland and the pole until the last mystery is unveiled."

> We shall do what we can next year, but when the three years assigned to us are up there will remain much to do. We have had misfortune but have accomplished a part of our work nevertheless. What you think of how we have met adverse conditions I do not know, and I do not write to plead any personal cause. But I feel strongly not only that Canada should explore the region to which she lays claims as far as the pole; it is true also that by doing so she makes good her claims. I shall remain ready to volunteer my services for this work, but if it shall seem that my record does not earn further support, then let another carry on the work, so [long as] he is Canadian in Canadian service.[90]

Doubtless, the prospect of discovering new land for Canada was quite appealing, if not irresistible, to Borden.

Stefansson believed that after the "*rough*" work had been finished, the work of specialists would become more necessary.[91] He even thought that when his work was finished he should return to civilization by the Northwest Passage and the Atlantic Ocean.[92] The Naval Service frowned on this suggestion as too time-consuming and fruitless in terms of exploration:

> It is not the intention of this Department to prolong the duration of the expedition beyond the next summer 1916. While it is desirable that the arctic regions should be thoroughly explored and that Canada should obtain full information as to the northern sections, the conditions at present existing are such that it is not advisable for the country to maintain parties on work of this kind. It is impossible to predict the conditions which will exist in a year from now but at the present time there is no doubt that it would be unwise to incur any unavoidable expenditures and that it would not be advisable to continue the expedition after next summer.[93]

In the light of this government policy, of which Stefansson was advised by mid-1916, his subsequent explorations and expenditures were directly contrary to the wishes of his superiors. In early 1916, Stefansson anticipated staying at least until the spring of 1917, but he was certain that his men could not stand the strain of prolonged exploration.[94] Many things had been left undone and he felt duty-bound to finish what he had initiated. In early 1916, he approached the National Geographic Society in Washington with this in view:

> I hope the Canadian Government will continue the work and I hope they will give me a chance to continue it. But the news of the terrible war which came last summer makes one fear that, even after peace has come, men's minds may be even more than ordinarily disinclined to the promotion of enterprises whose value cannot be seen by the mentally nearsighted. I feel that a deal of hard work has given me a moral right to the general field in which we are employed now (though I by no means own it), and that nine years have qualified me for it through a rather varied experience. I have an idea that the etiquette is that one who has in mind an exploring project should announce that fact. This brings me at last to the purpose of this letter; it is to ask you to announce for me in the manner you consider appropriate

that I intend, if we return safe from this expedition, to attempt organizing as soon as possible another expedition looking toward the further exploration of the general area between Parry Islands and meridian 180 reckoned from Greenwich. I believe this work should be done by Canada, in so far at least as concerns that region to which they have laid formal claim, but should the government consider itself not in a position to carry on the work further than has already been done by the present expedition, I expect to submit to your Society and to other geographic societies for approval and support a plan for the exploration of the above-mentioned area.[95]

To Stefansson, return to civilization would be a return to relative inactivity, for all he could look forward to was a series of lectures. "I would rather do more work than talk about what is already done—old age will do for that, if I live long, and if I don't live long it will be all one if I made money or didn't." He was intent, then, on staying in the north and raising another expedition as soon as he returned home.[96]

At the moment, though, he was primarily concerned with remaining in the Arctic as long as he possibly could, despite the Naval Service's policy. He began planning in earnest for a further ice trip for the spring of 1918.[97] He was still in the employ of a government that was anxious for him to come home as soon as possible. But, as the man on the spot, it was up to him "to make the final decision as to what was wise and what was foolhardy and expensive. If, on the very eve of an ice trip we should receive instructions not to make the trip, we would by not making the trip save only a small percentage of the year's expenses and have nothing to show for the work done and the money spent during the whole year."[98] It appeared then that he would go ahead, as he had in 1910, and virtually disregard any unwelcome notices from his superiors.

J. M. Tupper, Royal Northwest Mounted Police inspector, commanding the Mackenzie subdistrict, informed Stefansson in the presence of Constable Brockie that he had heard "rumours" on 11 November 1916 that Ottawa wished to recall him (Stefansson) before he made any trips to Wrangel Island, where the *Karluk* survivors had landed. Inspector La Nauze had been instructed to get such correspondence to Stefansson "no matter what the costs." But Stefansson apparently brushed aside Tupper's remarks and

intimated that he was not going out of his way to get the mail, and he was sent up here to explore and that until the Government gave definite instructions to stop he was going to explore; and went on to cite the case of some General who was besieging Vicksburg and who though he knew messages were on the way calling him off, delayed the messages and captured the place. Stefansson said he would not go as far as to cut the wires, or anything like that, but as long as he had no instructions sent him he was not going out of his way to get any.[99]

Until the receipt of specific instructions then, Stefansson, like Lord Nelson, would go his own way, to the consternation of Canadian officialdom.

What spurred him on, aside from personal ambition, were other "rumours"—news that his arctic world might be invaded by others whom he felt had no right to be there. The Norwegian, Amundsen, and the naturalized American, Bartlett, under the auspices of their separate governments, had announced plans to explore the Arctic. Stefansson felt he must carry out an obvious duty for the benefit of Canada, even if Canada was unaware and unperturbed about alien expeditions that might be injurious to her northern claims. "It is evidently up to us to do something this winter if our country is to be first in this field."[100] Besides, Amundsen and Bartlett had their nerve in proposing to come into Stefansson's domain for "I assumed that the etiquette of the past would hold and no expedition would enter our part of the Arctic so long as I intended to continue the work— which I intended after a year at home. But now it seems that if we are to do anything either for ourselves or for the government we must do it this year. It is now or never."[101]

Such was Stefansson's rationalization for an expedition he had already planned to conduct immediately, without taking a year off to organize a new venture. Now he argued that he had been forced by circumstance to become the custodian of Canadian interests—an act for which he felt sure he would receive the requisite backing in the near future. No real expense would be involved in continuing the program, he asserted, and "the danger is certainly no greater than millions are taking now in the war, and the object is the same personal achievement and the glory of the cause or country you represent—in this case Canada and the British Empire. Possibly we may increase the square mileage of the Empire lands as much as the armies."[102]

Much to the consternation of Desbarats and the Naval Service, Stefansson, without prior authorization, publicly announced in January 1918 that a new ice trip would be forthcoming.[103] In early March, the party left Crow Island, Alaska, for the eight-hundred-mile trip to Wrangel Island, north of Siberia. But fortune and ill health prevented Stefansson from going. He was confined to hospital at Herschel Island with typhoid fever and then pneumonia. The fact that he sent out the party nevertheless, under Storkerson's direction, incensed Desbarats, who made every effort to get word to Stefansson that the Naval Service would not be liable for unauthorized expenditure.[104] The ice trip had not been authorized and the Naval Service saw nothing in its instructions to Stefansson that justified landing another exploration across the Arctic Ocean, far to the west of Canada's sector of the Arctic Ocean, on Wrangel Island: "This is a departure from the original scheme, contemplates a lengthening of your absence, and thereby the date on which your reports will be available."[105]

Earlier, Desbarats had given Stefansson the benefit of the doubt believing that the explorer had not received his department's instructions of 17 November 1915. At that time, the government wanted all aspects of the expedition completed by the summer of 1916. The Naval Service had agreed it was proper for Stefansson to continue with his work that season.[106] But this new trip of 1918 was something else. Twice, on 14 April 1916 and 6 August 1917, Sir Douglas Hazen, the minister of the Naval Service and Desbarats's superior, had assured the Commons that the expedition would be over within a year.[107] Stefansson's new enterprise would make utter fools of the government. He must come back. Yet Stefansson managed to get his way by deliberately avoiding the issue though knowing full well— but not officially—the mood of the Canadian government.

Professing innocence of the Naval Service's real intentions, he presented them with a *fait accompli*. The Canadian government, to avoid embarrassment, could only regret that its instructions had not reached Stefansson, and announce that as a result an ice party had been sent out in the spring of 1918.[108] All that could now be done was to wait patiently for Stefansson to return to Ottawa, write his reports, tie up loose ends of the expedition, and forget the episode. Stefansson's final return south in the fall of 1918, following his recovery from a serious illness, was the beginning of a whole new round in his relations with Ottawa and Canada.

7

The Arctic Empire of
Vilhjalmur Stefansson

The Canadian Arctic Expedition was finished. It had been Canada's greatest arctic effort to date, towering both scientifically and financially over all previous ones. New lands had been discovered and claimed for the Dominion by Stefansson; he and the Southern Section had brought home invaluable data from Canada's little known northern latitudes. Between 1914 and 1918, Stefansson and his companions discovered the world's last major land masses, Brock and Borden Islands, Meighen and Lougheed Islands. His exploratory parties ran a line of hydrographic soundings one hundred miles northwest of Cape Isachsen, and redefined portions of the arctic islands' coastlines. Stefansson lifted the curtain on about 65,000 square miles of Beaufort Sea to the north of the Mackenzie basin, 10,000 square miles of the Arctic Ocean west of Prince Patrick Island, about 3,000 square miles along the northeast coast of Victoria Island, and more than 15,000 square miles of land and sea to the northeast of Prince Patrick Island. His five and one-half years in the Arctic was a world's record for continuous arctic service, and reflected a dogged determination. His drifting on ice floes, combined with a fierce drive to survive the unknown, and a faith that they would succeed, carried him and his parties hundreds of miles from the nearest land.

The achievements of the Canadian Arctic Expedition, fascinating and spectacular in their own right, had been played out against a background of internal political manoeuvrings. The expedition witnessed numerous attempts by Stefansson to maintain favour with Ottawa, and to win the support of the public at large. The politics of survival involved, in essence, Stefansson's attempts to win petty political squabbles with the other members of the Canadian Arctic Expedition, particularly Anderson who seemed especially unco-operative. Survival also meant—for want of a better phrase

—Stefansson's involvement in the politics of publicity. Finally, survival included a concerted effort to urge the Naval Service, already sensitive to the expedition's problems, to carry on the fight on Stefansson's behalf in Ottawa. At times all of Stefansson's attempts were inextricably bound together. If he could hold his own, or regain the initiative, his future in Canada could be promising.

For Stefansson, the enterprise had to succeed—and succeed it did, in a grand manner. Although he had incurred the wrath of Anderson's Southern Section and the belated displeasure of the Naval Service, Stefansson had used a host of techniques to keep his work going and to remain in favour with Ottawa and the public at large. He had won his battles with the elements and with the wide range of political considerations related to the expedition. Stefansson presented his case effectively, though there were misrepresentations about actual events and about his own prowess in exploration and survival. Anderson, involuntarily, had helped enhance Stefansson's image by fighting his commander at every turn. Anderson, as much as Stefansson, had overreacted, but only Stefansson had the ability to turn defeat into seeming victory.

Stefansson had fully realized the value of publicity and felt that "if our case is suitably presented to the public, conclusions will be that this has been a successful expedition."[1] He no doubt was aware of the political disadvantages of having a bad press and how to avoid this danger. Stefansson was assured a good press by the *London Chronicle* and its associated newspapers with which he had a formal contract, and he received broad coverage in North America, mostly favourable. The type of attention the august *New York Times* paid him in their editorials also pleased the explorer:

A VIKING GOES EXPLORING

In character of an ancient type, [he] is an explorer of the most modern, seeking to make a careful scientific examination of the country traversed rather than to go faster and further than others. These probably he was content with, these less sensational achievements largely because there is none of the other variety left unattained at either end of the earth, but he makes no moan that there is now no pole for anybody to find, and goes calmly on, half frozen most of the time and half starved much of the time, with never a thought of turning back till his appointed work is done.[2]

Stefansson's successful return from the Arctic had signalled a new round in his Canadian career. After his near-fatal bouts with typhoid fever, pneumonia, and pleurisy in 1918, he may have felt that his exploring life was all but over, despite earlier intentions to return to the north. But once he left the north, he was no longer content with writing about his experiences. In his own words, he wanted to become "Salesman for the North," not only to make money for himself, though this was a concern.

Stefansson did not regard the expedition solely as a money-making enterprise *per se*, and indeed, by his own choice, he received no salary. His experiences on the expedition would enhance his writing and lecturing career, to be sure, and here, as Stefansson was well aware, lay the real opportunities for financial gain.[3] But to dismiss his efforts and his penchant for publicity on such crass grounds obscures an important point. As head of the expedition that he had created, he was responsible for more than the management of men and supplies—which he did not do well—and the carrying out of a program of exploration—which he did boldly and magnificently. As an organizer and promoter he had to put forth the best image possible of the expedition, with a view to securing more funds and support for any future exploratory or other endeavours. Yet such a position held perils. The seeking of publicity put him in a bad light with those who assumed that such pre-occupation meant that he was indifferent to scientific ends. Stefansson perhaps was, more by experience and performance than by formal training, a scientist. He was also a first-rate intellectual and a talented writer. Yet, at this juncture he may have tried to be too many types of scientist, possibly over-extending himself. The blood of the renaissance man flowed in his veins. "I don't mean to be merely an explorer or merely an ethnologist or merely anything—I want to be what a friendly critic would call an 'all around' man and what a hostile one would refer to as 'a jack-of-all-trades, master of none.' "[4] His mind was filled with ideas about the north and its future. The Dominion was his laboratory; Ottawa, the north, and his own personality were the elements in his experiment. Success or failure depended on a proper mixture of each of these ingredients, but in large measure on Stefansson himself. By the end of 1918, he was at the zenith of his public career, with virtually all the world at his feet anxious to listen and learn; and to act—or so Stefansson thought.

Some of Stefansson's ideas were unique and novel, while others were not, but he had a supreme knack of taking apparently unrelated ideas and moulding them into all-embracing new theories. This was his particular genius. He was a man of wide scope and vision, who adopted many contemporary notions to form a complete theory of arctic development. Much of the credit belongs to others, as Stefansson admitted, but he felt his task was to shout out to the public what he had learned. Besides, as he told Gilbert Grosvenor, when one is among many who advocate a revolutionary idea, such as transpolar commerce by aircraft, credit would go to the individual who gets into print first.[5]

The publication in 1922 of what he considered his "favorite" book,[6] *The Northward Course of Empire*, capped his arctic and intellectual career. Most of the book's chapters had appeared in other publications such as *World's Work* and the *National Geographic Magazine*, but now all his ideas and logic were brought together in extremely well integrated form under one cover. In his own arguments, Stefansson incorporated the "scientific" conclusions of others, while indicating that he had derived his approach independently "from a consideration of the facts of the world we live in."[7] Most useful for his own ideas was a graph which appeared in an article, "The Coldward Course of Progress," by S. Columb GilFillan, professor of Social Sciences at the University of the South.[8] GilFillan was a geographic determinist who contended that higher civilization and empire-building were functions of latitude. A subtle racist connotation was implicit in the argument that the "Path of Supremacy" throughout history was directly related to mean temperature, for it pointed to northern nations as the supreme powers of the future. Stefansson wished to show that nations which lay in the higher latitudes, especially those bordering the arctic seas, would be the future empires of the world. It was a logical conclusion, if one accepted the trends and assumptions portrayed in GilFillan's graph.

For Canada to realize its potential for empire Stefansson felt that the prejudices that prevented national development had to be removed. Citizens and responsible politicians must be educated to look upon the north as valuable land that could be exploited to achieve supremacy. Otherwise Canada's natural path of history would be perverted. Antiquated notions must be exposed and obliterated:

> We have not come to the northward limit of commercial progress. There was many a pause but no stop to the westward course of empire until we came to the place where East is West. In that sense only is there a northward limit to progress. Corner lots in Rome were precious when the banks of the Thames had no value; the products of Canada were little beyond furs and fish when the British and French agreed in preferring Guadelope. But values had shifted north since then and times have changed. Times will continue to change. There is no northern boundary beyond which productive enterprise cannot go till North meets North on the opposite shores of the Arctic Ocean as East has met West on the Pacific.[9]

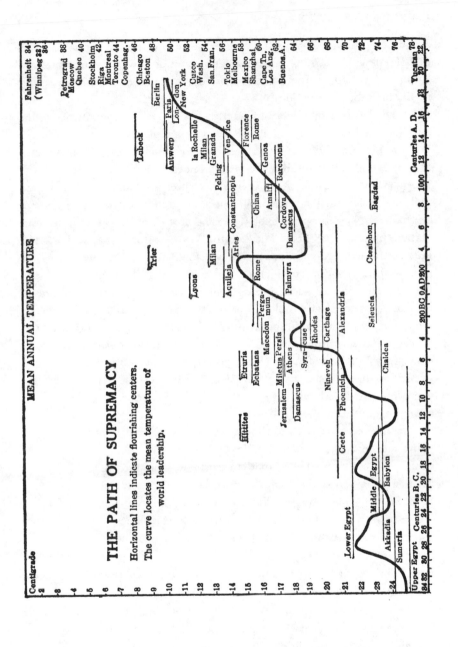

THE PATH OF SUPREMACY

Horizontal lines indicate flourishing centers.
The curve locates the mean temperature of
world leadership.

MEAN ANNUAL TEMPERATURE

Stefansson proclaimed himself a charter member of the "National University of Polite Unlearning," an institution one of his Harvard professors, Samuel McChord Crothers, had suggested as a means of dispelling popular myths and false information.[10]

The "Far North," Stefansson contended, was not unfriendly or hostile, but was "destined to be colonized in the same general way as were the Western prairies of the United States half a century ago, by the same type of people, and with a resulting civilization not fundamentally dissimilar."[11] The north was habitable. His own experiences and survival had proved that, and living in the north would become profitable when its resources and position were properly exploited. The north was, in Stefansson's estimation, not only "liveable" but "fruitful" in terms of its native flora and fauna. Although very little was known about its mineral resources, the north did have resources which could be offered the world. For example, the domestication of such grazing animals as the musk-ox could make Canada a world meat supplier. Canada's northern shoreline controlled a large portion of the arctic basin—in Stefansson's view the new Mediterranean—and when the Dominion understood its strategic position, Canada could establish herself as a world power, immeasurably enhancing the strength of the British empire. The pace of this advance depended on the strength of the "misknowledge" that had to be overcome, and the amount of "unlearning" that had to be done.

It was necessary both to show what the Arctic had to offer to men of vision and enthusiasm, and how enterprising individuals could tap and exploit its resources. The Canadian north was on the shore of a polar Mediterranean, a Mediterranean which because of insufficient technology until the 1920s had remained frozen and inaccessible. But now Stefansson saw in such technological advances as dirigibles, airplanes, and submarines —primitive as they may seem to us—the dawn of a new epoch for the Arctic and for Canada. These new machines could be readily adapted to service the top of the world and would become the vehicles of commerce in the future.

One of the earliest exponents of the use of the airplane in the Arctic had been Robert E. Peary, who as early as 1910 predicted the utility of the airplane in northern latitudes. In 1913, he became an honorary member of the Aero Club of America (founded in 1905), and from that time he urged the United States to attempt polar flying and become strong in the air generally.[12] Even though the airplane did not have the sophistication and capabilities of today's craft, Stefansson thought that transpolar air flights were both feasible and attractive. His genius, however, was to see the advantages of flying over the Arctic in terms of shortening distances and lines of commerce, as opposed to pure exploration. Airplanes could be used, but with their short range they would have to hop across the polar Mediterranean using a series of fuelling stations, such as Spitzbergen and Wrangel, and other islands still to be discovered which, in all probability, would be found by airborne exploration. Initially, Stefansson had little use for heavier-than-air craft in the arctic regions, believing that the submarine, if anything, would be the most natural and logical vehicle, until aviation developed further: "the airplanes had better wait until they can cross the Atlantic."[13] By 1919 they could; Alcock and Brown had shown the way. Flying over the Arctic would immeasurably cut down the time and distance between such diverse points as London and Tokyo by as much as 6,000 miles. His concepts anticipated the Great Circle air routes of today.

Equally important was the role of the submarine in the development of arctic transportation and commerce. This was actually Stefansson's special pet, partly because the idea, based on his observations of whales breaking their way through the ice to create breathing holes, was highly original. Others, too, had similar revolutionary ideas concerning submarine and under-ice work. Since the turn of the century, Simon Lake, for instance, had conducted experiments and had accumulated data on how an undersea cargo vessel should be constructed, including some novel devices: shock absorbers, upside down skis, and a snorkel for breathing.[14] Stefansson always made a point, though, of asserting—correctly—that his own concept had been arrived at independently. He did, however, request from people like Lake technical details to fill out his ideas. Stefansson would ultimately argue that a properly constructed submarine, based on the lessons learned during the Great War and using gyroscopic compasses, would be capable of under-ice navigation.[15]

> Under water a submarine can for a limited time maintain a speed of say ten knots, but at the much more economical speed of five knots a submerged journey of fifty miles is ordinary and one of two hundred miles not impossible even at the present-day stage of construction. This gives ample leeway for diving and passing entirely under the biggest piece of ice, coming up in free water on the other side. It may be objected that, from below, it is difficult to tell before rising whether you are going to rise in free water or under an ice cake. This is true, but the consequences are not serious. There is no danger of injuring the boat by rising against ice that is above it. The rise can be made very slowly, and naturally under-ice boats will have no conning tower, or other upward projection subject to injury.

Indeed, certain boats designed by Simon Lake carry a sort of toboggan on their backs so that when they rise against the ice they can steam ahead, sliding along its under surface, somewhat as a fly crawls on a ceiling, until finally the margin of the floe shall be reached when the boat will bob up into the open. Even apart from this the boat can rise and dive, rise and dive, as a whale does, going down each time it fails and trying again a few hundred yards ahead. . . . The most experienced man with whom I have so far talked was one who operated at times among ice to the north of Archangel during the war. He proposed a method of rising up through ice more spectacular than any that I had conceived but which he considered safe. The submarine he commanded had a bow fortified with the regular steel net cutter. His suggestion was that the boat should seek its greatest practical depth, say two hundred feet below the surface. It should then assume an angle of thirty to forty-five degrees and charge upward with a double speed attained by combining the forward thrust of the propeller with the acceleration obtainable by rapidly increasing the buoyancy of the boat so that it should fly upward somewhat as a cork does when released in water. The boat would then reach the surface with a velocity of perhaps fifteen or twenty miles per hour, which would give a sufficient blow to break ice of more than average thickness, especially in summer when it is moderately "rotten."[16]

Stefansson may not have completely understood the technical aspects of undersea navigation, but he did have the genius to foresee how such a development could be put to good use in the Arctic. The day would come, be it five or fifty years, when such inventions, he was certain, would turn the Arctic into a Mediterranean. Countries such as England, Japan, and Norway would become "neighbours across the northern sea."[17] Well within fifty years, Stefansson did see many of his prophecies become fact. In the 1920s there was a spate of arctic explorations and adventures involving the airplane, led by Admiral Byrd, Ben Eilsen, and Hubert Wilkins, to name only a few. In 1959, the nuclear-powered, sonar-equipped U.S.S. *Nautilus* silently traversed the Arctic Ocean; the same year the U.S.S. *Skate*, whose skipper had sought out Stefansson's advice before the voyage,[18] surfaced at the north pole. These events were in large part the culmination of ideas Stefansson had had as early as 1914 and of the abortive attempt in 1931 by his friend, Sir Hubert Wilkins, to try under-ice navigation using a modified submarine.

Yet, to make such notions attractive in 1919, Stefansson sincerely believed that the Arctic would have to prove that it had the commercial potential he ascribed to it. To this end, he launched a well-publicized campaign for the domestication of the musk-ox. Preaching was to be put into practice.

Before Stefansson came to believe in the domestication of species like the caribou, reindeer, and musk-ox, he devoted his energies to their protection and conservation. In 1914, for instance, he was anxious that the Dominion government through the offices of the prime minister, Robert Borden, and the influential Clifford Sifton, chairman of the Committee on Conservation, should prepare a broad plan for the conservation of the natives and fauna of the Arctic. Contending that he had "more definite information about the resources of certain districts than . . . anyone else," Stefansson urged the government of Canada to take prompt action.[19] Unhappy about the desperate situation of the disease-ridden and debauched Mackenzie Delta Eskimo, who had been exposed to civilization, Stefansson tried to ensure that the relatively untouched "prosperous, well-dressed, healthy, and contented Eskimos of the Coronation Gulf area be protected along with their means of support."[20]

Two main things were to be done. First, it was necessary "[to] protect these healthy people from the incoming of contagious and especially epidemic diseases now absent among them, and especially from those which medical science is, up to the present, unable to cope with such as measles and (to a lesser degree) syphillis[.]"[21] The conservation of the Eskimo, after all, was a conservation of natural resources, argued Stefansson, "for it is his presence alone that renders this section a source of possible profit to traders." Apart from humanitarian reasons, the only good Eskimo was a live one, for "[d]ead Eskimo trap no fur, and ill clothed Eskimo, like those of the Mackenzie today trap far less fur than they would otherwise, for, their cotton garments do not allow them to tend traps except in good weather."[22] Just as important, and virtually linked with the welfare of the Eskimo, was the protection of the caribou and other "food animals" from "wanton destruction such as was followed to exterminate those of the Mackenzie and Alaska within the last twenty years . . . (a) to ensure a permanent food and clothing supply to the Eskimo, and (b) to conserve for the people of Canada of all races a valuable natural resource of our country in a section which for the present, has no other considerable natural product of value."[23]

The Eskimo, though, had to face the prospect of increasing contacts with the outside world in all its unseemly forms. As Stefansson suggested, quarantine regulations and game laws were only a delaying action. This, the Canadian government had early recognized. The Eskimo inevitably would be caught in changes, for it was impossible to keep them and the animal species of the north in the grip of even an enlightened system of segregation. Before long, Stefansson became convinced that the Eskimo would have to adapt to the intrusion of the outside world. By using the resources on hand, he would be able to survive. The utility and future of the Eskimo were to figure largely in Stefansson's later plans regarding the domestication of native herds.

As time went on, Stefansson became more impressed with the possibilities of domesticating the musk-ox, rather than the caribou or reindeer. Earlier, he had advocated the protection and conservation of these northern animals. This theme, like his concern for the Eskimo before the onslaught of traders and missionaries, was, however, soon forgotten, or at least given a lower priority. In a 1917 memorandum to Sir Richard McBride, entitled "Possible New Domestic Animals for Cold Countries," Stefansson indicated that he was no longer really as concerned with conserving large northern animals as he was in breeding certain species and increasing their herd size for domestic purposes. In a sense, this was an aggressive sort of game conservation:

> The reindeer industry is now well established by the United States Government in Alaska and the herds will, in natural course, doubtless increase till most of the tundra is utilized for pasturage, unless a more profitable use of the ground is discovered. In Asia and Europe the tending of reindeer herds antedates history.
>
> In spite of the ancient character of the industry[,] reindeer are in most if not all places where they are now found, wild to the degree that they must be lassoed as semi-wild cattle of our large ranches must also be lassoed. In Alaska a dog not used to reindeer or a wolf will stampede and scatter an untended herd, and in some cases even herds that have an attendant, and animals are thus frequently lost even when they are not killed by wolves. In bad weather the herds are sometimes hard to control and in inclement springs a large percentage of the fawns die in spite of the best efforts of the herders.
>
> From these points of view the reindeer is, therefore, not an ideal domestic animal for the arctic lands. A further disadvantage is that a reindeer unlike a sheep is of no commercial value until after it is killed, except the few that are used as draught animals. True, reindeer are milked in some districts, but they are unsatisfactory as compared with most other milk animals.[24]

This early attitude about the shortcomings of reindeer as a domesticated animal makes interesting reading and leaves one to wonder why Stefansson, in league with the Hudson's Bay Company in the early 1920s, pursued the domestication of a species with known foraging eccentricities.

In 1917, Stefansson and his men were favourably impressed with the possibilities of the musk-ox which acted "more like domestic cattle than does the average Alaskan reindeer herd." The animals were essentially tame, and even when threatened by dogs or wolves they did not stampede or scatter, but grouped together for protection. Furthermore, in Stefansson's view,

> [a] full grown muskox gives three times as much meat, probably, as a grown reindeer of the same sex and two or three times as much fat. (as to the time it takes each to mature I do not have the facts) . . . A muskox gives three to four times as much milk as a reindeer. The milk is considered by the white men of our parties, to be better than cow's milk in taste. It differs less from cow's milk than reindeer milk does. It is clearly rich in fat . . . But the great advantage of the muskox over caribou is that, like sheep, they furnish a large amount of wool annually without having to be killed first.[25]

The animal might not be as good a draught animal as the reindeer, nor would its skins make good clothing, but musk-oxen were much more manageable in herds and required little attention, except at calving time.

Stefansson did not consider their domestication in terms of solving the more immediate needs of the Eskimo, but he did feel that such an industry would benefit the white man and the native alike:

> I shall not go into details of how the initial breeding animals could be secured, but it is a simple matter, whether on the mainland while they are not yet exterminated or in the uninhabited arctic islands. Simplest of all would be to set apart, say, Melville Island, as an experimental station. If it should not be deemed proper that I urge this matter publicly while in Government service, I hope to do so when the service is ended. When the southern part of our country becomes densely populated, and with our short Hudson Bay and British Columbia routes to Europe and the Orient, such a pastoral development of Arctic Canada as I have outlined above would become of great commercial importance. That the meat of the musk-ox would not find a ready market need not be feared. Few persons, as it is, could distinguish it from beef under most forms of modern meat cooking.[26]

Stefansson sincerely believed that musk-oxen could make the arctic tundra as valuable as sheep made the grazing areas of Alberta. The reindeer could not hope to do the like.[27]

So impressed with the possibilities of the musk-ox was Stefansson that he sent samples of the animals' wool to Prime Minister Borden,[28] and, amongst others, Sir Edmund Walker. Walker, a good friend, was quite enthusiastic about the prospects of developing such an industry in the near future,[29] and was to prove a very important ally to Stefansson's crusade. Stefansson also enlisted the support of the aging Theodore Roosevelt, former president of the United States, fellow explorer, adventurer, and sportsman, who wished the project well:

> as regards the future of the country. Our domestic animals are merely those of Asia, because it was in Asia that civilization first arose, and in consequence, as it penetrated other continents, men found it easier to use the animals already tamed, than to tame new ones ... It is a capital misfortune that the African land has not been tamed. It is a capital misfortune that the musk-ox has not been tamed.[30]

Roosevelt promised to do everything he could to back Stefansson's endeavours.[31] Unfortunately, he died a few months after this endorsement.

Stefansson's first opportunity to publicize the utility of domesticating reindeer and musk-ox came in the late fall of 1918, shortly after his return from the north. On 11 November 1918, a very auspicious day when enthusiasm and optimism for the Armistice may have spilled over for his proposals, Stefansson appeared before the Empire Club at Toronto's Massey Hall. There he proposed the creation of a reindeer industry in Canada similar to the one that had been continuously successful in Alaska since 1890. Between 1893 and 1915, for example, the number of herds established in Alaska grew from nine to seventy-six, while the number of Eskimos employed in the project rose from sixty-eight to 1,140. In that same period the number of reindeer owned outright by Alaskan Eskimos went from 2,841 to 46,683 and their income increased from $4,500 to $379,407. The valuation of the herd rocketed from $71,025 to $1,167,075. To the United States Department of the Interior, these and additional considerations represented an increase of "926 per cent for the 25 years, or an average annual gain of 37 per cent."[32] The spectacular success of the Alaskan experiment could, it would be argued, be duplicated in Canada. Essentially, Stefansson told his Massey Hall audience what he had spelled out in earlier letters to Canadian officials. He concluded—again arguing from analogy—

> that while this is about the most important project in my opinion, that

is now before Canada in her period of reconstruction after the war—
this particular possible development of the whole of Canada as a
grazing country—still the most interesting thing, I think, is the fact
that the climate of Canada is not at all disagreeable. It is by no means
prohibitive of further development. I take it as certain that just as the
people of the Euphrates and Crete and Greece and Italy and Spain
progressively made mistakes about the countries north of them, so we
still undervalue the country north of us, and civilization as high as
that which has developed in Ontario, is certain to be developed further
north than Ontario, to a distance that the wisest of us would be foolish
to try to estimate.[33]

The reception to this speech warmed the heart of the explorer, particularly the glowing remarks of Sir Edmund Walker. Said the president of
the Canadian Bank of Commerce:

It is not given to men of many parts of the world to bring into the
civilization of Canada a new element; but when Stefansson was born
in Manitoba of Icelandic parents he remained somehow sufficiently
near to the parental stock to bring to this country the feeling of
attraction towards the north as opposed to what he has himself been
speaking about—the average repulsion of the British stock towards the
north. I have spent part of my life for the last thirty years in trying
annually to put before the people of Canada the industrial possibilities
of this country; and I know that one of the things we have always
fought is that man is very much like the dog—he loves the fire, hates
cold, and hates the north. It is one of the most difficult things to make
Canadians believe in the value of their own country. What Mr.
Stefansson had said about the muskox and what can be done in our
northern country is no dream. It is a thing of the most tremendous
significance, and something we ought to weigh and make up our
minds as strenuously as he does. We have reached the time when the
packers of Canada and the United States will be going to the Argentine
to see what can be made of the vast herds of animals in that country.
We have talked quite glibly of having as large an area as the United
States, and we talk about having as large a population in years to
[come] as that country. We can never have that until we take hold of
the resources of this country on which man can exist. Mr. Stefansson
has presented a great subject, a great problem which should be tried
out by the Government. If it is a failure it will not cost as much as
other things in which mistakes have been made, while if it is successful

it will add to our food supplies for all time to come. (Hear, Hear) How can we doubt the north when we know that the sea in the north is more filled with pelagic life than anywhere else? There is life of the most vigorous kind all over that north country. We as a people have found out what northern blood means. Surely we have learned in that we are not like our friends to the South; certainly we have learned that the hysteric quality that does not lead so much to action, that has distinguished some of our cousins, has been more absent in this country; surely we know that the reserve and strength of character that is in our northern blood has meant victory in this war. We ought to be proud of the fact that we are northern people, and we have not to be afraid to breast the wave. We should take hold of the north, and of the one thing that is suggested by [Stefansson], which will not cost much to demonstrate, and which should be a great benefit to this country if successful.[34]

Stefansson had chosen his main backer well, for after Sir Edmund's remarks, there was a keen desire by other "strong Canadians" to endorse the project.[35] His timing seemed perfect, for the Canadian government had already recognized the virtues of establishing such enterprises under private auspices.

On 25 July 1918, while Stefansson was still in the north recovering from his illness, the Canadian government had granted sizeable grazing privileges in northwest Manitoba for thirty years, to a certain North American Reindeer Company (Inc.) of South Bend, Indiana. The order-in-council recited the following argument:

The introduction of reindeer into Alaska by the United States has resulted in an insured food supply for the natives and sufficient means of transportation; and within recent years a considerable quantity of reindeer meat has been available for export to Seattle and other Pacific coast points. It is considered that the northern areas of the Northwest Territories are exceptionally suitable for reindeer. The development of reindeer herds in the territory should be a great value in the matter of an assured food supply for the native population; the utilization of trained reindeer will provide means of transportation and permit . . . the effective exploration of the country; and eventually the reindeer herds should contribute substantially to the meat supply of the rest of Canada. However, the introduction of reindeer into northern Canada will necessarily involve considerable risk, and a large expenditure as well as expert handling and if pioneer work is undertaken by private individuals or corporations on an extensive scale, sufficient to insure a reasonable success, the Minister is of the opinion that such persons or corporations should receive encouragement from the Dominion to the extent of free grazing privileges for limited term.

The Minister, therefore, recommends that he be authorized to grant permits for free grazing privileges for reindeer, for a period not exceeding thirty years to any persons or corporations who establish bona fides of the enterprise to the satisfaction of the Minister of the Interior.[36]

Thus Stefansson had not only the requisite support from Toronto interests, but a ready-made commitment in principle by the Dominion.

Stefansson was convinced he was the only person who could carry his proposals to fruition. Later, when the time was ripe he would introduce Jafet Lindeberg into the picture.

Most of Stefansson's statistical information had come from Lindeberg, an Alaskan reindeer entrepreneur who was interested in inducing the Canadian government (or private Canadian or British concerns) to domesticate the reindeer in Canada.[37] Stefansson promised to do his best to further Lindeberg's reindeer plans, and he did so by publicly mentioning Lindeberg's eagerness for such a project. Stefansson was quite certain his own plans for the musk-ox would not interfere in the least with reindeer work—"in fact the two will go very well together."[38] In the meantime, he advised Lindeberg, who was anxious to sell his herds to Canada and who used Stefansson as his agent, to delay his dealings with the Canadian government. If Stefansson were allowed to present the scheme, the government could use him as one of its principal advisors.[39] Sir Edmund Walker had asked Stefansson to undertake the management of such a project if Sir Edmund and his friends were successful in securing government support, and Stefansson was certain Ottawa would give its blessing to such an influential clique of Canadian businessmen. The Conservative party, of course, had not forgotten the vital contribution of the erstwhile Liberal, Walker, and other dissident Toronto Liberals to Borden's campaign during the election of 1911. Lindeberg should wait in the wings until Borden returned from Europe which was the appropriate time to broach the subject to the government. Lindeberg was advised to use the ensuing time to import and train Eskimo herders, so that the Canadian government would have a ready-made package to buy.[40] The correct way to obtain the best support was to wait until the prime minister's return, and then gain his much needed backing.[41]

At the same time (the winter of 1918–19) while Stefansson was engaged in convincing Canadian authorities, he was actively promoting essentially the same scheme in the United States. No doubt he envisaged some sort of co-operation between the two governments to develop the pastoral regions of northern North America.[42] Furthermore, by dividing the effort, if he were unsuccessful in one country he could still hope to obtain some support in the other and thus avoid complete failure. While attending Roosevelt's funeral early in January 1919, and making speeches at the Yale Club, he made important contacts with some of the men whose departments would have a direct interest in the reindeer and musk-ox project. At a luncheon of the National Geographic Society on 11 January 1919, Stefansson also met an enthusiastic Governor Riggs of Alaska. The previous day he had had a thirty-minute interview with Franklin K. Lane, secretary of the Interior, at which Stefansson did most of the talking. Lane wanted him to take charge of the musk-ox project and meet the appropriate committee of Congress and to explain his plans, but Stefansson declined his offer of a job.[43] A few days later, on 14 January 1919, he apparently converted William C. Redfield, secretary of Commerce.[44] Such responses certainly brightened Stefansson's hopes that some sort of co-operation could be achieved between the two countries, at least with regard to the musk-ox. A joint musk-ox venture, however, apparently never went beyond the talking stage, though there is good evidence of the interest both governments had in the project and their willingness to co-operate on expenses.[45]

Actually, as became apparent to Stefansson later, he was able to make better headway by linking the musk-ox project with that of the domestication of reindeer. The latter already had been recognized as a viable industry. Hence, Stefansson began promoting both projects with equal vigour, even though it meant slower progress than would be attained by pursuing a single objective. Stefansson impressed Duncan Campbell Scott, deputy superintendent general of Indian Affairs, and Borden's minister of Interior, Arthur Meighen. Both men, according to Stefansson, were favourable to the reindeer proposition[46] and were asking his advice to push the matter through Parliament.[47] Lindeberg, waiting in the wings, was now writing to offer the Canadian government a ready-developed industry.[48]

Meighen was especially impressed.[49] Stefansson had evoked a vision of the commercial empire of the Canadian north. No person who had Canada's success and future at heart could help but be enraptured by Stefansson's broad strokes:

It may seem that much of the north is inaccessible and that transportation difficulties are an insuperable handicap, but this will seem so only to those who fail to realize the development of our West. It is a common thing when talking with the pioneers of Vancouver and Seattle to hear stories of how Easterners of forty or fifty years ago were stoutly of the opinion that the country would never come of value because it was "so far away from everywhere." Just as the Canadian Pacific and other railroads crawled slowly westward, so will other railways move north, and their pace will not be snail-like if we take to heart the lesson of the past and realize that these railways . . . are going to become outlets for vast natural resources. Of course, as long as we adhere to the blind dogma of the worthlessness of the north, it will appear obvious that the building of railways to the northward is merely a waste of labor and good money.[50]

Stefansson was confident, for example, that the railway from Edmonton to Fort McMurray would greatly enhance the transportation possibilities of the entire Mackenzie River system, a transportation system with the same potential for tapping the rich interior as the Hudson Bay route. Stefansson was resigned to the fact that many people would scoff at his schemes as grandiose and foolhardy, but "[m]atters of that sort are neither visions nor prophecy; they are merely calculations from reliable data."[51]

Meighen supported Stefansson's arguments to the point of arranging for him to address a joint session of the House of Commons and Senate to popularize the project. On Tuesday, 6 May, at 10.00 a.m., Stefansson faced the honourable members in the Railway Committee Room. This unusual public appearance, a powerful indication of the extent of Stefansson's growing influence in the Canadian capital, probably did more than anything else to bring him into the halls of official authority. Stefansson put forward his plans for the future of Canada and the world. Canada could help overcome the world's present and future food shortages. Northern Canada with her "undoubted resources" and a "million square acres of excellent grazing land" was "on the threshold of the same sort of steady development as that which has made our middle west one of the great food producing regions of the world . . . If we do it [i.e.: domesticate the reindeer and musk-ox] and do it on a large scale . . . we shall through these two animals within the next twenty years convert northern Canada from a land of practically no value, to the great permanent wool and meat producing country of the Western Hemisphere."[52] The inspirational and apparently sound nature of the presentation, coupled with Stefansson's personable style and reputation, and the obvious backing of Meighen, took hold of the assembled legislators. A dazzling glimpse at the potential of Canada's north was unfolded before them. Stefansson whetted the appetites of the aders of a victorious, optimistic, patriotic country by holding out new prospects for Canada in the postwar world. He gauged the result of his speech as a rousing success,[53] and he was correct.[54]

After measuring Stefansson's impact, Meighen sprang into action by recommending to the cabinet that a royal commission be established to look into the matter thoroughly. To his close friend, J. S. McLean, manager of the Harris Abattoir Co. (later Canada Packers Limited) of Toronto, he wrote privately:

> I am thinking of recommending to Council, the appointment of a commission to study and report upon the possibilities of developing the musk-ox and reindeer industry in Northern Canada . . . Recently I had [Stefansson] address the members of the Commons and Senate, and his speech made a pronounced impression. I have a lot of respect for the opinion of Theodore Roosevelt, which on this subject was to the effect that the domestication of cattle and other domestic animals as distinguished from the presently undomesticated animals, was merely accidental, and that the proper method of utilizing the north-land, is by taking possession of, and cultivating the animals native thereto, rather than by forcing the cultivation there, of animals native to milder climates. You are aware of course of the success that has attended the development of the reindeer industry in Northern Alaska by the United States.
>
> The project[,] in essence, is a business project. My idea is to have a report on it by a body of businessmen in whose personnel an element of the imaginative will have a place. Would you permit me to include your name among the recommended? Council may not agree with my proposal, but should my colleagues be persuaded I am anxious that you be a member of the commission. So far, I have written to no other, and, will treat your reply as confidential.[55]

Needless to say, McLean accepted the offer, but warned Meighen that "I know nothing of Musk-ox or Reindeer. I have never seen them except in a zoo."[56]

One wonders why the Canadian government embarked upon the course of creating a royal commission, when for all intents and purposes a government policy had been established on the question almost one year prior to the commission's creation and even before Stefansson's earnest campaigning. The North American Reindeer Company had received the Canadian government's blessing and support without any protracted investigation. No doubt it will remain another mysterious example of the workings of inner government. Perhaps the introduction of the element of the musk-ox, which had been declared a protected species in 1917, necessitated such an investigation. Only at a later stage, after Stefansson had devoted his time exclusively to the musk-ox, were the two species combined in a comprehensive plan. Needless to say, the royal commission was a convenient forum to publicize the domestication of the reindeer, and more importantly, the project closer to Stefansson's heart, the domestication of the superior musk-ox.[57]

On 20 May 1919, a royal commission was authorized to investigate the potentialities and viability of such industries "from a business and national standpoint," since, as the order-in-council recited, "there are good grounds for believing that the Canadian north may become a great permanent meat and wool producing area."[58] Stefansson could scarcely help being overjoyed; the government had appropriately recognized his efforts by making him one of the commissioners. The other members of the commission were James B. Harkin of Meighen's department of the Interior; and John Stanley McLean of Harris Abattoir; the chairman was John Gunion Rutherford of the Canadian Board of Railway Commissioners.

Stefansson could trust that most of the members of the commission were sympathetic to his aims. The only dark cloud on the horizon, from Stefansson's point of view, was the appointment of John Rutherford as chairman. Stefansson, rather indiscreetly, expressed himself as "heartbroken" over this decision, which to him was "a method of sabotage, of 'killing in committee.' I shall be greatly and agreeably surprised if this commission does anything."[59] Rutherford, according to Stefansson, seemed a "pessimist of the possibilities of the north and only mildly interested in our project."[60] He would have preferred someone more favourable, like Colonel J. S. Dennis, head of the C.P.R.'s department of Colonization and Development.[61] Nevertheless, with the commission, Stefansson had won his vehicle for official publicity, and it was an extremely useful step in his venture into the world of private business, for the establishment of the Musk-ox and Reindeer Commission imparted an air of legitimacy to Stefansson's ideas. As the expert, Stefansson was bound to be the key member, since his colleagues looked to him for advice and suggestions as to who should be interviewed. Naturally he was more than ready to provide them with such a list, and he personally recruited many of the witnesses.

The commission was appointed on 20 May 1919, but it was not until 24 January the following year that the first of the four public hearings was held; the other three, also held in Ottawa, being on 4–5 February, 29–30 April, and 12 May 1920.[62] In all, thirty-five expert witnesses appeared before the board.[63] Unfortunately, only the conclusions and recommendations were published, but not until two years later, somewhat indicative of the low priority that the newly elected Liberal government gave to the entire subject. The published findings appeared in a slim ninety-nine-page report, of which roughly fifty-eight pages were additional appendices. Such limited publication and belated distribution indicates that the commission was no better than a partial success.

For instance, the findings on the utility of the musk-ox were mixed and were more guarded than were Stefansson's original appraisals which, admittedly, had not been based on extensive data. This applied particularly to the supposed use of musk-ox wool. The commission did not fully sustain Stefansson's claims. Stefansson saw the domestication of reindeer and musk-ox as a means of making Canada's north one of the great meat and wool producing areas of the world. According to the commission's findings, though, the utilization of musk-ox wool was problematical:

> In itself the wool is of fair quality, but . . . no machinery has so far been perfected which will successfully separate it from the coarse hair of the outer coat, with which it becomes mixed when being shed.
>
> The shedding is a gradual process, the new wool taking the place of the old as this is shed, and there is, therefore, grave doubt as to the practicability of removing the latter until it has been properly replaced by the fresh growth.
>
> In this connection it will be noted that Professor Hornaday states that one of the musk-ox in the New York Zoological Gardens, from which the old wool was combed, died some three weeks later from pneumonia.[64]

Stefansson, of course, had never experienced this phenomenon simply because the wool he had gathered came from carcasses killed for food. These discouraging prospects severely discounted Stefansson's rosy picture of the future of the Canadian north and the place of the musk-ox in its development. The report conceded that the flesh of the younger animals was very palatable, and acknowledged the fact that musk-ox were "admirably" suited for domestication.[65] Yet it expressed a great present concern

1 R. M. Anderson in Copper ("Blond") Eskimo outfit, 1912.

2 Stefansson taking part in official ceremonies on board the *Karluk* shortly before she sailed, 1913.

3　Scientific staff of the Canadian Arctic Expedition at Nome, Alaska, 13 July 1913. *Front row, left to right* F. MacKay, surgeon (died on the ice of Chukchi Sea); Capt. Robert Bartlett, skipper of the *Karluk*; Vilhjalmur Stefansson, commander of the expedition; R. M. Anderson, zoologist and 2nd in command; James Murray, marine biologist (died on the ice of Chukchi Sea); Frits Johansen, marine biologist. *Back row, left to right* B. Mamen, meteorologist (died on Wrangel Island); B. M. McConnell, secretary; K. G. Chipman, topographer; (behind Chipman) G. H. Wilkins, photographer (afterwards Sir Hubert Wilkins); George Malloch, geologist (died on Wrangel Island); Henri Beuchat, anthropologist (died on the ice of Chukchi Sea); J. J. O'Neill, geologist; D. Jenness, anthropologist; J. R. Cox, topographer; W. L. McKinlay, magnetician and meteorologist.

4   K. G. Chipman outside James Bay
Hotel, Victoria, B.C., 1913.

5   R. M. Anderson and his wife,
shortly before the *Karluk* sailed.

6 The last photograph taken of the *Karluk* before she went down,
November 1913.

7 Stefansson's ice party leaving Collinson Point, Alaska, 16 March 1914.

8 Stefansson at Collinson Point, spring 1914.

SURVIVORS OF THE S.S. "KARLUK", OF THE CANADIAN ARCTIC EXPEDITION, RESCUED FROM WRANGEL ISLAND BY THE SCHOONER "KING AND WING"

9 Survivors of the *Karluk* rescued from Wrangel Island.

10 Northern Party cutting through a pressure ridge off the arctic coast of Alaska, March 1914.

11   Allan Crawford, who perished during Stefansson's private expedition to Wrangel Island, 1921–23.

12   Headquarters of the Southern Party, Bernard Harbour, 12 July 1916.

13   Monument to Stefansson, sculptured by Walter Yarwood, Arnes, Manitoba.

about the dwindling number of musk-ox and called rather for their conservation than their exploitation.[66]

As for the reindeer industry, about which Stefansson had greater reservations, the commission, impressed by the Alaskan experiments, suggested that a number of experimental herds be developed in the most suitable areas for the support of the Eskimos. Such industries could provide food supplies for future white entrepreneurs who might develop mineral and other natural resources in the north, and "lay the foundation for a possible future commercial meat industry."[67]

Essentially, then, the report was extremely cautious and conservative with its recommendations, something far removed from Stefansson's own attitudes and from the purposes for which he had initiated the committee.

By nature, Stefansson was not the type of man to move slowly, especially when he had the courage of his convictions. The first of the seven hearings was held a full six months after the creation of the commission; an inexcusable loss of time in Stefansson's eyes. His impatience was accentuated by his certainty, as early as June 1919, that the commission agreed with his "logical" ideas but were prolonging the investigation for formality's sake.[68] This manner of procedure—to him typical of bureaucratic red tape—was not to his taste. This was no time for experiment, but for action. Stefansson wanted to take the immediate initiative, without waiting for the final recommendations, which he sensed would be couched in very conservative language. By early March 1920, after the second round of protracted and tedious hearings, he could wait no longer.

On 8 March 1920, Stefansson applied for a lease which would enable him to create a "Reindeer Syndicate" to carry out the domestication of reindeer.[69] After he had the lease, he hoped he would be able to interest a "sound company" with "energy and discretion backed by sufficient capital"[70] to carry his plans through to their ultimate success. By this time, he was thinking of the Hudson's Bay Company rather than of his earlier associate, Jafet Lindeberg. Lindeberg had been hurt by the "complications" and delays in Ottawa. Like Stefansson, he had been overly optimistic, but had committed himself much further, purchasing the ship *Polar Bear* expressly for the reindeer venture he and Stefansson had worked out. "And now it is up to you [Stefansson] to get me the business so that I can make use of the boat."[71] Early in the royal commission's proceedings, Stefansson had scuttled Lindeberg's prospects, informing Rutherford that in the light of talks with meat packers and "others who have dealt with reindeer in Alaska" he was certain that no adequate number of reindeer could be secured in Alaska.[72] Stefansson contended that only some 2,000 head could be secured from Alaska with the permission of the American government and these would be available for domestication and breeding only in the Yukon and near the Mackenzie River. For some reason, Stefansson failed to mention to Rutherford Lindeberg's ready offer to supply up to 4,000 head if the Canadian government so desired.[73] Lindeberg certainly appears to have had the available stock, but his chances of securing a contract were severely handicapped by his associate's personal assessments of his capability and the Alaskan situation, and he never succeeded in interesting the Canadian government in his readiness to do business. Lindeberg was left in the lurch.

Stefansson realized that a conflict of interest existed between his membership on the Reindeer Commission and his application for a lease; therefore he resigned from the commission on 12 March 1920, feeling that he could do more good from the outside.[74] Perhaps this resignation would have been more proper had he handed it in before requesting the lease, or before he had contacted certain business concerns. Stefansson, it should be noted, had approached the Hudson's Bay Company sometime in December 1919, or January 1920—even before the hearings had begun.

The lease from the government was not granted until 1 June 1920.[75] In the interval, Stefansson was in England, armed with a letter of introduction from Sir Edmund Walker to Sir Robert Kindersley, governor of the Hudson's Bay Committee. On the afternoon of 25 March 1920, he attended a board meeting of the Hudson's Bay Company, which included Sir Robert, Charles Sale, the deputy governor, and Vivian Hugh Smith of J. P. Morgan. There he outlined his business proposals and answered questions.[76] He followed this by courting Charles Sale, the man he felt held the key to success. The powerful, ambitious Sale appeared fully aware of the potential of northern development,[77] and suggested that the musk-ox plans might even be attempted after one year if the reindeer project proved successful.[78] Stefansson naturally was elated, for he found very little convincing was necessary. The company apparently told him that all that was needed was to ascertain the policy of the Canadian government and the details of operation.[79]

Anticipating the formal arrangements with the company on 12 April, Stefansson made preparations to send Storkerson to Norway to secure reindeer and Lapp families; he proposed that his former arctic companion be made manager of the station.[80] However, Stefansson was betrayed by overconfidence. Two days later, on the 14th, he was curtly informed by Sale that "it [had become] apparent that annual outlays of a substantial nature would be required and we have also formed the opinion, contrary to our first impressions, that the project will entail various problems requiring time and attention which we cannot afford to give at this juncture."[81] Sale, whom Stefansson trusted implicitly, told the company's New York agent that Stefansson was unreasonable in striving to establish such a large venture in the same year; Stefansson had failed to consider the tremendous amount of work that would be required of the Hudson's Bay Company of making arrangements for such items as coal and supplies. "We cannot too strongly urge the utmost conservation at this time and the danger of engaging in any operations for which one cannot see clearly both the means and the end."[82]

This new position might have dashed Stefansson's project then and there, but instead, on the 15th of April, he began intensive first-hand negotiations to persuade the company to reconsider. He pushed ahead and secured promises that the company would enter into certain arrangements with him that year, provided Stefansson secured the lease for which he had applied. The Hudson's Bay Company would then incorporate a limited liability company under Canadian jurisdiction with a share capital of $200,000 divided into 200 shares, 170 shares being retained by the company or their "friends"; ten shares (i.e. $10,000) to be allotted to Stefansson "credited as fully paid in consideration for [his] services in obtaining the concession . . ."[83] Stefansson accepted the proposal with only minor modifications and no hesitation.

Now it was up to Stefansson to make good his part of the bargain. The lease was still pending. It would be forthcoming, but would need some pushing by Stefansson. The Canadian cabinet doubtless had more important matters before it, but Stefansson felt that for them to take an obstructive attitude would have been sheer stupidity.[84] Stefansson's main argument was to use the possible British investments as leverage. British investors, Meighen was informed, were ready to invest immediately in the Canadian project rather than in Russia where political turmoil was the order of the day.[85] Indeed, as Stefansson advised J. S. McLean, the Hudson's Bay Company had also founded a Hudson's Bay North Russia Company, with a capitalization of £100,000 (i.e. $500,000), to tap Russian fur and reindeer resources.[86] The time was right for Canada to act, argued Stefansson.

On 1 June 1920, Stefansson received his lease to the southwest portion of Baffin Island. Exclusive grazing privileges for his reindeer were allotted on the western portion of the island at 68° north—113,900 square miles in all. In addition, he was given the right to maintain and operate butchering, canning, tanning, or other reindeer-related establishments.[87] A little later, the government permitted Stefansson to transfer the lease to the Hudson's Bay Company, provided that stock of the new company might be bought by no one but Stefansson and legitimate shareholders of the company.[88]

The Hudson's Bay Company carried out its part of the bargain. The trustees of the newly formed Hudson's Bay Reindeer Company, Sir Augustus Nanton and Edward Fitzgerald, gave Stefansson, in consideration for his services *vis-à-vis* the lease and the transfer, ten shares of the capital stock, with option of buying a further twenty shares at par value not later than 31 October 1922. Also, after six calving seasons, he would receive a bonus of a further five shares fully paid for by the company. Stefansson was also to be employed by the Hudson's Bay Reindeer Company "in an advisory capacity to give expert advice and perform other special services of an advisory nature" with a relatively small salary. Finally, he had the option of becoming one of the directors of the company.[89] The lease was formally transferred by Stefansson to the company on 6 November 1920.[90]

This was quite an achievement for Stefansson. Within two years of his return from the Arctic, besides his many other activities, he had managed to impress his ideas upon one of the most respectable financial concerns in the world and had become a director in one of its most promising subsidiaries. His reputation as an arctic explorer and authority on arctic matters, his membership on the Reindeer and Musk-ox Commission, and the backing of some of the most influential men in Canada no doubt added weight to the Hudson's Bay Company decision. But everything thereafter was downhill.

Stefansson was eager to do everything in his power to make the company succeed, but, as he afterwards confessed, he was tied up with many other commitments—lecturing across North America, planning for the Wrangel Island expedition, writing his story of the expedition of 1913–18. He could not push the project "as it should have been pushed." Besides, the new company, like its parent, refused to rush headlong into such an untried project merely at Stefansson's urging.[91] He suggested that the newspaper publicity should play down the profit motive, and emphasize instead the public-spirited character of the Hudson's Bay Company.[92] Stefansson was moving too quickly perhaps for the Hudson's Bay Company and its subsidiary, who were not interested in publicity or other schemes. In the winter following the official incorporation, Jafet Lindeberg indicated he was now in deep financial trouble and was anxious to sell his reindeer interests in Alaska.[93] Stefansson urged the trustees of the company to seize the opportunity to buy Lindeberg's more than 33,000 head and packing plants and to expand their horizons into Alaska. But a meeting of the directors, without Stefansson present, decided it was "inadvisable to consider the acquisition [of the] companies mentioned or purchase their reindeer."[94]

Stefansson persisted in other directions, suggesting that the company expand immediately to take advantage of its position and Lindeberg's plight, and establish reindeer herds in the vicinity of the mouth of the Mackenzie River. As early as 5 November 1920, he put forth plans to expand to Wrangel Island, Ellesmere, and the Mackenzie.[95] The directors of the company took a dim view of such a scheme, for they "felt that there was as yet a good [deal] to do to get the present enterprise going."[96] Stefansson was not so much rash, perhaps, as he was somewhat naïve about the logistics of operating such ventures. Once again, Stefansson sought to force the pace. On 21 December 1920, he applied to the government for another lease, similar to his Baffin Island one, for grazing privileges for reindeer at the mouth of the Mackenzie River. However, this time he was unsuccessful. The Canadian government after "careful consideration . . . decided that at the present time it is not considered advisable to grant any further concessions of this nature."[97] The Canadian government was not willing to undertake such a scheme, because the recommendation of the Musk-ox Commission, tabled in September 1920, had urged caution and careful preparation prior to government support for grandiose reindeer industries in the north.

Stefansson did convince the directors of the Hudson's Bay Reindeer Company corporation to approach the Quebec government for a lease to an area of northern Quebec, north of the parallel of Fort Chimo, in the "general vicinity" of the Baffin Island project. As he explained to H. Mercier, minister of Land and Forests for the province of Quebec, the company needed a forested area adjacent to Baffin Island, which was devoid of trees. In other words, it might be wise to have a geographical area which would allow the reindeer to be kept in open country in the summer and driven into the woods in winter, as was done in Norway. Very little, Stefansson acknowledged, was known about the climate of Baffin Island, and although no one anticipated "absolute failure," it would be added insurance to have a treed area.[98] Stefansson and A. R. Holden of the Montreal law firm of Meredith, Holden, Haag, Shawnessay and Hewert, representing the interests of the Hudson's Bay Reindeer Company, met with J. A. Perrault, Quebec's minister of Colonization, Mines and Fisheries, and Premier L. A. Taschereau, to discuss the proposal. But Stefansson left the meeting exasperated, feeling that the provincial ministers were idiots and quite ignorant of what was being offered to them.[99] Perrault, in particular, was very negative and suspicious of the grazing request; he might have thought that the Hudson's Bay Company had some ulterior design upon the furs or game of the northern region of Quebec.[100] To be sure, the Hudson's Bay Company was not a Quebec favourite. At the Quebec City meeting, Stefansson tried to sweeten the bargain for the Quebec government by suggesting that the Hudson's Bay Reindeer Company should pay for any wild caribou incorporated into the reindeer herd, at a rate of about twenty-five dollars per head.[101] This caused Fitzgerald to react in horror at Stefansson's temerity in offering, without authorization, to commit the fledgling company to additional cash outlays. All that Stefansson and Holden should secure after "a straight-forward presentation of our case," Fitzgerald felt, was a lease similar to that already granted by the federal government—nothing more.[102] In any case, the application was rejected, though Stefansson continued to hope that something might be effected. He was still trying, long after the Hudson's Bay Company and directors of the company had given up hope. When it came time to ship the herd from Norway, there was some anxiety as to whether or not it might be necessary in an emergency to land the herd in Labrador. Stefansson thought that "there may be a silver lining to the cloud, for it may give us a chance again for a lease in northeastern Quebec . . . [I] imagine that an actual shipment of reindeer to that part of the Ungava Peninsula which is under the control of Newfoundland may have some effect on the mental attitude of the Quebec Cabinet."[103]

Stefansson had made certain general assumptions about northern Quebec when the requisite information, general and scientific, was actually lacking. The Quebec negotiations indicate that certain factors had never been seriously considered, namely the migratory habits of a herd accustomed to foraging in Norway. The Hudson's Bay Company knew this and Stefansson knew this too, yet the company was willing to take the word of a man who purported to be an authority on such matters but who had never visited Baffin Island himself.

The only first-hand information Stefansson ever received about Baffin Island was from his old friend Storkerson, whom the Hudson's Bay Reindeer Company had hired on Stefansson's recommendations. Storkerson seems to have had little experience with reindeer but was anxious to make a career of organized herding. His observations were certainly not scientific or detailed, and his trip to Baffin Island had a certain flavour of the optimistic, "get in quick" wildcatting of the pre-war years. Storkerson spent only one month assessing the flora and fauna and possible harbour sites of the area leased to Stefansson, an assessment which was only visual, for Storkerson had no training to undertake scientific investigation. The rash and hurried activities of Stefansson and his associate were in marked contrast to the deliberate operations of the Hudson's Bay Company and other directors of its subsidiary. The land Storkerson considered "forbidding and rocky," but a good harbour might be found at Amadjuak Bay where, he speculated, it could probably remain ice-free in the summer—because of a maze of outlying islands—until the deep winter. As well, Storkerson and Stefansson, like many others at the time, held that a reindeer is a reindeer is a reindeer, and that lichens are lichens. The area's vegetation left Storkerson deeply impressed, and he related to his former commander that,

> [t]here seemed to be an abundance of reindeer lichens growing on the face of the rock and the crevices and sheltered nooks so that from a distance of half a mile in places this mountainous land looked almost greenish-white on the dark background. Never before in any of the countries that I have travelled have I seen reindeer lichen in such profuse abundance on stoney ground . . . [Behind Amadjuak Bay] the vegetation is mainly reindeer lichens and grass. The grassland has the appearance of an ideal feeding ground [for] caribou and reindeer and is only about a distance of twelve miles from the bottom of Amadjuak Bay and therefore easily accessible . . . Grasses, mosses, reindeer lichens, and flowers are abundant all over the parts visited by me, so much so that I formed the personal opinion that Baffin Island as regards vegetation is better qualified as reindeer country than northern Norway where reindeer have been raised for centuries.[104]

Apparently this report delighted Stefansson, and the head office as well.

In January 1921, Storkerson reported to the Hudson's Bay Company in London, after which he was sent to Norway by Charles Sale to enquire into the purchase of reindeer stock. But, when it came to the actual work of buying the herd and recruiting herders, the Hudson's Bay Company authorized Francis Wood, who had worked with Grenfell, to undertake the task. Storkerson was to take over operations when the herd had been landed in Baffin Land. The Hudson's Bay people were probably convinced that neither Stefansson nor Storkerson knew much about buying reindeer, and placed their trust in an experienced buyer instead. Although Storkerson might have been the "best man" to manage the herd, the company was not ready to leave the purchasing to a man who had had no skill in that particular endeavour; the company was large, experienced in business, and considered such things should follow proper procedures. Storkerson's insistence that he control the entire field operation, including the purchase of the herd, was unacceptable to the venerable firm that was used to giving orders, not taking them. In their view, indeed, Storkerson had "developed ideas too advanced regarding his duties . . ."[105]

Storkerson saw Wood's appointment as undercutting his position; it was a "grave injury to me, for it casts reflection on my integrity and capability to perform what I, in the first place, was engaged to [do]."[106] With that he resigned because, he asserted, it had been "intended" that he should be in charge of the selection, buying, and transportation to Baffin Island of the herd, as well as becoming manager of the station.[107] Unfortunately for Storkerson, these intentions were never made explicit by the Hudson's Bay Company, which had its own method of operation. Stefansson later agreed with the company's procedures regarding the buying and transfer of the herd.[108]

Stefansson, who was half-way around the globe in California on a lecture tour, was stunned by the news of Storkerson's resignation.[109] He was too remote from the situation to do anything positive for Storkerson. Now he faced the prospect that the experiment on Baffin Island would be headed by strangers, not by Storkerson whom he had trusted to look after his interests. He requested Fitzgerald to ask Storkerson to reconsider,[110] but the company was not too anxious, concerned that such a person might cause trouble in the future, "[a]t [a] time when [it would] perhaps [be] very difficult to rectify."[111] Thereupon, Stefansson turned to Storkerson with a plea to withdraw his resignation, but Storkerson would do so only if he were given Wood's duties. This the company refused to do. To Stefansson, Storkerson's departure was the single mistake from which stemmed all the subsequent troubles of the Hudson's Bay Reindeer Company. What followed was a foregone conclusion to Stefansson: "The death knell of the Baffin Island Reindeer experiment was sounded, though we did not hear it at the time."[112] It is difficult to agree with this conclusion, for the very nature of the enterprise and the assumption surrounding its success spelled trouble, with or without Storkerson.

Stefansson had other worries besides. He sought the advice of Jafet Lindeberg in connection with the employment of Lapps on the Baffin Island project and, not being an expert himself, transmitted Lindeberg's knowledge to Fitzgerald of the Hudson's Bay Company: Norwegian and European Lapps were totally unsuited for the treeless regions of Baffin Island and would not know how to cope with this totally new environment. According to Stefansson, the only thing that had saved Lindeberg when he was a reindeer herder in Alaska was the presence of forested areas adjacent to the grazing regions.[113] But how importing Laplanders with experience in Alaska would meet the needs of managing reindeer herds in treeless country is a puzzle. What Stefansson unwittingly implied was that no matter who was hired to look after the herds—Laplanders imported directly from Europe or Laplanders with experience in Alaska—they would all face the same problem and have to improvise solutions for the winter migration of reindeer. Yet, even though Baffin Island was essentially an unforested country, Stefansson set great store in importing Laplanders who had been in Alaska; otherwise, he believed, there would be disaster.[114] This gloomy assessment, indeed, was correct in the long run, but his advice and arguments made no effective solutions for the problem.

The stage was now set to begin operations. The Hudson's Bay Company chose a man they considered to be an "experienced and competent leader," Ole Johneson. During the summer of 1921, six hundred and eighty-seven deer were purchased in Norway, and the services were secured of Johneson and six Lapp families as herdsmen. While in quarantine, before loading on board the *Nascopi*, the herd was checked over and cleared by an expert pathologist from the Canadian government. But, by the time the *Nascopi* reached Bugten i Alten in September, sixty of the reindeer had died or were lost before loading aboard. A further seventy-seven had perished on the journey across the Atlantic, despite the numerous precautions taken for their physical comfort.[115]

The arrival of the *Nascopi* at Amadjuak Bay on 1 November 1921 was no signal for rejoicing either:

> The country was covered with snow, and seemed to consist of nothing but rocks, cliffs and stones. There was scarcely any signs of vegetation except for a little reindeer moss here and there.
>
> On arrival it was found that by mistake a house had not been built to accommodate Captain Mikkelborg, Ole Johneson and his family. However, a small one roomed house belonging to the Reverend Doctor Fleming was utilized. It was in a derelict condition but it was made habitable.
>
> ... In spite of the endeavours of the herdsmen, the herd on landing commenced to scatter in all directions in search of food. Instructions were given to the Lapps to do their best to keep the herd together, but they report that they were unable to do so, because the animals would take no notice of the dogs.[116]

The scattering of the unmanageable herd meant that they were at the mercy of the elements. By June 1922, only two hundred and ten deer were left; by September of the same year only one hundred and eighty, including eleven new calves.[117]

Steps were taken to look for better feeding grounds in the areas Storkerson had indicated as favourable, but the herders and the station manager, Captain Mikkelborg, agreed that the better pastures were near the coast. All were very critical of Storkerson's report:

> In the summer [of 1922] a journey was made to Mt. Mingo on exactly the same day that Mr. Storkerson travelled there two years before to make his report. Captain Mikkelborg was accompanied by one of the Lapps who was accustomed to herding reindeer in the hard north country. The pastures were found to be unfavourable. Reindeer lichen were very scarce, and the scanty, boggy grass contained very little or no nutriment. The feeding grounds were only sufficient to provide for a small herd during the summer, and offered no chance for the animals laying in fat for the winter.[118]

Storkerson, it was claimed, "not being conversant in the herding of reindeer," could not differentiate between the three types of moss on Baffin Island: Iceland moss, black moss, and Elk moss. "In Baffinland the first two mosses are very scarce, particularly the Iceland moss. The Elk moss is more plentiful, but of this the reindeer only nibble the tops ... The Caribou will live on it, but the reindeer will not consume it as food."[119] Not only could the herd not establish a proper balanced dietary routine because of this shortage of the right type of forage, but the forbidding climate took its toll: "In the summer they [the reindeer] may live, but in the winter it is worse, because the snow gets so hard that the reindeer are not able to break through to get at the food. When it gets really cold we cannot break through with a stick. It is as much as one may get through with an iron shovel."[120] Frank Melton, who succeeded Mikkelborg as post manager in September 1922, concluded in his reports to the parent company that there was "no possibility of the venture ever developing into a profitable business in Baffin land." He suggested that the remainder of the herd be moved to the east side of Hudson Bay in the vicinity of Richmond Gulf in northern Quebec:

> from what I have learned of this country it [Richmond Gulf] appears to be ideal, both from herding and for transportation facilities, being within easy reach of any railway that may terminate in the Hudson's Bay, this itself would be a great advantage should the business ever reach a commercial stage, there is also timber, which if not suitable for building purposes, would be a great saving in fuel, which is one of our most expensive items in this country ... whatever policy the reindeer

company adopts, they should have a resident manager whose only duty is to look after their interests, superintend the herders, and be at all times within reach of the herd, it would also be far less expensive for them to have their business under the control of their fur trade department, if this was done, a small herd fenced, could be made almost self-supporting even in this country.[121]

This was a rather gloomy outlook for an industry that was supposed to achieve instant success, complete with packing, slaughtering, and transportation facilities within two or three years. Such adverse reports concerning one of his pet projects made Stefansson livid. To him, all the difficulties experienced by Mikkelborg and his helpers appeared to be merely excuses to cover up their incompetence. True, Baffin land was cold and stormy, but the temperatures, he was certain, were no worse, if not better than Manitoba. The whole fiasco to him underlined the folly of letting Storkerson go, for the same gales that had intimidated the Norwegians would have been to Storkerson a chance to go out and enjoy the weather. Stefansson would not accept the alibi that the herd needed some sort of taiga to fall back on during the winter season; nor would he believe that the type of reindeer moss was unsuitable.[122] He was ready to accept the food prejudices of men but not of reindeer. Sheer incompetence, timidity, and the wrong sort of herders were for him at the bottom of the fiasco. Stefansson claimed that the Lapps employed in the enterprise were coast Lapps, unfamiliar with reindeer, who had been selected by a person to whom they owed money, and to whom they had turned over a portion of their salaries.[123]

Authorities are not entirely in agreement as to which type of lichen was most prevalent in southwest Baffin Island. The Hudson's Bay Reindeer Company stated that the reindeer preferred the Icelandic type but found only an abundance of Elk moss which was not to their liking. According to Diamond Jenness, there was an abundance of Icelandic moss, but a scarcity of *Cladonia rangiferina*, which would have had enough nourishment to sustain the beasts.[124] Another more recent work suggests that during winter forage, reindeer will eat all three, all of which are deficient in nutritive value,[125] and rely mainly on the products available in summer foraging to sustain themselves through the winter. But Baffin Island could in no way offer such summer foraging.

It was unfortunate perhaps that the reindeer were landed in November, after an exhausting trip across the Atlantic. No one can tell just how much wear and tear was inflicted upon the animals who, in all likelihood, could not store up enough food within themselves to meet the rigours of winter. What they may have needed most—and this is speculation—was an initial food supply nutritious enough to regenerate their wintering abilities. Instead, faced with the hard snow and the type of food available, many died of starvation. The divergent views even as to the species of lichen present in the area underscores Stefansson's lack of accurate knowledge about the flora of Baffin Island and the foraging habits of the reindeer, certainly not enough on which to base a commercial operation. As late as 1967, the Canadian government's report *Mackenzie Reindeer Operations* acknowledged the need for more research on the relationship between the delicate physiological makeup of the reindeer and their environment and the level of utilization of tundra vegetation in the care and feeding of such animals.[126]

For all intents and purposes, the experiment on Baffin Island was over after the first year. The herd either had been depleted by starvation or had run off with the wild caribou, and only one-third still survived. The governor and committee of the Hudson's Bay Company turned down Stefansson's reminder that the company should live up to the terms of the lease and land 1,000 reindeer by 1 November 1924, and it rejected his suggestion that he approach the minister of Interior in Ottawa to secure an extension of the lease stipulation.[127] By now, Stefansson was fighting a losing battle against a company which had had heavy losses and refused to take further risks until it was certain about the premises of any future enterprise. While the Hudson's Bay Company remained tolerant of Stefansson personally, it was very cool in rejecting his proposals for salvaging the project. By late 1925, all capital invested in the reindeer company having been lost, in addition to several sums advanced to the company to keep it from sinking, the value of the Hudson's Bay Reindeer Company shares had fallen to zero.[128] A year later, Stefansson was asked to surrender his shares in the defunct company to enable its affairs to be wound up; it appears that the old company wished to use the organization and machinery of the Hudson's Bay Reindeer Company to establish "further experiments in districts bordering Hudson's Bay."[129] Stefansson relinquished his shares, while expressing the hope that, if the new scheme were successful, he might be associated with it.[130]

The scheme was finished. Stefansson's reputation as an expert on arctic development took a slide downhill in public and professional circles, though he disclaimed responsibility for the failure. He continued to believe that if Storkerson had been allowed to manage the herd, the project would not have failed, although long afterwards, in his autobiography, he was also prepared to concede that Storkerson had probably "misjudged the character of the vegetation on the Baffin Island range."[131] It is doubtful, however, whether the Hudson's Bay Reindeer Company would have succeeded even in a limited fashion if Storkerson had been the range manager, for there was too much working against the fledgling company. The selection of Baffin Island was a mistake, and this made all the other moves, such as the choice of the manager and Lapp herders, ineffective. While Stefansson only acknowledged late in life that the selection of the Baffin Island range had been an error,[132] the Hudson's Bay Company reached that conclusion much earlier, in fact by 1926: "Whilst failure may have been the result of several causes, we were certainly unfortunate in the selection of the grazing lands, and that error made success impossible."[133]

Who was to blame? Storkerson bore some share of the responsibility, for though he was not a trained botanist, his reports were coloured to please his principals. On those reports, also, hung his chances of a future livelihood. What the project needed most was an independent expert associated neither with Stefansson nor the Hudson's Bay Company. Stefansson, himself, was certainly no expert on reindeer or the eastern Arctic. Even worse, he had not employed scientific principles in this matter. He may have been logical in his use of the existing yet woefully incomplete information, but he was not scientific in checking its accuracy for himself. No one had bothered, as has been done since the establishment of reindeer herds in northern Canada under government auspices, to study vegetation and reindeer from a detailed, scientific point of view. Stefansson knew he was groping in the dark when he wavered over the effect of a treeless region on a species used to certain patterns of existence. When he attempted to secure a portion of northern Quebec, another area with which he was totally unfamiliar, he merely underlined the dubious nature of the experiment. In some areas in which he became very active both financially and publicly, he was more promoter and popularizer than expert scientist. Some thirty years later, a member of the Bureau of Northwest Territories and Yukon Affairs summed up the fiasco this way:

> I don't think there is any doubt that the failure of this enterprise must be attributed in large measure to inadequate study and preparation.
>
> Our main concern in regard to reindeer is to develop herding as a native industry suitable to the conditions which prevail in the territories. Information from other countries is interesting and sometimes helpful but nothing takes the place of actual experience and persistent effort to find out what can be done without any extravagant forecasts. We are gradually accumulating data based on facts. The

problems involved are becoming clearer. These are receiving constant study.

Dr. Stefansson seems to have a wide fund of fact and fable about the northern regions of the world . . . However, it is not possible for one in his position to come to grips with the administrative difficulties in carrying forward northern projects and for this reason his views tend to be rather broad and sweeping.[134]

8

The Misadventure of
Wrangel Island

Stefansson's crusade to educate, or more precisely re-educate, his fellow man had brought him personal prestige and success in Great Britain, the United States and, especially, Canada. The halls of power beckoned to him and, after his return from the Arctic in 1918, he experienced a feeling of real influence amongst businessmen, politicians, statesmen, and bureaucrats. He had realized that, to be listened to, he would have to prove the validity of his hypotheses through practical application. Initially he and his ideas were accepted in the highest circles, for he had carefully cultivated people in Canada, the United States, and Great Britain who shared his optimism and admired his prowess. The Hudson's Bay Reindeer fiasco, however, had tarnished his image and uncovered a serious shortcoming within the man.

Stefansson seemed to have a naïve, mysterious inner faith that, despite obvious difficulties and lack of planning, after a project was off the ground improvisation could take care of the details, or the details could take care of themselves. In a sense, this had also been his approach to the Canadian Arctic Expedition. The reindeer concept had been bold, and would perhaps have been economically sound if the homework had been done,[1] but under the circumstances of 1920–21 it was too rash and impractical.

The whole affair helped dislodge Stefansson from his pinnacle of influence with business and governments. The Wrangel Island episode was even more important in undermining his political influence because it alienated his base of power, the government of Canada.

Wrangel Island, lying one hundred and ten miles due north of Siberia, was discovered in 1849 by Captain Kellett, an Englishman, and for many years bore the name of Kellett Land. Less than twenty years later, in 1867, an American, Thomas Long, sailed close by in the whaling bark *Nile*. Long did not know that the island had been discovered by Kellett and placed upon admiralty charts. Supposing it to be a discovery of his own, he suggested it be called Wrangel Island in honour of Baron Wrangel, then governor of Russian Alaska. Between 1822 and 1824 Wrangel, on behalf of the Russian government, had conducted northern sledge explorations from the mouth of the Kolyma River. These were in response to rumours that a land mass existed beyond the mainland. Captain Long, familiar with Wrangel's unsuccessful efforts, felt that it would be appropriate to name the island in the baron's honour.

The first official landing on the island was made by Captain Calvin Hooper of the United States revenue cutter *Corwin* in August 1881. At this time, Hooper raised the American flag, deposited a record of his brief stay, and claimed the island for the United States. Another American revenue cutter, *Rodgers*, landed a few days later. Yet nothing was done to cement the claim. The island remained derelict until 1911, when a hydrographic party from the Russian ice-breakers *Taymyr* and *Vaygach* erected a navigation beacon on the southwest portion of the island. Finally, in 1914, the crew of the wrecked *Karluk* of the Canadian Arctic Expedition eked out an existence on Wrangel Island for six months. On 1 July 1914, the survivors ran up the Union Jack, supposedly claiming the island for Canada and the British Empire.[2]

Although the notion that the island had been formally claimed for Canada in 1914 was encouraged by Stefansson,[3] it seems very unlikely that anything of an official nature had been done. Contemporary evidence, including photographs and their identification, show that the raising of the flag in 1914 had nothing to do with a formal claim. The celebration of Dominion Day had been the occasion. On the reverse side of a photograph, showing the Union Jack waving over Wrangel Island, appears the following inscription: "The celebration of Dominion Day (1 July 1914) at Roger's Harbour, Wrangel Island."[4] William L. McKinlay, one of the *Karluk*'s marooned crew, wrote on that day, "Nothing much doing today. Very warm."[5] Moreover, Bartlett, the captain of the *Karluk*, categorically denied that the flag raising was intended to take possession of the island. At no time did he report to the Canadian government that the island had been claimed for Canada.[6]

Stefansson had been commander of the expedition to which the *Karluk* was attached, but he had not been part of the shipwrecked party. The vessel, a prisoner of the ice, had drifted away while he was absent. Stefansson had received his knowledge of the island at second-hand, after many an informal talk with Jack Hadley, a survivor of the disaster. Hadley painted a rosy picture for his commander, outlining the strategic and commercial prospects of Wrangel Island. Yet, an unresolved mystery still surrounds Hadley's report, for it appears that Hadley either had misled Stefansson, or that Stefansson grossly exaggerated Hadley's opinions in using them as a reliable eye-witness "source." Certainly, Hadley's opinions of Wrangel Island, as quoted by Stefansson, did not coincide with his views during his stay there in 1914. The island Hadley described in his diary for July-August 1914 was certainly no paradise. Yet Stefansson was able to produce Hadley's glowing account and published it in *The Adventure of Wrangel Island*.[7] In fact, the provenance of that Hadley "manuscript" appears suspect for a number of reasons. The English used in the account was certainly not typical of a man who, for all intents and purposes, had a difficult command of the language.[8] Moreover, the published account only appeared a year after Hadley's death,[9] though Hadley might have dictated some observations to Stefansson. No one, save Stefansson, vouched for its authenticity. According to William McKinlay, an expedition scientist, Hadley had little use for his commander.[10] If this was so, and if Hadley did make the statements attributed to him, then there is a good prospect that he deliberately misled Stefansson. Nevertheless, Hadley told Stefansson what he wanted to hear.

In any case, the apparently resource-filled island fitted into Stefansson's concept of what his Arctic should be: a polar Mediterranean from which Canada and the British Empire would derive renewed economic and strategic vigour. The world's centre of activity would drift northward from the more temperate latitudes toward the pole. The northward course of empire was now being applied in a strategic sense.[11] Aiding him powerfully, as he was well aware, was the international situation in the north Pacific. The victorious Allies and the United States were now in Siberia, bent on checking the emergent militant Soviet state. As well, the Americans distrusted Japan's intentions in the Pacific and in Siberia. Stefansson reasoned that it would be in the best interests of Britain, the Empire, and the United States to secure Wrangel Island and that these countries would welcome such a move.

Accordingly, Stefansson made tentative approaches to the Canadian government in 1919, apparently with the blessing of Sir Robert Borden.[12] It was not until the fall of 1920, however, that he began his campaign in earnest. In September and October of that year, he approached the new prime minister, Arthur Meighen, and a number of high-ranking individuals in the Canadian government: Loring Christie, legal adviser of the department of External Affairs and one of the most influential policy-makers in the Meighen government; W. W. Cory, deputy minister of the department of the Interior; and J. B. Harkin, Commissioner of Dominion Parks and an expert on polar problems. Canada, he told these gentlemen, must enjoy freedom of movement in the Arctic. Stefansson scoffed at Canada's complacent reliance upon the sector theory, first enunciated by Senator Poirier in 1907.[13] "It is no more inevitable that every land north of Alaska should belong to Alaska than it is that a strip of coast from Skagway to the vicinity of Prince Rupert shall belong to us, which it does not."[14] Once such a nonsensical notion as the sector theory was dropped, Canada would be free to acquire valuable islands such as Wrangel. As for Wrangel, it

> should be British territory because during the next great war and, indeed, in the course of peaceable development of the next two or three decades, there will be traffic across the polar basin from Europe to Japan, by way of the polar ocean, certainly with dirigibles and submarines and probably aeroplanes. This distance from England to Japan by a great circle drawn through the polar ocean is not much more than a third as great as the distance from England to Japan by way of Montreal and Vancouver. The perpetual daylight of summer will not only make this route feasible in time of war but also advantageous in times of peace. As naval bases for our submarines and as way stations for aircraft we need a chain of islands across the polar basin.[15]

To Stefansson's way of thinking, Wrangel Island also offered a stepping stone to the undiscovered riches that the polar basin had to offer. Only one problem remained—formal possession.[16] Even the raising of the British flag in 1914 and six months' occupation by the *Karluk*'s crew were insufficient. That claim had lapsed in 1919, according to Stefansson's interpretation of existing international law.[17] It remains unclear as to how Stefansson arrived at this concept of a five-year "time limit" regarding unofficial territorial claims. Stefansson had appeared as a witness before the Technical Advisory Board on northern islands on 20 November 1920. There he told the board of Knud Rasmussen's, and presumably the Danish government's, negative attitude toward Canada's claim to Ellesmere Island. From a reading of the minutes of that November meeting, it becomes quite obvious that Canadian officials were apprehensive about Canadian claims in the Arctic and that they, too, were working under some sort of "time limit" assumption. Basing their report on Oppenheim's *Treatise on International Law*, they recommended that Canada immediately take measures—in the form of additional expeditions, and what eventually became the annual Eastern

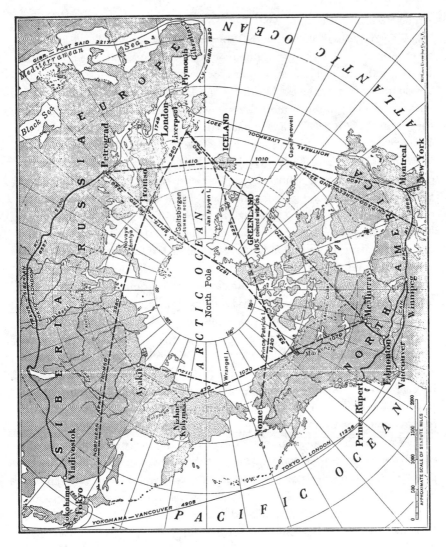

MAP 5
STEFANSSON'S
ARCTIC MEDITERRANEAN:
AIR ROUTES

Arctic Patrols of the RCMP—to secure the eastern portion of the Arctic.[18]

The only way the claim to Wrangel Island would be safeguarded, Stefansson argued, was by continuous occupation. If Canada were to follow up original discovery with exploration, and especially by commercial development such as the establishment of a Hudson's Bay Company trading post or a similar trading enterprise, she would then have the best claim to the island.[19] But if Canada remained inactive, others would occupy Wrangel Island. To add a sense of urgency to his pleas, Stefansson alluded to various newspaper reports that the U.S.S.R. had leased the northeastern corner of Siberia to a syndicate of American capitalists, presumably the Liebes trading company of San Francisco. These rumours were eventually confirmed by the Soviet representative in New York. To Stefansson, the leasing of an area immediately south of Wrangel Island was an implicit threat to Canadian pretensions there, because such a firm could well occupy the island as part of their lease.[20] Moreover, in the long run, the granting of such a lease would strengthen the claim of the grantor, in this case the upstart U.S.S.R., as demonstrating its sovereign authority.

To Arthur Meighen, who was already impressed by many of Stefansson's ideas, he argued that Canada was faced by two strategic problems in the north—Ellesmere Island and Wrangel Island. Because of the hesitant attitude of Denmark, it would be sufficient for Canada merely to "assert its claim to Ellesmere Island openly and decisively." The most pressing single polar problem of Canada, in his opinion, was Wrangel Island. A solution could be an exploratory expedition there, led by himself.[21]

From the beginning, however, the Canadian government, by now becoming wary of Stefansson's tactics, exhibited reluctance to follow the proposal, and the wheels of government were to turn slowly for Vilhjalmur Stefansson. As early as 25 November 1920, Sir Joseph Pope, under-secretary of state for External Affairs, advised Meighen against taking any action. Pope indicated that the tenuous Canadian claim rested upon the fact that Wrangel had been sighted by an Englishman who had never landed there.[22] He disregarded the action of *Karluk*'s crew in 1914 on the simple grounds that they had had no authority to claim the island. Though Stefansson was insisting that the gesture had been valid and binding, his instructions in 1913 had only authorized the expedition "to take possession of and annex to His Majesty's Dominions any lands lying to the north of Canadian territory which are not within the jurisdiction of any civilized power."[23] In no way could "north" be interpreted to include Wrangel Island. Pope, in fact, concluded that the island in question was "not even in the Western Hemisphere, as the 180th median of longitude falls upon it. Essentially, it is an Asiatic Island." He drove home his department's verdict by reminding the government that any claims Canada might have to the island were of an unsubstantial character "and could only result in weakening our legitimate claims to the Arctic islands contiguous to our own territory . . ."[24]

Still the government dallied and these strong warnings went unheeded. On 19 February 1921, Meighen conveyed the following message to Stefansson: "I have discussed the matters which you laid before me today and desire to advise you that the government proposes to assert the right of Canada to Wrangel Island, based upon the discovery and exploration of your expedition."[25] These "matters" of which he had apprised Meighen were reports that Mr. Angus Brabant, the fur trade commissioner of the Hudson's Bay Company "had a strong inclination to put a post on Wrangel Island." Brabant had postponed any action because his company did not feel sure the island was British territory. Stefansson tactfully brought this to Meighen's notice. The prime minister presented the Hudson's Bay Company's problem before a meeting of the cabinet which, within a matter of hours, arrived at the decision to push ahead with the Canadian claim to Wrangel.[26]

Armed with such assurances, Stefansson next set out to enlist the official support of the Hudson's Bay Company in London. Earlier he had tried, through his position within the Hudson's Bay Reindeer Company, to expand its operations to Wrangel Island, but had been discouraged. Now he returned with a seemingly powerful gambit—the blessing of the Canadian government. Mentioning that Brabant had been enthusiastic about the idea of a post on Wrangel Island, Stefansson thought it wise to remind the company of the interest displayed by its competitors. Now that the war was over, its chief rival in the western Arctic, N. Liebes and Company of San Francisco or some other trading concerns, was bound to revive plans to place a post on Wrangel Island. Stefansson confided that the Canadian prime minister and minister of the Interior were fully cognizant of the danger. In fact, the Canadian government felt it would not be proper for them to ask the Hudson's Bay Company to establish the post but, said Stefansson, they welcomed such action by the company.[27] Having more or less prodded the government into making a pronouncement by means of the company, Stefansson was now using the government's position to proselytize the company.

The company, interested in expanding its fur-producing territory, reacted favourably at this juncture.[28] But this was of little consequence for within ten days Meighen executed an about-face and Stefansson's plans had come to naught. On 1 March 1921, Meighen curtly informed the explorer that the government's approval had been withdrawn, and that its previous position should be disregarded.[29] On the preceding day, an annoyed department of External Affairs had prompted Meighen to squelch the project. Loring Christie, slighted because of the administration's disregard of his department's conviction that the disadvantages far outweighed any possible advantages, took Stefansson's arguments severely to task. He reminded Meighen that Wrangel's commercial value was purely "speculative" and based solely on Stefansson's assessment. Besides, Stefansson's arguments, based upon the Hudson's Bay Company need, could be set aside because trading concerns such as the Hudson's Bay Company could secure fair commercial privileges even if the island were occupied by another power. Furthermore, Christie attached no strategic or military importance to the island and was quite willing for it to be acquired by either Japan or Russia.[30] Faced by the conflicting advice of the explorer Stefansson on the one hand, and of his civil servants Pope and Christie on the other, Meighen yielded to his official counsellors. In effect, cooler heads had prevailed and Stefansson's hopes that the Canadian government would underwrite his project had been thwarted.

The department of External Affairs and its attitude were not solely responsible for scuttling Stefansson's project. Stefansson had raised strong doubts and hostilities towards himself there early in the game, as a result of the 1913–18 expedition. His forceful methods, which they regarded as impudence, his reputed publicity-seeking, and his unpredictability inspired resentment on the part of important officials in government. Even Harkin, whom Stefansson believed to be a strong supporter of his cause,[31] had severe misgivings about the explorer. On 2 March, the day after Meighen's note, Harkin advised his superior that, since Stefansson was "an exceedingly difficult man to handle," the department of Interior should guard against antagonizing him at all costs and make every effort to humour him. He even suggested it would be expedient to inform Stefansson that he was the prime candidate to command a secret expedition currently being planned as a means of asserting Canada's sovereignty over the northern archipelago. Stefansson had been lobbying for this appointment since his return in 1918, and this prize might appease him over the frustration of his hopes for Wrangel Island. In fact, the rumoured appointment could be used to retain Stefansson's friendship until this expedition was under way, then he should be sent north "as soon as possible where he would not be able to damage the Canadian cause."[32]

Actually, the government, still anxious to continue its program of polar exploration, was proposing to place the expedition either under

Stefansson or under the British polar explorer, Sir Ernest Shackleton. Harkin's fears as to Stefansson's reactions are an eloquent commentary on the attitude that even a sympathetic member of the administration held towards Stefansson:

> There is a grave probability that, if any aid or recognition is given the Shackleton expedition either (or both) the United States and Denmark may receive advance information from Stefansson . . . because Shackleton proposes to explore the identical regions that Stefansson also proposes to explore. Stefansson was the first person to specifically call attention to the weakness of Canada's claim to the Northern Islands. No one else is more familiar with the weakness of our case. He is aware of Canada's plan for remedying that weakness. He therefore is in a position to ruin the Canadian scheme by tipping off the facts to the United States, or Denmark, or in fact any other country that might have ambitions to acquire new territory. Stefansson is a Canadian in the sense that he was born in Canada but that is all. It would therefore be unwise to bank on his Canadian loyalty too much. The Canadian expedition has been developed in the line of keeping him with us through self-interest.[33]

Plainly, while Ottawa was formally being indulgent towards Stefansson, nothing he could say or do could allay the deep mistrust of him exhibited behind his back.

So unsure was Ottawa of entrusting another expedition to Stefansson, and so apprehensive was the government about giving the command to Shackleton instead, that the cabinet split on the question. The only solution was to cancel the expedition outright. Stefansson claimed that Shackleton, anxious to do polar exploration, had double-crossed him by spreading false rumours that the commander of the 1913–18 foray was no longer interested in exploration. At one point, even Desbarats's superior, the minister of the Naval Service, was supporting Stefansson's rival, and Stefansson had to look to Meighen to carry on his fight in the cabinet. But the resistance was too strong and the only solution to this predicament was to do nothing.[34] Shackleton claimed the government had made an early promise to him,[35] but Meighen had dodged this by advising the British explorer that he, the prime minister, had been advised that Shackleton could not make the necessary preparations in time.[36] This, however, was untrue, for Shackleton had men and a ship ready to go.[37] Shackleton, even if he had been trying to outmanoeuvre Stefansson, was shabbily treated by the Canadian government—or at least by Meighen.

Stefansson was not the sort of man to be checked even by government. Thwarted in his first plan, he secretly set about securing Wrangel Island as a private enterprise. The Canadian government should accept its responsibility. To achieve these ends, the Stefansson Arctic Exploration and Development Company, a Canadian company, obtained incorporation on 23 June 1921. Stefansson had raised some money and enlisted four young men as his agents—Allan Crawford, a University of Toronto student and son of a professor there, and three eager, and devoted Americans—to carry out the company's prime objective, the occupation of Wrangel Island. Two of the Americans, Lorne Knight and Fred Maurer, were former Canadian Arctic Expedition members, while the third, Milton Galle, had been Stefansson's secretary. Crawford, the Canadian, was chosen as the nominal leader of the expedition because Stefansson was afraid the undertaking would not be considered British unless a British subject were at the helm.[38] When the time came to apply for government backing, Stefansson was to insist that patriotism and the empire were always uppermost in his mind.[39] His mission was to show the Canadian government the error of its ways. Charges that he hoped to acquire a lease to the island with a view to subletting it (as with Baffin Island) were unfounded, he asserted. His development company was, in effect, a front "to camouflage our real plans." He had talked of commercial development only to allay suspicions.[40]

This, however, was not the whole truth. To all intents and purposes, Stefansson had given up the life of an active explorer. The Canadian government had dashed his hopes of leading another expedition. Since Stefansson's income now was largely derived from public lectures and from royalties from his books, and because his Hudson's Bay Reindeer Company was faring poorly, it was not surprising that he should have been thinking in terms of a good investment for the future. Indeed, to his good and trusted friend, Orville Wright, he later speculated that he could "sublet the island to some fur company for enough to get a handsome annual return on the money so far invested."[41] Stefansson wanted a greater share of profits than from the reindeer scheme. As he told a close friend and old schoolmate, F. Paysant, the Hudson's Bay Company had allotted him only a few shares in the Reindeer Company; his concern, aside from the imperial considerations, was "of profitting personally" rather than see all the profit go to the Hudson's Bay Company.[42]

By occupying Wrangel Island with an unofficial party, Stefansson was pursuing both his hopes for private gain and the best strategic plan for gaining official support for his enterprise. As he suggested to Paysant, the main idea in sending the men to Wrangel Island was to establish the fact of British, as well as Canadian, occupation of the territory. Therein, he hoped that he would be rewarded:

> This would give me a chance to say to the British Government that but for my occupation of the island it might next year have fallen into the hands of either Japan or Russia and that they should, therefore in gratitude to me give me a lease on the island. I have no doubt this argument will work, for Sir Auckland Geddes, the British Ambassador, has already told me that it seems to him reasonable and that he knows the temper of the present British Government is such that they will be ready to recognize the validity of exactly that kind of argument.[43]

Stefansson was determined to secure the island for his company, no matter what the circumstances. He transmitted private orders to Crawford on 15 August 1921, that the island should be claimed "in the name of King and Empire," as a continuation of the "right to the island already established by the Stefansson Canadian Arctic Expedition of 1913–18." The flag raising, photos, and deposition of a record of the event, he warned Crawford, "should be done *no matter if men of our or any other nations are already on the island.*"[44] Stefansson had to think of his business interests too.

Stefansson's junior partners fulfilled this task immediately after the *Silver Wave* deposited them on Wrangel Island on 16 September 1921. But, in carrying out Stefansson's bidding, Crawford had been indiscreet. He raised the British flag in front of the predominantly American boat crew, who returned to Nome charging they had been duped. During the winter of 1921–22, the grumblings of irate Alaskans to the American state department reached the ears of the *New York Times*.[45] Stefansson thereupon announced the news of the "adventure" in the New York paper before any other versions could cloud the issue. His report was soon followed by American press notices that an agitated state department was planning to claim the island. But these remained only rumours. The entrepreneur remained confident, knowing his disciples had been safely in occupation of the island for the past six months. In effect, he was the master of Wrangel Island.

By this time, the Canadian government had changed hands, Meighen having suffered defeat from Mackenzie King. For Stefansson, here was a new opportunity, a new man to impress, another chance to gain official Canadian support. On 11 March 1922, just before the story broke in the *New York Times*, Stefansson wrote to Mackenzie King to emphasize "the need of adopting at once a definite policy towards the polar regions in gen-

eral and in particular towards Wrangel Island."[46] He called King's attention
to the fact that the latest maps issued by the Intelligence Division of the
United States indicated that the northern boundary of Canada was at
Lancaster Sound and Barrow Strait and that, by inference, the islands
north of that did not belong to Canada. Although the islands that he had
discovered were Canada's by right of discovery further action was necessary.
According to Stefansson's understanding of international law, Canada's
claims to the northern archipelago would lapse by June 1922; the 1914
claims to Wrangel Island, he contended, had already lapsed in 1919.[47] He
pleaded with the government to abandon its passive reliance upon sectoral
claims and to begin a new and vigorous policy of actual occupation. To
illustrate the necessity for actual occupation, Stefansson envisioned the
probable fate of Wrangel Island had he not had the foresight to occupy it:
"I take it for certain that had the Japanese moved into Wrangel Island
and had we then protested, an international court would have awarded the
island to the Japanese in view of the fact that our claims had lapsed and
we had shown no definite intention of confirming our rights by continuous
occupation."[48] Fortunately, however, the Stefansson Arctic Development
Company had saved the day. But now the company was in dire straits, for
it had acted privately and was at the mercy of the American state department which might, at any time, intervene on behalf of the Alaskans whose
interests his associates had challenged. The project needed the cloak of
official protection—recognition by the Canadian government.

Mackenzie King, new to his role as prime minister, was hardly in a
position to give a forthright answer. He turned to more experienced heads
for advice. What should he do? The venerable Sir Joseph Pope indicated
that the views of his department remained unaltered; the sooner the
administration dissociated itself from such a "far fetched claim" and such
"fantastic pretensions," the better.[49] Nevertheless, King, Charles Stewart,
and W. W. Cory, the minister and deputy minister of the Interior respectively, and the director of the Northwest Territories Branch, O. S. Finnie,
met with Stefansson on 2 May 1922. The conversations were sufficiently
encouraging. On the following day, Stefansson submitted a formal proposal
regarding Wrangel Island. Making no mention of compensation or a cash
settlement, he asked that an exclusive, long-term lease be granted to his
company or to himself.[50] In view of this encouragement from such influential officials, coupled with the knowledge that a lease would be forthcoming
within twenty-four hours after receipt of word from the government to go
ahead,[51] Stefansson felt he was about to achieve his goal. To all appear-
ances, the new Canadian government had reversed its predecessor's stand.

Or was Ottawa playing the same old game until the issue could, in some way, be resolved without alienating Stefansson or jeopardizing the international situation?

In fact, the attitude of the department of the Interior at this time was essentially the same as that of External Affairs and for basically the same reasons.[52] All agreed that, *if and when* the government gave the go-ahead, they would not oppose the issuance of the lease. However, such a development would be regrettable. Once the die was cast, however, the government would have to stand behind the act in every way. If such a contingency arose, the department of the Interior claimed that it should "be provided with the funds sufficient to complete immediately its program for maintaining Canadian sovereignty in the north instead of spreading it over a number of years as is the present intention."[53] Yet, like the department of External Affairs, this department was supremely confident that the present administration knew its true feelings and would never allow such a folly to transpire.

Then the impossible happened. During a debate on the Naval Service estimates on 12 May 1922, Meighen, now leader of the opposition, questioned the government on its policy toward Wrangel Island:

Mr. Meighen: Will the Ministers state what is the policy of the Government towards the Northern islands with particular reference to those covered by the Stefansson Expedition 1913–18, laid claim to on behalf of Canada, and to Wrangel Island.

Mr. Graham [minister of Militia and Defence]: It is a delicate matter to state the policy of the Government on that question.

Mr. Meighen: Has the Government any policy?

Mr. Fielding [minister of Finance]: What we have we hold.

Mr. Meighen: I would recommend the Government never to fall away from that principle.

Mr. Graham: Some People have failed to do that.

Mr. Meighen: The Government failed once, but I think if they had the same thing to do over again they would act differently.

Mr. Graham: The old Government.

Mr. Meighen: Yes, the old Government my Hon. friend was in. It is well known there is a dispute as to Wrangel Island. The question of the proper attitude of Canada towards the Island is doubtless before the

Government. This vote has to do with these matters and I am asking if Government is in a position to say what its views are with relation to the retention of Wrangel Island or the continuance of Canada's claim thereto; and the same words apply to the other islands covered by the expedition.

Mr. Graham: The policy of the Government, as I understand it, is as just expressed by the Minister of Finance—what we have we hold.

Mr. Meighen: Well, have we Wrangel Island?

Mr. Graham: Yes, as I understand it, and we propose to retain it.

Mr. Fielding: We had it in December, and we have not let it go.[54]

The fat was in the fire; the government had made its policy statement before the House of Commons. Whether King had anticipated such a turn of events is not clear, but he heaped coals upon the fire, for he was now forced to back his ministers and declare that "the Government certainly maintains the position that Wrangel Island is part of the Property of this country."[55] By doing so, the government hoped to out-manoeuvre the opposition and to escape the charge that the Liberals had failed to uphold national and imperial interests. But the random remark was to leave responsible civil servants muttering incoherently—and Stefansson quite pleased with the turn of events.

It seems reasonable to assume, however, that King did not mean what he had said in parliament, for his government took no action to give Stefansson his lease. Instead, Stefansson was kept at bay until King could extricate himself and his government. Yet King's statement had created an official position and Canadian policy began to encounter international opposition. On 15 July 1922, an embarrassed Colonial Office forwarded a note from the Soviet government agent in the United Kingdom to Governor General Byng. The Soviet note, dated 2 June, was obviously inspired by King's declaration. The Russian government appeared disturbed, intimating that Wrangel Island had been discovered by a Russian officer in the 1820s. The Russian flag had been hoisted there when a hydrographic expedition (1910–15) had been sent out by the Russian admiralty, and that, in reality, there never had been any question but that Wrangel Island was a Russian possession.[56] For its part, the Colonial Office expressed serious concern over the Canadian position and sought an explicit policy statement.

Mackenzie King was perturbed, not sure of himself or of the position his government should maintain. Recant, or follow through and fight—

either course was politically explosive. King enquired anew "whether any action on his part was required and, if so, what step should be taken next." The departments of External Affairs and the Interior made their intransigence known. Christie, sensing that the government's hand was being forced by an "impudent" adventurer, explained that his department's negative attitude was shared by others. The department of Trade and Commerce had never supported the idea as economically feasible. As for the island's strategic possibilities, neither the Air Board nor the Naval Service Department had, in his opinion, recommended the acquisition of the island. The naval strategists, like their colleagues in External Affairs, were aware of the changing power balance that was taking place in the Far East. To recognize Russia as owner of the island might contribute to the restoration of the balance of power there. The United States would be denied the establishment of substantial influence and advantage in the Siberian region; at the same time, Russian interest might be allowed to grow in the northwest Pacific to partially offset a truculent Japan. Christie could even foresee American support for Russia, but for different reasons. Washington, no doubt, would reason that if Canada acquired the island such action would enhance the British strategic position and, by association, that of its former ally, Japan. The United States might therefore feel pressed to prefer a claim. However, a hostile United States was the last thing Britain desired or Canada could afford, so "the matter should be dropped altogether, and . . . the Government should decline to give either support or recognition to Mr. Stefansson's venture."[57]

Meanwhile, T. L. Cory, legal advisor of the Northwest Territories Branch of the department of the Interior, also supported this opinion. Nevertheless, he felt constrained to advise King that Canada's claim was in accordance with existing international law: "If, for example colonists establishing themselves in an unappropriated country declare it to belong to the state of which they are members[,] a simple adoption of their act by the state is enough to complete its title, because by adoption the fact of possession and assertion of intention to possess, upon [which] the right of property by occupation is grounded, are brought fully together." This precept, Cory acknowledged, would give Canada its best claim to Wrangel Island. He went on, however, to emphasize the folly of pressing a Canadian claim and the possible disadvantages Canada and the Empire would derive from its acquisition. By claiming the island, Canada would anger the United States which, most likely, would "rush a party into the Arctic and settle on some of our Northern Islands in retaliation" before Canada could strengthen her tenuous hold upon the Arctic archipelago.[58]

King returned Cory's memorandum without comment, ignored the British query, and proceeded naïvely to advance a worried Stefansson $3,000 intended solely for the relief of his expedition. This aid was not to be taken as an indication of formal support for the enterprise.[59] Stefansson, apprehensive about the condition of his party on Wrangel Island, had petitioned the King administration for $5,000 to cover the chartering of a ship and supplies. His own money and credit exhausted, he hoped to secure an advance, "details of repayment, etc., to be settled later."[60] The government was banking on the probability that Stefansson, who had sunk an enormous amount of his own money into the scheme, would thankfully take this humanitarian scrap, remove his men from the island, and drop the matter in gratitude. This proved to be an error in judgement on the part of the government. The relief ship, the *Teddy Bear*, only sailed in September and failed to reach its objective because of the lateness of the season. Yet the American state department was aroused since Stefansson deliberately advertised the journey not as a rescue mission at all but as evidence of the Canadian government's determination to aid Stefansson's occupation. Stefansson always maintained that the ship had been a "supply ship"[61] and that the $3,000 allowance was "to help us continue the Wrangel Island enterprise."[62] This assertion, however, was certainly not the policy of the Canadian government.

Because Stefansson took such pains to make it appear that his enterprise implied formal recognition on the part of Canada, the United States decided to enter the fray. On 27 September 1922, the United States ambassador to Great Britain forwarded a memorandum to the Foreign Office dealing with the "national status" of the island. This American note did not advance any specific claim, but merely reviewed the history of the discovery and explorations of Wrangel Island, significantly emphasizing the American participation in 1881, the fact that the *Karluk*'s crew had been rescued by an American vessel, and finally that Crawford's crew, which included three Americans to begin with, had been transported to the arctic island by the American sloop *Silver Wave*.[63] The American note came at the height of the Chanak crisis and was put aside; the Colonial Office did not inform Canadian officials of this development until the more pressing Chanak affair had been dealt with. On 5 November, the Duke of Devonshire, secretary of state for the Colonies, indicated to Lord Byng, the Canadian governor general, that consideration of the status of Wrangel Island might be warranted.[64] Finally, late in February 1923, the impatient Colonial Office counselled Byng that Great Britain had to be advised of the official Canadian attitude toward the island.[65] King could not afford to procrastinate any longer. So once again the prime minister turned to his ministers and their deputies for a definite answer.

Pope, Loring Christie, and Charles Stewart thought it best that the Colonial Office be advised that Canada did not consider it expedient to put forth any specific claim.[66] There, it was hoped, the matter would end to the satisfaction of both the Soviet Union and the United States. But this unequivocal advice was not adopted. The persistent Stefansson appeared able to convince the Canadian cabinet that, strategically, the empire as a whole would gain immeasurably. Byng, on behalf of the administration, was advised to inform the Colonial Office that Canada would not press a claim, but it was hoped that Stefansson would be allowed to make a personal statement about the strategic importance of Wrangel to imperial authorities.[67] The explorer himself had recently been stressing this possibility and the Canadian government took advantage of this opening. The Colonial Office had never even hinted at an interest in the matter, but King turned the tables to his government's advantage by arguing that the question was really an imperial rather than a Canadian one. Thus he hoped to rid himself of a persistent and troublesome individual and place the onus for the retention or abandonment of Wrangel Island upon British authorities. Also, by making the matter an imperial affair, King ensured that the acquisition of Wrangel Island would not be a Canadian action and hence need not occasion retaliation in the Canadian sector by the United States, Denmark, or any other country.

Devonshire, probably assuming that authorities in London were more competent to handle the problem, accepted Byng's proposal that Stefansson be allowed to cross the Atlantic.[68] Stefansson's pet project gained another lease on life. King could now wash his hands of the affair. He had rid himself of the matter from a Canadian standpoint by simply sending Stefansson to England, dumping the problem in the British lap.

By way of insurance, Stefansson had approached various Washington officials in March 1923. His attempts to influence the State department were a failure,[69] but his friend and schoolmate Theodore Roosevelt, Jr., the assistant secretary of the Navy, turned a sympathetic ear and, through Roosevelt, Stefansson was able to meet several American admirals.[70] Of these, the most enthusiastic was Admiral Moffett, chief of the United States Bureau of Aeronautics. Wrote Moffett, "I am familiar with what you have written and what you have done in regard to Wrangel Island. I'm only sorry that one of my fellow countrymen did not have the vision to do what you did. I am in entire agreement as to the importance of Wrangel Island

and its future use."[71] Stefansson was to receive similar flattering remarks in conversation with such eminent advocates of air power as General Billy Mitchell.[72] The explorer was delighted by this support, but it placed him in a rather awkward position. As he confided to his loyal friend Orville Wright, if he had had "any notion the Americans wanted Wrangel Island, I should probably have gone to them rather than the Canadians," especially after the Canadian authorities had sloughed the matter off on the British. Now, he informed Wright, he would have to be content with seeking out responsible and influential Americans in Washington to aid with the acquisition of Wrangel Island, should the British renege.[73]

Though Stefansson was doubtful of the American interest in developing the island, he strove to interest a general board of the United States Navy on 7 May 1923, when he was invited to appear before it. When queried as to the political and commercial possibilities of Wrangel Island and the island's possible use as a stepping stone for an arctic air route, Stefansson handled such questions adroitly. He pointed out, somewhat inaccurately, that the 1914 expedition which had raised the flag on Wrangel Island had been commissioned to take possession on behalf of the king of England and reaffirm prior British rights to the island, but that the effect of such claims had lapsed. He belittled the argument that the 1914 claims had been reaffirmed by the 1921 expedition: "The boys ran up the British flag, but I don't think that counts." Stefansson went on to relate how disheartened he was that some Americans, and noticeably the Hearst papers, had charged him with "grabbing American territory . . . I have lived in the United States since I was a year old, and it never had occurred to me that I was doing anything with which Americans would find fault. I thought Americans would prefer it to be British rather than Japanese." Stefansson promised the Navy board that he would do what he could to acquire Wrangel Island for the United States, should the British relinquish their prior rights. "Of course, I don't own it, and I cannot give it away, but there might be something I can do."[74]

The arctic explorer and adventurer had thus found himself, in his own words, "trying to cram down the throats of the British something they do not want and for which the Americans show at least a reasonable appetite."[75] It was to be one of his policies henceforth to attach the island to the United States, whose claim, in his opinion, was second to Britain's. This was not to suggest that Stefansson sought to undermine possible British rights, for nothing is further from the truth. All Stefansson was really worried about and hoped to insure against was a possible deliberate abandonment by the British of Wrangel Island to the Russians. This would have betrayed the United States claim. It would also have destroyed his personal enterprise.

Such was Stefansson's position as stated to the Duke of Devonshire during his visit to England:

> Although I am a British subject by birth, I have lived in the United States all my life . . . I know how anxious America is to get Wrangel Island. While I want to evade nothing in my urging that the Empire shall continue possession, I want to urge also that we publish also no decision which will lessen their chances to make good their claims . . . It would seem an exceedingly uncomfortable situation for me personally, to have spent all I had and all I could borrow in making sure of our rights on Wrangel Island if the result were to profit us not at all and in some way injure the United States, which country . . . next to the British Empire—I should have liked to serve.[76]

Even as he was writing, the British government was on the brink of reversing its stand. The Foreign Office may have continued in its doubts, but British military authorities had reappraised the situation and reached a more favourable conclusion. By the Washington Conference of 1922, the United States had been placed in a weakened position in the Pacific *vis-à-vis* Japan. Great Britain, too, had been adversely affected, for not only had she lost a powerful ally in Japan but she too was handicapped by the restrictive nature of a number of the treaties. British air and naval authorities, like their American counterparts, were intent upon finding any toehold in the Far East which would offset their weakened position. Might Wrangel Island not, in some limited fashion, bolster the British strategic position?

Stefansson arrived in England convinced that he must convert the British strategists and politicians to his way of thinking. He began his campaign by contacting experts in both the Admiralty and Air ministry; through these meetings, he became intimately acquainted with the energetic Sir Samuel Hoare, secretary of state for Air, and Colonel L. S. Amery, First Lord of the Admiralty, a staunch imperialist.[77] Both men, it seems, took Stefansson's cause under their wing and were instrumental in guiding British policy in this instance. The results were not disappointing.

The Admiralty concluded that, although Wrangel was of no great immediate value, either strategically or commercially, "the island is the only territory in a vast area to which Great Britain has any claim, and the Admiralty considers that it would be short sighted policy to surrender our claims to it."[78] Not a strong recommendation for retention but, nevertheless, a reassuring one. For its part, the Air ministry was of a similar opinion: "From a service point of view the Air Staff does not consider that Wrangel Island can be of value at present, but . . . they feel that its retention would prove a valuable adjunct to the development of British air policy." This conclusion was reached after a number of factors had been reviewed by the Air staff. It decided that regular meteorological observations from a station in the vicinity would be of assistance to long-range weather forecasting, particularly for Canada; in addition, the establishment of a wireless telegraph would further aid meteorological reporting and assist the navigation of aircraft using any projected polar route: "It is almost unnecessary to add that the station would be of inestimable value, if not actually indispensable to the working of an air route through the Arctic Circle." With the development of long-range heavier-than-air craft, the report pointed out, the island could serve as a maintenance and refuelling depot.[79] The Air staff, like Stefansson, shared the conviction that a polar air route, say from London to Tokyo, would cut flying distances by as much as three thousand miles.

But these optimistic responses met with firm opposition from the Foreign Office, which naturally examined the problem from a political point of view. For one thing, Mackenzie King's administration had finally turned thumbs down on Stefansson, indicating Canada's lack of interest in the affair. Also, on 25 May, two days after Stefansson had set foot on English soil, the Soviet government had sent a formal protest note to the Foreign Office. Although the issue had been raised previously, the Soviet government now felt constrained "to approach the British Government requesting it to use its good services with the Canadian Government in order to put an end to these raids."[80] The agent, a member of the Russian trade delegation, also informed Britain that the Soviet Union was adopting measures "for the prevention in future of the violation of its sovereignty over the island in question." With the Baldwin government toying with the idea of recognizing the Red regime and establishing trade relations, the Foreign Office thought it quite unwise to do anything to upset the U.S.S.R. The Soviet note was followed by an American inquiry on 4 June which, although no American claim was enunciated, made it clear to the Foreign Office that the State department was not indifferent to the fate of Wrangel Island.[81] The question of Wrangel Island therefore was referred to the whole cabinet, where it would undergo close scrutiny.

Stefansson's position had weakened considerably and he set out in earnest to educate and convert unimpressed or hostile members of the British ministry.[82] Yet, for all his endeavours, Stefansson could not win the full backing of the British cabinet. From his partisans, Stefansson learned that those ministers who had an opinion to express all supported his views, although they wished to move cautiously in view of Canadian "lukewarmness."[83] Out of consideration for Canadian sensibilities, as well as to forestall unfriendly action on the part of the U.S.S.R., Lord Robert Cecil suggested it would be best "to continue occupying quietly as we have done —privately."[84] Stefansson's plans had been dealt a heavy blow and he knew he could only accept the cabinet's decision or face outright rejection. The Baldwin administration would not even go as far as the Canadian government had done in the year previous for, warned by that experiment, it refused to advance him any money for another rescue mission. Aware of the earlier "rescue" attempt, they wished to avoid anything that might turn it into an official imperial expedition. By the end of July, Stefansson knew he had to "go it alone," a prospect that his combative pride and stubbornness welcomed.

The British cabinet's decision was vindicated within two months. The British had been anxious to ascertain the United States reaction in the event the United Kingdom was to press a claim.[85] It was thought too risky to broach the question directly to the State department. Instead, a number of discreet and unofficial inquiries were made. On 15 August, the British chargé d'affaires in Washington, H. G. Chilton, reported that the American government would protest and that the United States was "considering the possibility of creating an air base on Wrangel Island."[86] Still later, on 21 September 1923, Group Captain Christie, the British Air attaché in Washington, reported to Chilton that:

> at your request I have made one or two private inquiries amongst Army and Navy Officers, one of whom had been recently in personal touch with Stefansson both here and in London [presumably Archibald Roosevelt] and I gained the impression that the British-Canadian claims to Wrangel Island are considered very weak. Apart from the earlier landing of the U.S.S. *Corwin*, American whalers are stated to have used the Island from time to time in recent years; the fact that Stefansson's party of occupation consisted of 3 Americans and one Canadian is also being emphasized. One informant indicated to me that suggestions had been made within Navy Circles that the British-Canadian claim should be supported in return for the occupation of certain small islands outside the Treaty Zone in the Pacific by the U.S.A. which might be of strategic value to the U.S. Navy, but that this scheme had not materialized owing to the attitude of the Japanese.

Apart from any political considerations, the opinion was fully expressed that Wrangel Island from the geographical aspect obviously belongs to Russian Siberia.

I have gained the impression from my conversations that [while] the U.S. Government would contest a British-Canadian claim, [it] would not, however, press its own case, but would probably support Russian sovereignty. I imagine U.S. Naval officers . . . still harbour suspicion of co-operative intentions on the part of Great Britain with Japan against the operations of the U.S. fleet in the North Pacific Ocean.

It is not unlikely that the incident might be followed by American occupation of some other islands to the immediate North of the Canadian Dominions, for instance in the neighbourhood of the Parry Islands. In this connection, General Mitchell once dropped the remark to me that one of the American Geographic societies has proposed a scheme to him for a survey of the Arctic Islands in the North of Canada by aircraft.[87]

Thus, for Great Britain to do anything to encourage official support would stir up a hornets' nest in Washington. The only diplomatic action the British had taken was to inform the U.S.S.R. that Stefansson's relief attempt was private and unofficial, that the question of ownership of the island was in no way raised, and that any Soviet attempt to interfere with the rescue of Crawford's party would be frowned upon by Great Britain.[88]

Stefansson, proceeding alone, eventually scraped up enough money from private subscribers in Britain to pay for a relief expedition—comprised of twelve Alaskan Eskimos, and, significantly, one American—who were to continue the private occupation of the island by his company. On 3 August, the *Donaldson* departed from Nome to deposit this second colony on Wrangel Island. It returned to Nome on 31 August, bringing bad news: the party of fourteen had been landed but, of the original colonizers, only the Eskimo seamstress, Ada Blackjack, was found alive. Three of the men, including Crawford, had perished on the ice somewhere between Wrangel Island and the Siberian mainland; the fourth, Lorne Knight, attended by Ada Blackjack, died of scurvy. Like Hadley before them, they had found the island desolate, scarce of game and fuel, and certainly not self-supporting; Stefansson's methods could never apply to this region.[89] But Stefansson could not admit this publicly and suppressed such evidence which could undermine his credibility. Stefansson contended in his autobiography that, according to Knight's diary, the men did not leave Wrangel Island because of a shortage of food.[90] However, both Crawford and Maurer, the men on the spot, decided in January 1923 that they could not survive for any length of time. "In fact, as early as last spring [1922] I [Crawford] considered it [leaving Wrangel Island] and when I saw how sparse seal and bear were, I decided it was unwise to stay here with the dogs all winter . . ."[91] Fred Maurer had written to his wife that "[t]he chief reason for our leaving is the shortage of food. There is not adequate food for all, there being only ten twenty-pound pokes of seal oil to last until next summer."[92] Stefansson's reaction to Maurer's letter was as follows: "I thought it less painful to relatives to realize that [the] immediate tragedy was accidental breaking through ice and not starvation[.] [I]t seems to me starvation incorrect and reflecting too much on [the] competence of [the] boys. Tell Crawfords [that] [Fred] Maurer's letter to his wife as she told me yesterday shows that trip to mainland was undertaken to carry news to me and not because of imminent food shortage."[93]

The British government grew totally disenchanted with the whole episode and considered itself lucky that it had not been an official party to the disaster. Almost overnight, Stefansson's "Friendly Arctic" had become "The Unfriendly Arctic."[94] The Canadian government in particular came under fire, for a large segment of the press and Crawford's parents held the government, together with Stefansson, responsible for the death of young Crawford. The aggrieved parents received front page coverage as they proceeded to attack the stunned Stefansson. (In a token gesture, the Canadian government, on the advice of the Monuments Board of Canada, dedicated a plaque to Allan Crawford in 1925. For years it hung in the entrance to the old Public Archives building on Sussex Street, Ottawa, even though the "historical" event took place outside Canadian boundaries. When the new Archives was built this plaque, as well as the one commemorating the men who had lost their lives in the *Karluk* disaster, was quietly stored in the basement.)

Now that his activities were coming under fire from all sides, Stefansson knew he was fighting a losing battle. Baldwin's administration could not be drawn into further comment and it wisely ignored his pleas for compensation. He found little consolation in unofficial reports that the United States had reluctantly entered the squabble. "If the foreign departments of the United States and Great Britain were to flip a coin for the possession of Wrangel Island, I should not care much whether it turned up heads or tails. I have done all I can for the Empire and now it is up to others."[95] But this was only a temporary reaction. Though Stefansson claimed it was up to others now that Great Britain had given him the cold shoulder, he attempted once more to persuade the State department to underwrite the enterprise.

Stefansson's sale of his company to Carl Lomen, the "reindeer king" of Alaska, was certainly an attempt to involve the United States and to strengthen the American case. Equally, it was a way to relinquish his responsibilities, and let someone else shoulder the burden which had placed him on the verge of bankruptcy.[96] By this time, Stefansson was deeply in debt for, in addition to the $17,000 he had sunk into the Wrangel Island promotion, he received news that his Hudson's Bay Reindeer Company had fallen through.[97] As the arctic explorer explained to Lomen, the sale would spare him another year of negotiations and would lead to eventual American ownership of Wrangel Island.[98] Financially exhausted and weary, Stefansson relinquished his company's interests in May 1924.[99] Now it was up to the reindeer king to carry the torch. Lomen's efforts during the fall of 1924 and in the spring of 1925 to persuade the State department to take action also were stopped dead in their tracks. The official State department position was thoroughly noncommittal. The United States government stated that its policy regarding Wrangel Island "did not go . . . beyond a reservation of all American rights in respect of the island; a readiness to discuss its status with the British Government."[100] Publicly, however, the United States government, time and again, declared that because of its nonrecognition of the Soviet regime, among other things, it was not prepared to make any statement with respect to the status of Wrangel Island.[101] In the end, however, Lomen was promised compensation from the United States government[102]—which was more consideration than Stefansson got from either Canada or Great Britain.

In any case, the fate of Wrangel Island never had rested with the United States. As long as nothing overt was done to claim the island by the British or Canadian governments, the American government seemed content to leave the problem alone. The Anglo–Soviet conference, held in London in July and August 1924 with the new Labour government of Ramsay MacDonald, brought about a final diplomatic solution. Prior to that conference, the Foreign Office had canvassed the various interested departments once more, and they reiterated that Wrangel Island was of little strategic or economic significance and that "His Majesty's Government would be unwilling to adopt an attitude calculated to create difficulties with the Soviet Government unless substantial interests were at stake."[103] This was basically the same position that the Conservative government had taken in 1923—that Britain's interests in Wrangel Island were minimal and that the U.S.S.R. now had sufficient power to force a decision on the island. The British position was made known to Canada, and presumably to the United States. The colonial secretary simply inquired whether the King administration had "any observations to offer" but he knew in advance what sort of answer he would receive. Canadian officialdom was sick of the whole issue; Mackenzie King, for his part, had managed to side-step for two years. On 18 July 1924, the same day that the inquiry was made, Byng hastily, and no doubt with relief, despatched a telegram stating that the British attitude was shared by the government of Canada.[104] When the issue reached the conference table in London, Mr. Ponsonby, in his reply on behalf of the British delegation, declared that: "His Britannic Majesty's Government lay no claim to the island of Wrangel." To which his Soviet counterpart, Mr. Rakovski, replied: "I am glad that one of the points, although a small point, which caused misunderstanding between the Soviet Union and Great Britain has been removed and I would suggest that this should be recorded in the minutes of the Conference."[105]

This pronouncement was made on 6 August 1924. Within three weeks the Russian warship *Red October* was removing the twelve Eskimos and one American who had been making their home on Wrangel Island since 1923. To justify its action, the U.S.S.R. claimed that the party had been operating on Russian territory without a licence and without proper authorization.[106] The American schooner *Herman*, on its way to rescue the party at the identical time, failed in its attempt to reach the island, so an unwanted confrontation between the Russians and the Americans was avoided.[107] According to the press, the American vessel had been beaten back by arctic gales after managing to reach Herald Island, forty miles east of Wrangel. The *Red October* spirited the colonizers to Vladivostok where their American leader, Charles Wells, died of pneumonia.[108] The Eskimo survivors, eleven in all, eventually were returned to their home in Golovin Bay, seventy-five miles east of Nome.[109] Carl Lomen protested to the State department, asking it to intervene. However, Evan E. Young of the State department advised Lomen to file a formal private complaint against the Soviet government protesting the *Red October*'s activities. Lomen did so to the tune of $30,000. It is interesting to note that the United States government, upon the failure of the U.S.S.R. to recognize Lomen's claim, promised to pay Lomen $46,630, $16,630 of which was interest, as compensation for losses incurred in his colonization venture. All one can conclude from this is that the United States had promised Lomen its support, but had changed its mind and decided to make up Lomen's loss in recognition of a mistake or failure in policy. Lomen himself reported that the colonization attempt he had adopted from Stefansson had the backing of secretary of state Hughes: "I had already seen Secretary of State Hughes before we went there, and he urged me to . . . hold the island."[110]

As a result of this alleged territorial violation, the U.S.S.R. was led, in April 1926, to incorporate the sector principle into her own national legislation to protect her arctic interests, basing the statement upon a Russian imperial decree of September 1916. Wrangel Island became an integral part of the U.S.S.R. within the sweeping claim now put forth by the central executive committee of the U.S.S.R.:

> All discovered lands and islands as well as those that may in the future be discovered, which are not at the date of publication of this decree recognized by the Government of the U.S.S.R. as a territory of a foreign power, are declared to be territories belonging to the U.S.S.R. within the following limits:
>
> In the Northern Arctic Ocean, from the northern coast of the U.S.S.R. up to the North Pole, between the Meridian 32° 4′ 35″ east longitude from Greenwich, passing along the eastern side of Vaida Bay through the Triangulation mark on Kerkursk Cape, and Meridian 168° 49′ 30″ west longitude from Greenwich passing through the middle of the strait which separates Ratmanov and Kruzenstern of the Diomede group of islands in the Bering Straits.[111]

The Soviet sectoral claim, like the Canadian, has never been accorded international recognition. However, since 1926 the Russians, their claims uncontested, have occupied, colonized, and developed Wrangel Island and islands similar to it, to their own benefit. To the Russians, the incorporation of Wrangel Island was a stage in the growth of Soviet internal control over the territories of the czars and signalled the frustration of another diabolical capitalist scheme of encirclement.[112] Soviet authorities, interestingly, do not condemn Stefansson's actions in this episode, perhaps out of respect for his status as a "friend" of the Soviet Union. Instead, excuses are made for him, "for he was not experienced in the problems of international law and was misled by the anti-Soviet statements and speeches of the English and Canadian press."[113]

9

Exit Stefansson

For Stefansson's Canadian career, the Wrangel Island debacle was a mortal blow, signalling his fall from grace in the halls of power. This time he had stepped on the world stage and had involved Canada in an international poker game which might have occasioned a reversal of efforts to consolidate the arctic archipelago. Canada's assumption of authority over the archipelago had been temporarily weakened by Stefansson's actions. Indiscriminate remarks by various Canadian officials, including Mackenzie King, and vigorous efforts and manoeuvres by Stefansson had kept the matter in the public eye and caused a flurry of concern among members of the international community. If King had rejected Stefansson's scheme, the matter would quietly have come to an end during the summer of 1922. Instead, the prime minister withheld a clearcut decision until he had roused the ire of the Soviet Union and the apprehensions of the United States. Canada had mishandled the affair and Stefansson had helped to create an international incident. To his credit, the wily Mackenzie King conveniently turned the tables and had argued that the matter was really an imperial affair.

Apart from Stefansson, Canada, Great Britain, and the United States were all content to see the island recognized as Russian, but a peculiar chain of events (chiefly Stefansson's meddling) had complicated the matter, breeding apprehension and distrust. Canada, when her government did give the matter serious thought, concluded that the island was not worth keeping, both because of its limited value to Canada and because recognition of her claims there might have put in question her own tenuous claims to the arctic archipelago. The Anglo–Canadian claim to Wrangel Island was dropped in favour of the principle of contiguity, and of the practical goal of promoting amicable relations with the Soviet Union and the United States.

Again, as in the reindeer project, a lack of detailed planning, incomplete data, and second-hand reporting, sometimes deliberately falsified by others, sealed the fate of the project. Over-eagerness and an unscientific approach were once again at bottom. Stefansson on occasion had forced the issue. Yet, in no way could his actions benefit the Dominion. Ottawa now realized that Stefansson was embarrassing, hence dispensable. Since his return from the Arctic in 1918, Stefansson's "track record" in Ottawa had not been an enviable one. The Geological Survey, the department of the Interior, External Affairs, and the Prime Minister's office all had had their fill. Stefansson had alienated too many administrative elements too often.

To assume that the Wrangel Island tragedy or the Hudson's Bay Reindeer Company failures were solely responsible for his demise overlooks a number of other salient points which seem trivial, but nevertheless contributed largely to his fall from favour. At the same time that the reindeer and Wrangel Island affairs were unfolding, Stefansson was involved with other parts of government. The problem boiled down to this: could the Canadian government afford to tolerate such a disruptive element as Stefansson? That would mean the alienation of a band of loyal civil servants. Or would Stefansson, who claimed to be just as loyal, be made to realize that his presence in Ottawa was no longer desired? This predicament had to be resolved.

The disagreements between the Geological Survey-Naval Service elements of the government and Stefansson revolved around the publication of the results of the 1913–18 expedition. There were a number of reasons for Stefansson's tardiness in discharging his obligation to wind up the affairs of the expedition. But none of these was really valid, and his delays were not taken very kindly by the government departments involved. Stefansson had none but himself to blame for the predicament in which he eventually found himself after 1918. Naturally, the government was aware Stefansson had contracted to give public lectures after his return to civilization, but it had expected him to fulfil certain duties, namely the completion of a "full report," and only then begin to lecture.[1]

Desbarats, in 1918, was intent upon tying up the loose ends of the expedition, and there were many of these on Stefansson's side, particularly regarding the lands he had discovered and explored north of Prince Patrick Island. This was, naturally, of prime importance to the Canadian government which had put so high a priority on discovery, and was concerned to establish its title beyond question to such lands; the government had to be able to confront any foreign encroachment with an indisputable claim. However, as an annoyed Desbarats complained:

> We have really no definite location of these lands nor any idea of their extent. We have your first report announcing the discovery of the lands and giving a position which did not correspond with the charts. It is quite possible of course that the older definitions were not correct. We lack information entirely as to the whole exploration, having merely received fragmentary reports which it has not been possible to piece together so as to give a connected history of the work done by the expedition. It would seem that your parties have covered a good deal of territory and have made a number of trips into the new land which you discovered, we have little information as to the results that have been obtained from the information which has been gathered. We have no information which would allow . . . our laying . . . a chart of the lands which you have discovered . . .[2]

Under the circumstances, it was very important both for reasons of official government policy and for the sake of Stefansson's professional reputation that he produce the fullest possible statement of his discoveries to complement the Southern Party's publications, which were well on their way to completion.[3]

But Stefansson had other ideas. He preferred to embark on his lecture tour immediately and to leave the Canadian government waiting until he had decided it was time to publish the official reports. According to Stefansson, who was still recovering in St. Stephen's Hospital in the Yukon in 1918, the lecture tour was to be for the benefit of the Red Cross, whose efforts during the war, which was still raging in Europe, should be aided.[4] The Canadian government knew virtually nothing about his plans. Yet Stefansson confided to John Greenough, President of the American Geographical Society, that Ottawa had allowed him to begin his lecture series "sooner than would be the case in ordinary course because my entire share of any profits (above current expenses) is to go to the Red Cross."[5] Stefansson was confident that he could satisfy Desbarats with a three page summary of the highlights of his explorations.[6] If the government persisted, then he would cancel his arrangements provided they did not injure financially his lecture manager, Lee Keedick.[7] He reminded the government, however, that if they took this course he could not guarantee his performance for them.[8] Certainly, Stefansson was growing less diffident with his employers, and this might have been construed by them as impudence and arrogance.

Stefansson probably wanted to ease himself out of the government's grasp, hoping his preliminary reports would suffice to meet their terms and that a plea of giving patriotic lectures for the Red Cross would make them more sympathetic and less insistent. It certainly would give greater legitimacy to his lecture tour and aid his career. But the truth of the matter was that neither the Canadian government nor the Red Cross knew about these supposed arrangements—the latter not until it was informed of Stefansson's plans by Rudolph Anderson, watchdog. In any event, it was against Red Cross policy "to permit any such lectures or to permit the name of the Red Cross to be used in connection with lectures, commercial enterprises, etc., of any kind."[9] Stefansson's statements to the Canadian government and the press then were "entirely unauthorized."[10]

As yet, Desbarats did not know this, and Anderson kept the news to himself for several weeks presumably to allow Stefansson more rope. The only card that the deputy minister had to play was the old argument that such a tour

> [w]ould defeat the objects of the government in manning, equipping and financing the [expedition]. The object of this expedition was to obtain information for the benefit of the people of Canada and I must repeat its main task was to record this information in proper shape, so that it can be published and laid before the public, the object of the Department would be entirely defeated if Canada would obtain no return for its expenditure in the efforts it has put forth in this expedition.[11]

Desbarats's own department would certainly be in a very embarrassing situation if Stefansson did not submit his findings in full for publication. The department of Marine and Naval Service (formerly the Naval Service), under whose auspices the Canadian Arctic Expedition had been organized, conducted, and largely financed, and which no doubt was anxious to conduct any future polar expeditions, had virtually nothing on paper to show for its time, patience, and large amount of money:

> The Southern Branch of the expedition is getting its reports into shape and they will soon be available for publication. The reports will give a large amount of information and show that this branch of the expedition has done much good work. If the report of the northern branch is lacking and no information is published regarding the work accomplished by that section the inference will be clear that there is nothing to say on the subject and nothing worth publishing has been accomplished by the northern part of the expedition. You would be

the first one to regret such a result, and it would, undoubtedly, lead to a severe attack on the government and yourself.[12]

The minister of Naval Service was insistent that the report be completed as soon as possible so that the department's involvement would be vindicated.

But the confident, self-willed Stefansson was not to be bullied. He immediately turned about and scolded the government, particularly Desbarats, for being so shortsighted:

I . . . took it for granted that the government would be glad if I could capitalize the prominence of the expedition in the public mind and turn all the receipts into patriotic and useful channels. If I was wrong in this, it is because I do not understand the attitude of the government. I thought all energies of our people were (and ought to be) bent on winning the war (I have seen it frequently so stated) and I was assured by lecture managers that considerable money could be secured for the Red Cross in this way.

. . . I equally fail to understand [the Government's] attitude towards the increase and diffusion of knowledge—I fail to understand how the people of Canada will lose any of the fruits of our work by hearing a narration of some of [the experience] from the mouths of men who did the work. If it is duly announced, as I have always taken it for granted it would be, that the government is lending one of its servants to the Red Cross for the purpose of securing increased funds for work of patriotism and of mercy, and if it is announced that the information given is the property of the people of Canada, then I fail to understand how any aims or ends of the government or people of Canada are being interfered with. It is well known that few besides specialists ever consult government technical reports. Besides, it is impossible to represent technical results in a popular lecture. I feel sure that were one of the members of the expedition to tell a popular audience how to build our snow houses so as to be comfortable, how we dress so as to be always warm and dry though no artificial heat is available for the drying of clothes, and how we secure our food as we go and thus free ourselves from the limitations of former travellers who thought they needed to haul their food with them—if one of us explained these and similar things, doing so would probably capture the interest of many who would not otherwise consult the formal reports, and the total publicity of the technical results therein contained would be increased. Certainly such results would divert no one's attention from the knowledge secured by the expedition or from the credit due the government for supplying it.[13]

Stefansson's assumptions about the government's position were completely unfounded and he could not understand why the government was so determined that the results should be published under official auspices. Would he not be aiding Desbarats by seeking a wider forum? Certainly it would do himself no harm. Stefansson acknowledged that he was obliged to follow government orders, and that if the government decided he must give up his idea of lecturing for the Red Cross he would obey.[14] But he implied it would be with bad grace, and the government's face would be blackened for discouraging such patriotic work on Stefansson's part.

Desbarats might have been put off by such arguments, but, when he found out that Stefansson's plan of support for the Red Cross was not acceptable even to the institution in question,[15] he was in a much stronger position to persuade Stefansson to live up to his end of the bargain. The explorer had accepted a job with the government and he should follow through by providing the sponsoring agency with the information it wanted and to which it was entitled. Dissemination of information should be through regular official publications, not through lecture tours. The rebuke to Stefansson was harsh but deserved for, as Desbarats pointed out, "I explained this to you about two years ago when I sent instructions not to continue your explorations in Arctic regions but to return south, as the government considered the needs of the war were paramount and that any available funds should be devoted to war purposes."[16] Stefansson had let down the government and the war effort from 1916 onward, or so Desbarats implied. The government had sacrificed everything for the war effort and would not now tolerate being lectured to by Stefansson. Furthermore, now that he was in the south he could not pretend ignorance of the government's real position. By November 1918, Stefansson realized he could not beg off the responsibility for winding up his work with the government if he wanted governmental co-operation for any further ventures, upmost of which was the musk-ox project.[17] Subsequent disclaimers on his part regarding the Red Cross business can only be viewed as self-serving.

Stefansson now asked Lee Keedick, his lecture manager, for a postponement of the tour, arguing that it would be dangerous to lecture and write simultaneously, for it would result in his spreading himself too thinly and weaken his individual efforts:

For my personal success it is absolutely essential that I have time to get my scientific work in shape . . . My first magazine stories cannot appear before March (1919) and need not appear before April. My book will not appear before next fall. You have already seen what folly it is to try to compete with war, and [during] the period of readjustment till the treaties of peace will be signed[,] the public will be full of interest in the shifting of the boundaries of states and in the establishment of republics after monarchies, I urge upon you, for all these reasons, as great a postponement of the lectures as possible. For myself, I would not care if I lost money—I think we shall gain money —by waiting till my scientific work is in shape.[18]

Stefansson acknowledged the predicament he was in, but argued that it was more in Keedick's interests than his own to delay the lecture series. But Keedick would have none of this and, like the Canadian government, was determined to make his performer abide by the contract he had signed in 1913.[19] Stefansson had placed himself in a very difficult position, especially since his lecture tour would take him far away from the centre of his influence, Ottawa. He had bitten off more than he could chew: to write a popular book on the expedition; complete his duties for the Canadian government; give a series of lectures; and simultaneously to promote the musk-ox venture and, a little later, the Wrangel Island project. It required a delicate touch to balance all these activities, and as time went on Stefansson, continually complaining about his self-inflicted tasks,[20] was left to extricate himself by his own devices. Stefansson tried unsuccessfully to break his contract with Keedick, claiming that his lecture manager was discrediting him by issuing untruthful promotional material.[21] He also argued that his respiratory system was being adversely affected by lecturing and that he was not well.[22] Keedick, for his part, in January 1922, sued Stefansson for breach of contract and Stefansson responded with a counter-suit of $20,000 claiming injury to his professional reputation.[23] The court decided in favour of Keedick.[24] After the incident, Stefansson went on lecturing, despite his professed "malady" allegedly aggravated by lecturing. He placed himself under the direction of the Ellison–White organization, known as the Affiliated Lyceum and Chatauqua Association, which paid for his law suit.[25]

Stefansson was too busy with these other matters to be able to give the government a first-rate summary of the expedition, and Desbarats apparently was willing to release Stefansson when he submitted a brief ten-page typed manuscript. Stefansson went through the motions of submitting this final report, but he told Desbarats that he would not attempt a summary of the previous four years' work as it seemed to him that any "clerk" could extract material from the files.[26] Other projects were of more importance to him, especially the popular narrative for the Macmillan Company.

Stefansson was also worried about the possibility of each specialist in the Southern Section writing his own report of his scientific findings. If this happened, he, as commander, would be left with nothing to report beyond his own activities. He considered this unwise from a scientific point of view. He also believed it was a deliberate personal slight by former members of the Southern Section, a derogation of his position and right as commander to report on the expedition as a whole. Referring to the case of the geologist, O'Neill, Stefansson complained about his own position by going to Borden as soon as the prime minister had returned from his labours at the Paris Peace Conference:

> The attitude of the Survey is that Mr. O'Neill is a highly trained geologist, and there was no other highly trained geologist on the expedition. They say that their professional standards require that they publish nothing except the work done by specialists. My reply to this is if this attitude had been maintained by other Polar expeditions, such, for instance, as Scott's first expedition or Shackleton's, there would have been no geological results published by them.
>
> It has been a matter of practice, however, upon the return of every Polar expedition, that all geological information gathered by any member has been put at the disposal of some such specialist as a university professor in geology and then published yielding results which are commonly considered to be notable contributions to science.
>
> Should our expedition adopt the attitude of publishing the information secured by such specialists . . . it will result in the suppression of much valuable knowledge. This attitude appears to me to be a sort of "labour union spirit" where those not members of a technical craft are looked upon as scabs, and their valuable results disregarded by mere reason that they are not members of a union.[27]

Stefansson gained the prime minister's promise to look into the entire matter,[28] and his position in this new row was supported by Desbarats when the latter was queried by Borden.

Desbarats, in fact, pointed out to Borden that the Southern Section's disinclination to recognize Stefansson's authority, as first affirmed in the order-in-council of 22 February 1913, had been carried over after the expedition had returned. This spirit was still hampering the publication of the official report. Although some headway had been made, Desbarats implied that the attitude of the Geological Survey was the main stumbling block. He suggested that Stefansson be appointed editor of the expedition's publications to supervise the project inasmuch as "the full responsibility for the expedition was placed on Mr. Stefansson." Alternately, he suggested that a small committee be established, with Stefansson as one of the members, to ensure the publication of the report. Although R. G. McConnell, deputy minister of the department of Mines, "gave qualified support to this project . . . no action has been taken by the Geological Survey."[29] The Geological Survey offices, it appears, would only do their work independent of Stefansson, or not at all. At this stage, a feud appears to have arisen not merely between individual members of the Geological Survey and Stefansson, but between the two government agencies, the Geological Survey and the Naval Service.

Certain members of the Arctic Biological Committee, of which Anderson was a member, were given vague responsibilities for publishing the reports. The committee was fearful about allowing Stefansson to write the narrative of the entire expedition for "it was important that a fair account of the work of the [Southern] party should be given."[30] Stefansson may not have liked what the Survey men would write, but it is obvious that the Geological Survey men feared Stefansson would tamper with their reports to benefit his own ends.

At an early meeting in Desbarats's office, guarantees had been given that the Southern Section would have its own narrative, but somewhere along the way Anderson gained the impression that Stefansson wanted to write the entire report.[31] Anderson had overestimated Stefansson, who certainly was not behind this alleged manoeuvre. In fact, entangled as he then was, Stefansson would have welcomed Anderson writing an expanded, fuller narrative than the one he had already published;[32] and he had earlier advised that Anderson's report be written along the lines Anderson ultimately suggested. Anderson should write a narrative of the journeys and field trips of the Southern Section; the scientific results *per se* of Anderson's group should be written by the scientists themselves.[33]

By mid-1919, this rather silly publication controversy had settled down, and the technical and scientific reports were.being prepared for publication. Yet little was being done by either man with the publication of the official narratives. Although it was part of his job, Anderson was reluctant to publish his scientific findings. Stefansson was too preoccupied with his private affairs: lecture tours, lobbying in government circles, and writing his unofficial version of the adventure, *The Friendly Arctic*. The latter, of course, allowed Stefansson far greater freedom to express his own views than any publication under government auspices. When it was released, late in 1921, it proved to be a bombshell in Ottawa.

The Friendly Arctic, a title suggested to Stefansson by Gilbert Grosvenor of the National Geographic Society,[34] was Stefansson's version of the 1913–18 expedition, its trials and tribulations and, of course, Stefansson's multitude of achievements in the face of adversity and near mutiny. In essence, it was his rationale and justification for his actions. The topics ranged from the confrontation at Nome, the Collinson Point episode, and the many wranglings over priorities in terms of ships and supplies, Stefansson's exploits, and his theories on arctic matters. Anderson and other members of the Geological Survey were painted in less than rosy colours, and Anderson's initial reaction to the book was predictable: Stefansson had made many libellous and underhanded statements, which placed him and the entire Civil Service under a cloud.[35]

Answering Stefansson, Anderson believed, would merely play into his hands by giving him the publicity he was after. On the other hand, there were many reasons why Stefansson should be answered and exposed.[36] "The important thing now is the inquiry, a Royal Commission if possible," said Mrs. Anderson, who shared her husband's sentiments. "We shall have to pulverize Mr. Stefansson but he deserves it for doing such things."[37] The Andersons were confident that they would triumph:

> Steffy does not realize that he is fighting the Canadian government when he fights Rudolph. He [had] better study the condition of the country before starting a thing like this . . . [T]here is no room at the present time in Canada for VS and Rudolph at the same time unless Steffy reforms. He may. He is not a good "villain." And he is brilliant to do anything if he wants to do it, [but] he must be taught to play fair.[38]

But little official notice had been taken by the upper echelons of the Geological Society. So Anderson and Jenness hoisted their standard on their own initiative[39] and soon they were supported by J. J. O'Neill, who was now a professor of geology at McGill University.[40] O'Neill considered Stefansson a smooth-tongued diplomat whose goal was self-advancement through publicity at the expense of genuine scientific activity. The newspapers and the Canadian Press knew a good story when they saw one. Anderson asked for a "full government inquiry" into the affairs of the last expedition, charging that Stefansson unjustly accused the scientific staff of "attempted mutiny" and "insubordination"; and that the whole expedition was really "at bottom, a newspaper and magazine exploiting scheme" paid for by the people of Canada. In fact, Anderson charged, Stefansson had been insubordinate in attempting to change the complexion of the expedition, and evading all government notices to return to civilization. Moreover, he implied, Stefansson had been derelict in his duty because he pursued a policy of "wild extravagance," buying extra ships, supplies and dubious services, which cost the Canadian government and taxpayers more than $500,000 when the expedition was originally to have cost $75,000. Stefansson's publicity about living off the country was an ironic joke, for his "foraging was done on the people who pay the taxes."[41] These were strong charges, but they certainly were nothing new, for as far back as 1916, when the Southern Section had returned, similar charges had been "leaked" to the press. Between 1917 and the airing of Anderson's charges in 1922, similar stories and rumours had been bandied around Ottawa. Some of them were directly attributable to Anderson. And, when one looks at the real story of the Canadian Arctic Expedition, these charges had more than a little truth to them.

One could argue that *The Friendly Arctic* was a reply to these earlier stories, and sympathize with Stefansson for being the victim of calumny. True, Stefansson loved and sought publicity, but he had taken a fair share of abuse. Some of his closest friends, including Sir Robert Borden, suggested he ought to lay his cards on the table and turn on his critics. Anderson, who was a novice in the realm of newspaper publicity, had sown the wind and would have to face the prospect of reaping the whirlwind. Anderson had certainly held nothing back when he spoke or wrote to innumerable individuals about the expedition and Stefansson. He was almost beside himself in 1918 when he wrote to Dr. Isaiah Bowman, editor of the *Geographical Review* and secretary of the Explorers' Club in New York, about the impending election of Stefansson as president of the latter organization. Anderson's remarks, which bordered on libel, labelled Stefansson a coward, a publicity seeker, a liar, a "bounder," and an "international Socialist"; all of which were anathema to himself as a man of principle, "of honour as an ex-soldier of the United States, an officer and . . . a gentleman, a man and a Mason."[42] Such extreme vilification could only be tolerated for so long even by Stefansson, who was tolerant about most matters. Stefansson wanted, naturally, to achieve fame by publishing an account of the expedition, but he could not afford to let his detractors escape. Silence about the key issues could inspire additional condemnation.

Stefansson unburdened himself of these doubts and asked the advice of both Desbarats and Borden who were, admittedly, sympathetic to him. Yet he saw no way of avoiding the many controversies that abounded between 1913–18. Nevertheless, before the book went to press, he sought advice to salve his conscience about his subsequent course of action "to tell everything as frankly and fairly as I could" rather than "to tell a dozen lies to cover up the original one."[43] Desbarats, Borden, and several others,[44] agreed with him. Borden went so far as to write a glowing introduction for the book.

When Anderson suggested to Borden that he had been unwise in writing the introduction to *The Friendly Arctic*, Borden rebuked him forcefully saying that his preface

> had relation to the achievements of the expedition therein detailed. I cannot recall conversation respecting the difficulties that arose between Mr. Stefansson and other members of the expedition, except one occasion. Mr. Stefansson explained that certain charges had been made against him, and he felt some hesitation in putting forward his side of the case . . . He asked my opinion as the course I should pursue, and I advised him that he should set forth the circumstances as he understood them. It seemed to me advisable that this should be done for the sake of historic accuracy, and in justification of the action he had taken.[45]

Borden was still a powerful, highly respected individual, a man of complete integrity and honesty. Stefansson knew this and he had been overjoyed when Borden had consented to write the preface to his book.[46] Such support would give the book and its author the stamp of authority and legitimacy. Anderson, no doubt, was convinced that Borden had been hoodwinked by Stefansson, but he would get nowhere with the former prime minister.

Anderson had to look elsewhere for the counter-attack on Stefansson. He could direct an appeal through the press, for the president of the parliamentary press gallery informed him that the newspapers of Canada would be glad for someone to take Stefansson to task, and would be willing to offer him their services.[47] This might have been the case, but probably Anderson would have been exploited, producing sensationalisms comparable to Stefansson's own. In the long run, no one could benefit, except the press. The government, particularly the higher echelons of the Geological Survey, feared this prospect and were anxious to avoid public airing of the differences. The day after the newspaper charges appeared (14 January 1922), Anderson, Chipman, and Jenness were instructed that no more interviews were to be given to the press until the minister, the Honourable Charles Stewart, decided "what action is to be taken on behalf of our men."[48] The Geological Survey wanted to reply to Stefansson on a scholarly level without the full glare of publicity.

Rather than have the battle fought in the newspapers, Camsell, deputy minister of the Geological Survey, thought it best that a former member of the Southern Section should write a critical review of *The Friendly Arctic* for an internationally respected geographic journal. He implied that someone no longer connected with the Branch would be preferable and he approached J. J. O'Neill for the purpose. O'Neill sympathized with Camsell for:

> I, for one, do not care to have an application for some important position refused on the grounds that I have a reputation of being an insubordinate, cantankerous person, whose outlook is very narrow, and who may be expected to show the white feather if called upon to volunteer for any apparently hazardous task: such is the reputation Mr. Stefansson has seen fit to impute to the members of the Scientific Staff.[49]

But even though O'Neill felt he had been wronged, he would not speak publicly. The only ones who had the courage to protest were those very same people who were being silenced by their superiors. Stefansson, who may have had an inkling of their quandary, could not have planned it better had he set his mind to it. Everything seemed to be going his way, and everything seemed to conspire against his "enemies."

The former members of the Southern Party, some still in the employ of the government, chafed under the inactivity of their superiors. Before long, Anderson, Chipman, O'Neill, and Jenness sent a strong note to Charles Stewart, minister of the Interior, protesting the allegations in *The Friendly Arctic* which, they claimed, injured their "personal honour" and professional reputations, and demanded that a formal investigation look into the matter.[50] To make certain that their petition would not be swept under the carpet, as their last protestations had been, they made sure in March that their plight once again reached the ears of the *Ottawa Morning Journal*.[51] But it was really to no avail for, as Stefansson himself well knew by this time, no one wanted the dirty linen of the past paraded before the public.[52] If anything, the actions of Stefansson's opponents, designed to force the government's hand, infuriated the latter. Anderson and his cohorts were prohibited from making further public statements by their minister, Charles Stewart, who told them to return to their proper duties.[53] According to Mrs. Anderson, the only reason Stewart gave for not granting an inquiry was that "it was an impossible situation for two government departments to engage in a fight with one another. Stefansson is shrewd. Isn't he shrewd?"[54]

The only way left to assail Stefansson had been to attack him in the scholarly press, particularly through the respected journal *Science*.[55] The new round began in July of 1922 with the appearance of a long letter by Jenness in *Science* disputing many of the allegations made in *The Friendly Arctic*.[56] The letter, of course, put the Southern Section in the best possible light, centring around the problem of whether Stefansson was in complete command of both Sections, or whether the Southern Section had been created as a separate entity. In addition, using some documentary evidence, Jenness was able to cast doubt on Stefansson's ability to live off the country. If he had had Stefansson's own diaries, Jenness could have made a more convincing exposé. Although he did not alter them, the text of the instructions, as he related them, were made up of three different paragraphs which, in the original document, were separated by pages of instructions. Yet the sentences selected, when gathered together, gave a different impression to that which they conveyed when read with the rest of the instructions. Jenness's letter, as written, cast doubt on Stefansson having been made supreme commander.

Although other individuals attacked Stefansson in one fashion or another in other scholarly journals,[57] Jenness's article was the one which infuriated Stefansson most and made their relationship tense and full of mutual suspicion. Stefansson was so upset he had a local lawyer write a threatening letter to Jenness, which the latter ignored.[58] Stefansson's reaction to the article so delighted his detractors that they could confidently assert that they were "perfectly satisfied" that Stefansson had been answered appropriately.[59]

Stefansson decided not to enter the fray, but he let his own supporters carry on the cause. For example, his friend William H. Hobbs of the Department of Geology, University of Michigan, reviewed *The Friendly Arctic* in *The Journal of Geology*. Of all the reviews of the book, Hobbs's is the most partial, denigrating Jenness's aspersions on "this ultra-modest explorer," Stefansson.[60] His non-involvement in the academic debate was a wise move for, although he had been wounded and his reputation besmirched, Stefansson did gain some advantages. His enemies were doing his job for him much better than he could—and he admitted it.[61] Silence on their part might have been golden for the members of the Southern Section. Their actions may have blown Stefansson's prominence out of all proportion, at least in Canada. *The Friendly Arctic* was not a best seller in Canada or Great Britain, although one can be sure the controversy generated after its publication may have helped its sales. "The City of Cleveland alone has bought more of my books than all of the British territories put together," lamented Stefansson in 1922 to Stephen Leacock.[62] If anything, then, the actions of the former members of the Southern Section did not damage his prestige. They helped promote it instead and, in the process, they became doubly infuriated. With international attention focusing more and more on Stefansson and the Wrangel Island business, which had not met disaster as yet, every little scrap of publicity helped.

But now it was Stefansson's turn to take the offensive, not against Anderson, who really posed no threat to him, but against Diamond Jenness, a fellow anthropologist. Jenness had caused some concern with his rebuttal in *Science*, but he now posed a greater threat to Stefansson. In his pending final report on the physical characteristics of the Copper Eskimos, Jenness once again severely took his former "commander" to task, questioning not only his conclusions, but his methodology and basic truthfulness about the Copper Eskimos' location as outlined in *My Life With the Eskimo*.[63] Jenness had been assisted by Franz Boas of Columbia, Dr. Hootes of Harvard, and Dr. Sapir of the Victoria Museum.[64] The Southern Section's attacks on him were of no consequence, because no formal inquiry would ever be established to air their grievances. But Jenness was another matter. He worked in a field where Stefansson had some claim to competence. Stefansson's international scientific reputation in matters of ethnology, the reputation he cherished most, was now at stake. Stefansson, however, claimed his main concern with Jenness's conclusions was to stop another controversy from reaching the official level and thereby lowering the work of the expedition in the esteem of worldwide scientific circles.[65] He could ignore attacks on his proficiency in scientific areas such as geography and oceanography, but this was the absolute limit. Stefansson's opposition in this case was quite serious, for it might have ruined the entire series of publications.

This, rather than the squabbling between two scientists of decided views, was the significant issue. The deputy minister of Mines, Camsell, was informed that Desbarats, deputy minister of Marine, was tempted to

stop the funding for the publication of the reports "in view of the controversy being carried on . . ."[66] Stefansson insisted that Jenness was determined to carry on the fight in the official report. The ethnologist, who had
been used to criticism, feared that such views finding their way into official
publications might give them the stamp of authority. Unless certain pas-
sages in the report were revised, Stefansson announced he was ready to
charge Jenness with "deliberate misrepresentation." Stefansson was even
willing to let Jenness question his theory concerning the white origins of
the Copper Eskimos, so long as this was done in a "truthful and legitimate
way." Stefansson told Jenness's superior, Charles Camsell, that he would
be satisfied if Jenness admitted that, first, his own forays in the Copper
Eskimo country had not been as intensive as Stefansson's; second, that he
had not seen the Prince Albert Sound Eskimos,[67] and, finally, that his
generalizations could not be so absolute.[68]

Jenness refused to back down, and was incensed that Stefansson had
been allowed to see his report before it was published, when the explorer
had no legal or moral authority to do so. Jenness asserted: "Mr. Stefansson
spent about six weeks among the Copper Eskimo and met about forty
percent of their number. I spent upward of 18 months and saw 70%. To
insert the statement asked for by Mr. Stefansson would be a direct un-
truth."[69] Not only that, but such a statement would undermine Jenness's
contention regarding the possible origin of this native group, and would
give Stefansson's original hypothesis as much validity as his own. Jenness
was no fool. To admit anything else would downgrade his own conclusions.

If Jenness would not revise or eliminate some of his remarks, Stefansson
insisted on his right to reply in his own report.[70] But by now such threats
were not given serious attention by the Geological Survey. They may have
gained the impression that Stefansson would never complete his end of the
bargain. In any case, he could be kept at bay by not being given a chance
to get in the last word. The manoeuvre was simple enough: hold off the
publication of the narrative of the Southern Section. Anderson had indicated he was not averse to this.[71] Furthermore, with the rebuttal in
Science, and with the publication of Jenness's report under official auspices,
what more could be asked for? The narratives were of secondary importance to the Geological Survey as compared with some of the scientific
reports. Stefansson would not be permitted to get in the last word, because
Anderson refused to supply the second-to-last word. The waiting game
began and outlasted Stefansson. No changes would be made in Jenness's
report.[72] Stefansson, however, was determined to have the last word and
promised that it would be "a very vicious last word," but he would never

be given the opportunity. The Geological Survey was confident that his flickering star would be extinguished. Stefansson, indeed, was "hurting," to use his own words, and indicated his desire for a truce.[73] But it was too late, for Stefansson was no longer a man to be worried about.

As time went on, Stefansson ceased to feel any particular obligation to the Canadian government to see the project through. He smarted at the abuse hurled at him in Parliament after the Wrangel Island affair, especially after he had served faithfully in the Arctic for eleven years without salary.[74] The other publications went forward while the government continued to plead with Stefansson to be reasonable and let bygones be bygones for the sake of the general reading public.[75] Stefansson would not budge, though by now he considered it might be wiser "to get some impartial historian to write the story of the expedition on the basis of the documents[.]"[76] By 1925, the government considered it "quite useless" to take the matter any further, and resigned itself to the fact that neither Stefansson nor Anderson would publish the official narratives; Stefansson because he insisted on having the last word, and Anderson because he did not want to play Stefansson's game.

It is true, though, that Stefansson in 1931 (when a different government was in power in Ottawa) had the temerity to suggest he would undertake the project if the government would "make a definite grant for this purpose" seeing that he, unlike Anderson and the other scientists, had to earn his living "without salary or support from anybody."[77] But it was now too late; his cry of self-support fell on deaf ears and his suggestion was rejected utterly.[78] By his own admission, Stefansson was earning between $20,000–$30,000 a year in 1920, mainly from his lectures on the north. The explorer-lecturer pointed out that this was his just due for twelve years of unpaid service in the Arctic.[79] However, that had been his own choice. Stefansson had speculated on the long term returns and the freedom of action that had accompanied his unsalaried position. It is likely that Ottawa officials in 1931 would assume that nothing drastically had changed Stefansson's financial position. Besides, why should the Canadian government subsidize an individual who had been so successful in the past because of opportunities afforded by the same agency?

Stefansson's official narrative was never published. The department of the Naval Service had nothing to show for its efforts, unlike the mass of Geological Survey expedition reports. Recognition for the Naval Service's part in the expedition came in the form of a short black-bordered notice which only appeared once, ironically enough in Jenness's volume on the Copper Eskimo:

> This volume is one of a series of reports dealing with the results of the Canadian Arctic Expedition, 1913–18, which was led by Mr. Vilhjalmur Stefansson under the direction of the Department of the Naval Service. The Geological Survey of the Department of Mines was also interested in the expedition, sending several specialists with it, and is issuing part of the technical volumes of the series of reports. Copies of this volume, paper-bound, may be obtained for fifty cents apiece from the Department of the Naval Service, Ottawa.[80]

Hardly worth the effort.

To R. W. Brock, under whose leadership the original Southern Section was planned and who now was a dean at the University of British Columbia, the whole situation had grown lamentable:

> I do not suppose that there ever was a polar expedition out any length of time, that did not have this sort of row. The difference is that in almost all cases, when they got out they returned to normal, laugh and forget and stand up for each other. This case is the exception to the rule, and is damaging to all concerned.
>
> No good to anybody, but only harm to all concerned, will result in pursuing the matter further. It has gone too far already. No one is interested except the principals, and they have each had their say and gotten in their blows. Let it go at that. I do not think for the personal vanity or private satisfaction of one or a few individuals, the officials or any others should be dragged into this dirty mess, or that the country should be put to the unnecessary expense of an investigation. In the end, the individuals, the parties and the expedition will be judged on one thing only and that is the scientific results they present to the public.
>
> The squabble has taken up far too much of their time and has been given too much publicity already.
>
> I am perfectly clear as to the instructions to Stefansson and the Southern Party. They have both been right on some points and wrong on others. That is one main reason why no good can come to anyone pursuing the matter. Some dirt will stick to each one of them. So far as any outsider takes any interest in the matter his sympathies will

incline to one side or the other as it does now, but the main reaction will be, what it has been with both you and me, annoyance with the lot. "A plague on both your Houses." There may be something to be said against Stefansson—but I can vouch for this in his favour, when he got back he wished to make up with Dr. Anderson and to be fair with him and let bygones be bygones. I know that from the earnest way he asked for my assistance to bring it about.

His references to the trouble in the Friendly Arctic were unfortunate, but [Stefansson] had been goaded to the explosion point. However, he still desired to be fair, for he tried to get the manuscript to me to look over. Unfortunately, I was out of reach . . . Had I seen it, I know he would have accepted my alterations, which would have been satisfactory to all concerned.

If there was anything to be gained by continuing the controversy, if anyone needed vindicating, or if there were an official inquiry, I would be forced to break silence. But such is not the case. Because a few dogs insist on fighting, it is not incumbent on every cur in town to get into the scrap.[81]

Brock's assessment may have been a fair one, but since he was no longer in government service he could afford the luxury of speaking frankly. To the men in Ottawa, however, there existed a real and practical problem: how to resolve the issue. Government officials, particularly those of the Geological Survey, also were anxious to end the squabble, but Camsell believed this would be impossible: "I am anxious as anyone to avoid any controversy . . . but from my recent experience I am inclined to think that Mr. Stefansson is not inclined in the same way. It is regrettable that these differences will continue to rise, but we have no control over Mr. Stefansson's actions."[82] If anyone had to go, Camsell's tone suggests that it was Stefansson who was considered expendable.

Stefansson was in trouble with both the Geological Survey and the Canadian government in the spring of 1923. By the autumn of the same year, he had been placed in a very uncomfortable position with the news of the Wrangel Island tragedy. Although he was not present in Ottawa for more than a few days at a time, by now even his spirit was being exorcised from the capital.

With the Wrangel Island fiasco, the mud-slinging campaign against him, by Mrs. Anderson in particular, began in earnest. Throughout the fall of 1923 and the spring of 1924, she was pouring out her feelings in letters to Mrs. Crawford, mother of young Allan Crawford who had lost his life in the service of the Stefansson Arctic Development Company.[83] Previously, such points of view had only been spread by word of mouth in the closed civil service circle of Ottawa, but now the whispering campaign reached out to other areas—fuel for a closely knit hate-Stefansson club. Some of the rumours could never be substantiated—but, intermingled with them were elements of truth which could only tarnish Stefansson's reputation. Even had they been complete fabrications, the important fact that they were being spread, and that many people by now were receptive, was sufficient in itself. Ottawa was told that Stefansson was a reprehensible, publicity-seeking liar, a plagiarist, a rebel, and a cheat who was expelled from Harvard for selling examinations to students he was tutoring; he was a man who turned on those, especially missionaries, who had befriended him, a man who had deserted his Eskimo wife and son.[84]

Rudolph Anderson carried on in similar fashion but on a more subdued key.[85] The Anderson crusade continued well into the 1950s; they collected clippings on Stefansson and his activities, and disseminated such material, with comments, to intimates and associates within the government employ and elsewhere. As far as can be ascertained, nothing came of their efforts. By 1952, even Mrs. Crawford was tired of the whole affair simply because it had come to naught, especially after an arctic island had been named after Stefansson.[86]

The reasons for the long and bitter Anderson campaign are obscure, but their efforts were redundant and quite unnecessary. Le Bourdais, a close associate of Stefansson in the 1920s, maintained that the Anderson-Stefansson controversy was the "Feud that Froze the Arctic."[87] The feud, according to Le Bourdais, paralysed the Canadian government, making it unable to continue a strong program of northern exploration and interest in the northern latitudes. This is not entirely accurate. The Canadian government had, by the mid-1920s, cooled toward Stefansson for other reasons than Anderson's hostility.

Too many other parts of government had been alienated. Stefansson never again received the trust, respect, and influence he had generated in his earlier relations with Ottawa officialdom. It was more important to close ranks rather than occasion interdepartment conflicts and cause dissatisfaction and wounds to government servants.

Stefansson's days in the halls of power were numbered. Ottawa did not think it worth sacrificing good, loyal men to appease an individual whose personality and manoeuvrings were becoming a nuisance. Stefansson had to go. By this time he had not only incurred the wrath of the Geological Survey, whose alienation was deep-seated, but also the displeasure of those groups which had for so long been his main support—the government and the politicians. He made a hasty and quiet retreat.

Yet, even when he tried to get away from it all by going to Australia after the Wrangel Island misadventure, his newspaper critics there, emboldened by his fall, carried on:

"Our Friend Stefansson"

Canadian literature that has drifted my way suggests that our late visitor Stefansson is a many sided man. I would call him nothing less than an Hexagon, and he may even be an irregular crystal. The latest addition to my collection is an article cut from a Toronto paper. It deals with the wanderer's explorations in the deserts of Australia, he having gone there to disperse the illusion that there really [are] "deserts." A misty impression is left that he succeeded, and this Australian [mystery] is now cleared up in some way like the sources of the Nile. It is added that Stefansson hopes to go to the African Sahara and put it likewise in a new light which nobody has heard of before.[88]

10

Conclusion

There was no deliberate government policy to ostracize Stefansson but, as he became more insistent in his demands and activities in Ottawa between 1918 and 1923, it became plain that government cooperation with him must be predicated on Stefansson's toning down his manner and softening his posture. It was not in Stefansson's nature to retreat, or to subordinate himself to others. What must be done was obvious to him: forsake his Canadian career. Stefansson had overstepped himself in his postwar years in Ottawa as government advisor and northern propagandist. He had underestimated the political realities within the Canadian bureaucracy and had assumed he could get his own way in the formulation of government policies.

Stefansson may not have realized the intensity and duration of feeling against him. By 1924, he did know that he had overstayed his welcome in Ottawa. Never again was he directly associated with any official Canadian projects—meagre as they were. He could never understand why Mackenzie King, his "old Harvard friend," or other politicians avoided him.[1] Forgetting the incidents that had embarrassed and sometimes mortified the Canadian government, he thought the main reason for these snubs—aside from the lobbying of the Anderson "clique"—was simply that Canadians did not appreciate the potentials of their Arctic and had ignored Stefansson's efforts to raise their awareness.[2]

From 1924 until his death in 1962, Stefansson's connection with Canadian affairs was relatively obscure. Lecture tours occasionally brought him before Canadian audiences. His later Arctic-related endeavours were carried on in the United States but received little notice in Canada.

Ottawa tolerated him, but did not entrust him with any further information that might, even in the slightest, embarrass the Canadian government. For example, Major General J. H. MacBrien, Commissioner of the Royal Canadian Mounted Police, supplied Stefansson with some information in 1933 on the Force's efficiency and ability to function in cold climate. Stefansson wished to show that cold was not a noticeable handicap to individual or collective performance. The Major General, at Stefansson's request,[3] sent a questionnaire to the members of the Force asking for their opinions and personal experiences,[4] and passed the results on to Stefansson. Much to MacBrien's consternation he was reprimanded even for this:

> as the information which you have collected and supplied to Mr. Stefansson was given without expectation of being published, permission to publish same should be withheld. The consensus of opinion seems to be that members of the Government Service should not be drawn into any controversy on this subject and that the views expressed by the Police officials represent their own personal outlook and were not based upon scientific observation.[5]

Such caution was now the rule when dealing with Stefansson. When in 1938 he requested material for an article he was writing for *Foreign Affairs*, the director of one branch of the department of Mines and Resources told his staff to beware. "You have read enough of Mr. Stefansson's material to be fully aware that his interest is primarily in advertising himself and that he has very little up-to-date knowledge about what is going on in the Canadian Arctic. Under the circumstances I think we should be very careful about what we send him."[6] It seemed that, in the eyes of the government service, Stefansson could not be trusted. By the 1940s, even his earlier work was being denigrated within Canadian government circles. The *Arctic Manual*, prepared for the U.S. Army during World War II, was felt to be sorely out of date in Canadian and American circles.[7] "Even women have been travelling around parts of the country that were the scenes of his early travels."[8] If women could do that, then what could one really say about Stefansson's exploits? The innuendo is there. To their way of thinking, Stefansson had nothing to offer the Canadian government in terms of ideas or concepts. His new work was denigrated as being old hat: "The usual Stefansson theory of the Polar Mediterranean!" was all that could be mustered in assessing his *Arctic in Fact and Fable* (1945).[9] Obviously Stefansson was regarded by the Canadian government as an anachronism that should be politely but cautiously tolerated.

Stefansson's experiences in the Canadian North, sometimes self-exaggerated and self-deceiving, reinforced his rather simplistic conviction that to succeed, to be great, he must live by his wits and be ready to meet all challenges. Once a person had committed himself to any task, he had to be successful at all costs, even if on occasion it meant resorting to questionable methods. Life he regarded, and often spoke of, as a "game"—or, more correctly, a succession of games that had to be played to the full and taken to victory. As long as man used his innate talents to the full, he was bound to achieve his goal handsomely. Even if he lacked the requisite training or, for that matter, the essential information, he still could rise above the ordinary. In a way, his career was like mounting a set of building blocks, for Stefansson was able, step by step, to cultivate the right men in the right places; he improved his status from an unknown, inexperienced ethnologist, to a respected and influential arctic explorer, to the adviser of governments and theorist of international stature. One must remember, too, that Stefansson was not alone in his ambitions for self-fulfilment, for he lived in an age where fame and rags-to-riches stories were part of the American ethos. Like many of his peers, he was convinced such aspirations were no more than natural, the correct path to follow. In the eyes of many, however, the brash attitude that accompanied his efforts to realize his potential only sullied his aspirations and lowered him in their esteem.

Having been wounded and poorly treated by the Anglo-American Polar Expedition, Stefansson was determined to be his own master, and began learning the finer points of how to conduct an arctic expedition of his own making. All enterprises—and arctic expeditions above all—must have adequate sponsorship, meaning an intensive promotional campaign to attract public interest and the requisite financial backing. By gaining the support of people who counted in Canada and the United States, and by presenting them with a promising ethnological objective—the little-known Eskimos of Coronation Gulf—and a novel, inexpensive method of exploration which involved living off the country as far as possible, Stefansson was able to gain the ear of the American Museum of Natural History and the Geological Survey of Canada. Ultimately, the latter connection was to be his entering wedge into close dealings with the Canadian government.

In some ways, the expedition of 1908–12 did Stefansson more harm than good. He did some very excellent ethnological work amongst the Copper Eskimos, but his stubborn determination to stay in the field until he had proved himself, even after the American Museum had withdrawn its support, was to prove a bad precedent. The Museum's recantation after the news of his discovery of the Copper Eskimos convinced him that a good press was the secret for keeping an expedition going. The force of publicity attached to his discovery of the people of Coronation Gulf could and did change his American sponsor's mind. Publicity became to Stefansson the key, or at least a short cut, to success. It helped him to achieve instant world notice and paved the way for another expedition.

In seeking support for that next expedition, which was to become the 1913–18 expedition, ethnological pursuits, which Stefansson wanted to continue, became secondary by force of circumstance; a reduced priority for his own scientific specialty was the price he had to pay in his eagerness to command a first-class, amply-financed expedition. He succeeded beyond his expectations, interesting the Canadian government to support the entire enterprise. He had whetted Prime Minister Borden's appetite to send a fairly impressive expedition to the Arctic that continued and intensified the Canadian government's northern program.

Yet, although the expedition of 1913–18 was to be Stefansson's most famous, it was replete with hostilities and misunderstandings, which were not all of Stefansson's doing. R. M. Anderson believed that it was his duty to thwart Stefansson, even to the point of misusing his own authority. Despite his feats of exploration and the excellent work of the Southern Party, Stefansson's determination and his fear that the expedition would not be a public success forced him into questionable tactics. In this, he gained the undying hostility of the personnel of the Geological Survey in the north and afterwards in Ottawa.

Stefansson was not deterred, though, by what he considered as minor setbacks, and he looked beyond exploration for new vehicles to achieve further greatness. He hoped to put to practical use some of the findings and theories arising from his northern experience. His earlier exploits, pioneering efforts, sheer brute perseverance, and his contacts with some of the most influential men in North America, opened up new vistas for himself and, he hoped, for Canada too. His endeavours to promote interest in the Canadian north were commendable but, in retrospect, they appear to have been quite premature and therefore unrealistic. The methods Stefansson employed led many to believe he was a charlatan. Ambition and drive had made him a success, and success inevitably brought power and influence. If not used astutely or responsibly, power in the Actonian sense, and an overweening urge to be great, can debase an individual's finer qualities as has been the case with so many great men of history.

In the process Stefansson became less of a scientist, in the strict sense, and more a publicist and promoter. In his haste, he was prone to be superficial in his scientific work and observations, leaving the spadework, "details," and finer points to others. Some inner undefined faith told him that a true genius need not concern himself about detail and mundane day-to-day matters. After a logical theory or argument was put forth and accepted, the trivial aspects or the details would naturally take care of themselves. Pure reason, intuition, and vigour would overcome any form of resistance. This process can be seen at work in the 1913–18 expedition, the Hudson's Bay Reindeer Company, and the Wrangel Island incident. The last two, in particular, cast doubt on Stefansson's credibility. Both were based on insufficient data and evidence and were complicated by his impetuosity. Stefansson always claimed he was in pursuit of the truth through scientific investigation but, when he forsook pure scientific pursuits, the truth sometimes suffered. He appeared oblivious of this metamorphosis.

Although Stefansson was a genius in many respects, he had great shortcomings when it came to dealing with others. This became especially obvious after 1912 when his career made him a "public" man. Throughout his Canadian career, he displayed a lack of tact, an insensitivity in understanding other people's points of view, and a poor ability at judging character. In the expedition of 1913–18, he not only alienated people such as Anderson and Chipman, who were on the "other side" of the main issue in dispute, but he placed trust and respect in persons—Storkerson and Wilkins for example—who had few kind things to say about their commander.

More important, Stefansson was politically naïve. He may have understood the political realities to which Canadian government responded, but his boundless faith told him he could overcome opposition even from this quarter. If he could get the leaders to stop and listen to his vision and logic, he felt sure he could help them mend the error of their ways. He was clever, perhaps too clever. He was also too naïve to survive in the Ottawa environment which ultimately rejected him. In Stefansson's view, Canadians were narrow-minded and shortsighted when it came to the Arctic. Yet he could not remove this blind spot. The undying hostility of the Andersons and the reaction of Ottawa officialdom to his methods and, to them, his overbearing attitude, were not merely symptoms of narrow-mindedness. Civil servants and politicians were tired of being repeatedly told that they were fools— and this was the message they saw in Stefansson's lectures and publications. Civil servants were tired of Stefansson's tendency to step over their heads to the top echelons of the Canadian government. They resented his habit of intruding himself in important areas of policy-making with advice that was counter to their own. Politicians resented his efforts to force the pace when they were too cautious for his liking.

Perhaps the fundamental conflict was one of temperament. Stefansson wanted to involve the Canadian government in northern development, but it had to be in his way and on his terms. A country which traditionally had thus far handled its own pioneering endeavours and development following collectivist and statist approaches could not quite accommodate itself to his individualistic character. In a sense, Stefansson failed to understand this, and was unable to adjust his "style" to the tone and outlook of Ottawa.

Stefansson's departure from Ottawa, after the Wrangel Island affair, signalled his failure to convert the Canadian government to his program. Ottawa adopted a low-key approach to the north and the attendant problems of sovereignty and commercial development. Stefansson's "feud" with Anderson was not the singular cause which froze the Canadian Arctic, as claimed by Le Bourdais. Many other factors led the Canadian government to follow a quiet approach to the effective occupation and gradual development of its northern regions. Plans for more scientific and exploratory expeditions were dropped for less grandiose, less expensive projects. To a degree, Stefansson's influence had been negative—it helped to alter these programs, to stultify further expeditions for some years.

The Canada of the 1920s was too busy developing along other industrial and commercial fronts to be really concerned about the Arctic. Other prospects, thrown open by the railway building boom of the pre-war years and the development of the power, forest, and mineral resources of the Shield in the 1920s and the 1930s, were more lucrative. Today, it is quite evident that the Arctic could never be exploited employing ordinary standards developed in a more southern clime. More research than even Stefansson could have imagined is still necessary in understanding the unique problems of the Canadian north. With the Liberal government of Mackenzie King coming to power, Stefansson's ideas were out of joint with the main current of contemporary Canadian development. Borden and Meighen, his former patrons, were no longer steering the Canadian ship of state and, by 1923, Stefansson had proved he could be an embarrassment and a source of trouble. Having caused a disconcerting international incident and having vexed a host of public servants in the departments of External Affairs and the Interior, the Geological Survey, the National Museum, and the prime minister's office, Stefansson had to go. Otherwise, several branches of the Canadian bureaucracy would be impaired in their functions, and the trust of a number of loyal and diligent civil servants might be lost. They might not have been as intelligent and far-sighted as Stefansson, but in the long run they were considered more vital. In trying to become a private policy adviser to Canadian governments, Stefansson simply took on more than the sum of his talents could manage.

The atmosphere of the United States was more congenial and could afford an environment more suited to Stefansson's aptitudes for education and publicity. There, he shifted his perspective from the Canadian north to the problems of polar regions in general and the American Far North, in particular, emphasizing the economic and strategic significance of Alaska in the American empire. In the process, he became probably the greatest expert in the United States on the Arctic. In Canada, however, Stefansson would continue to be regarded with suspicion. He never, it appears, fully understood why.

APPENDIX

Recommendations of the Reindeer and Musk-ox Commission*

1 THAT steps be taken either by the use of aeroplanes or otherwise, to ascertain at the earliest possible date the approximate numbers of MUSK-OX still in existence in Northern Canada, and the localities in which they are to be found.

2 THAT the policy of preventing any further slaughter of these animals, either by natives or by white men, except in cases of dire necessity, be rigidly enforced.

3 THAT a station be established in one of the northern islands, where musk-ox now exist and where young animals may be readily obtained for purposes of domestication, with a view to later bringing considerable numbers to some point further south and more readily accessible, at which their development from a national economic standpoint may be carried on and extended.

    Needless to say, the success of this undertaking will, from its inception, depend entirely on the personal and technical qualifications of those who may be entrusted with its management.

4 THAT small experimental REINDEER herds be established in a number of such localities as may, after searching Departmental investigations, be found most desirable in points of vegetation and otherwise.

5 THAT in the selection of the localities for these stations, the needs of the natives in the matter of food supply be given the most careful consideration.

6 THAT where suitable arrangements can be made, the various missionary bodies be requested to co-operate in an earnest effort to ensure the success of the undertaking, not only by influencing the natives to protect the animals, but also by encouraging them to learn how to handle and care for them, that, as in Alaska, they may become herders and eventually owners of herds.

---

*From *Reindeer Commission*, pp. 36–38.

This will involve the gradual working out of a system similar to that so successfully followed by the United States Government in Alaska, whereby small numbers of reindeer are given to the natives in recognition of the interest and industry which they show in the work.

7   THAT at least one experienced Lapp deer-man should be detailed to each herd, this being necessary, not only to avoid mistakes in handling the deer, but to ensure that the instruction given to the natives is of a sound and practical character.

8   THAT . . . a number of Lapp deer-men might be induced to come to Canada and bring their herds with them, steps be taken at once to ascertain the exact conditions in that regard.

9   THAT if these conditions are found to be as represented, negotiations be entered into immediately with the view of securing as many of these desirable people as possible, in order that their services may be utilized in the development of the reindeer industry in such areas as may be approved for that purpose.

Your commissioners do not feel that they would be justified in recommending at the present time, any definite policy with regard to the granting of further grazing leases to persons desirous of securing such concessions.

Your commissioners approved the grazing lease granted in 1920 to Mr. Vilhjamar [sic] Stefansson on Baffin Island, because the local conditions as regards isolation are, in that case, such that it should be reasonably possible to enforce the limitations imposed by the lease with regard to the absorption of wild caribou in the reindeer herd.

Owing to the fact that on the mainland such enforcement would be quite impossible, especially in the case of large, and, therefore, only very partially domesticated reindeer herds, the reindeer would either become altogether wild, or the caribou, if not deliberately exploited for gain, be driven to seek other pastures, thus interfering with their regular, periodical migrations, and in all probability, causing them serious injury.

The granting of leases on Victoria island or Banks island would also involve the large herds of wild caribou which annually cross from the mainland, and many of which remain on these islands from year to year.

The information at the disposal of your commissioners is not sufficient to warrant them in expressing any opinion as to the feasibility of fencing off any of the peninsular areas on the northern portion of the mainland, so as to permit of their being leased for grazing purposes without damage to the wild caribou.

In this connection it should be remembered that in those areas in

Alaska to which the reindeer were brought, the wild caribou had been previously almost altogether exterminated.

For the reasons above set forth, your commissioners would advise:—

10   THAT great caution is exercised in the granting of grazing leases, and that no such leases be considered until after a most careful Departmental investigation of the local conditions and possibilities.

Altogether apart from the proposed introduction of domestic reindeer the vast herds of wild CARIBOU which undoubtedly still exist in the interior mainland area, repeatedly referred to in this report, constitute a valuable national asset, the importance of which, if properly dealt with, can be enormously enhanced, and your commissioners therefore respectfully recommend:—

11   THAT an earnest effort be made to ascertain as soon [and] as closely as possible the numbers and movements of the Barren Land caribou, especially those on the mainland and on the islands adjacent thereto; as also the numbers and movements of the caribou of other varieties, particularly those in the Yukon Territory and in northern British Columbia.

12   THAT a comprehensive survey be made of the vegetation and other conditions having a bearing on the support of herbivorous animals in the interior area, with the object of securing information as to the comparative value of the various districts for grazing purposes; the extent to which these natural pasture lands are now being used by the caribou; the approximate numbers of additional caribou or reindeer which might reasonably be expected to find sustenance in the different districts.

It will be obvious that in securing accurate and reliable data on these points, the migratory habits of the caribou and the length of time required to reproduce the reindeer moss after it has been eaten down, will have to be closely studied.

13   THAT special attention be given to the enforcement of such regulations as will effectively prevent the wasteful or useless slaughter of the wild caribou, either by natives or others.

14   THAT an intelligent and systematic campaign be inaugurated, having for its object the extermination of wolves, wolverines and such other animals as prey upon the caribou.

15   THAT at each of the Reindeer Experimental Stations, the establishment of which is recommended herein, provision be made for the domestication, on intelligent lines, of such numbers of young wild caribou as may be conveniently handled with the reindeer herd.

ABBREVIATIONS

AGS	American Geographical Society
AMNH	American Museum of Natural History
CAE	Canadian Arctic Expedition
CP	Chipman Papers
DIAND	Department of Indian Affairs and Northern Development
HBRC	Hudson's Bay Reindeer Company
MC	Mavor Collection
MG	Manuscript Group
NGS	National Geographic Society
PAC	Public Archives of Canada
PM	Peabody Museum
RG	Record Group
RMA	Rudolph Martin Anderson Papers
SC	Stefansson Collection
SEWC	Sir Edmund Walker Collection
VS	Vilhjalmur Stefansson
WIMF	Wrangel Island Main File

NOTES

Chapter 1 Introduction

1. Hortense Myers and Ruth Burnett, *Vilhjalmur Stefansson, Young Arctic Explorer*, Childhood of Famous Americans Series (New York: Bobbs–Merrill, 1966).
2. Translation from the "Introduction" by Dr. G. A. Agranat, ed., in E. A. Ol'khina, *Vilhjalmur Stefansson* (Moscow: Academy of Sciences of the U.S.S.R., 1970), pp. 5–7.
3. Henry B. Collins, "Stefansson as an Anthropologist," *Polar Notes* 4 (November 1962) : 8–13.
4. For example: Stefansson, "Observations on Three Cases of Scurvy, Meat Diet in Health and Disease," *Journal of the American Medical Association* 71 (23 November 1918) : 1715–18; "Man Can Live on Meat Alone," *Physical Culture*, August 1919, pp. 23–24, 64–65; "Adventures in Diet," *Harper's Magazine*, pt. 1 (November 1935) : 668–75; pt. 2 (December 1935) : 46–54; pt. 3 (January 1936) : 178–79. Also, a number of controlled studies were conducted on Stefansson during the 1920s to determine the effects of a meat diet on the human body, most of which substantiated Stefansson's own investigations and theories. See Dr. Clarence Lieb, "The Effects of an Exclusive Long-Continued Meat Diet, Based on the History, Experience and Clinical Survey of Vilhjalmur Stefansson, Arctic Explorer," *Journal of the American Medical Association* 87 (3 July 1926) : 25–26; "A Year's Exclusive Meat Diet and Seven Years Later," *The American Journal of Digestion and Nutrition* 11, no. 8 (1935–36) : 473–75.
5. See Vilhjalmur Stefansson, "Food of Ancient and Modern Stone Age Man," *Journal of the American Dietetic Association* 13 (July 1937) : 102–19; Charles H. M. Williams, "An Investigation Concerning the Dentitions of the Eskimos of Canada's Eastern Arctic," *The American Academy of Periodontology* (1942), pp. 34–37.
6. Earl P. Hanson, *Stefansson, Prophet of the North* (New York: Harper, 1941); also, D. M. Le Bourdais, *Stefansson, Ambassador of the North* (Montreal: Harvest House, 1962), pp. 173–91.
7. Trevor Lloyd, "Vilhjalmur Stefansson," *Polar Notes* 4 (November 1962) : 8.

8. Carl Berger, "The True North Strong and Free," in *Nationalism in Canada*, ed. P. Russell (Toronto: McGraw–Hill, 1966), p. 21.

9. Morris Zaslow, *The Opening of the Canadian North, 1870–1914* (Toronto: McClelland Stewart, 1971), pp. 262, 280.

10. The list of works concerning arctic sovereignty is formidable. Among the most important are the following: Yvon Bériault, *Les Problèmes Politiques du Nord Canadien* (Ottawa: Université d'Ottawa, 1942); V. K. Johnston, "Canada's Title to the Arctic Islands," *Canadian Historical Review* 14 (March 1933): 24–41; W. F. King, *Report Upon the Title of Canada to the Islands North of the Mainland of Canada* (Ottawa, 1905); V. L. Lakhtine, "Rights over the Arctic," *American Journal of International Law* 24 (1930): 703–17; D. H. Miller, "Political Rights in the Polar Regions," in *Problems of Polar Research*, ed. W. L. C. Joerg (New York: American Geographical Society, 1928); Elmer Plischke, "Territorial Sovereignty in the Arctic" (Unpublished manuscript specially prepared for *Encyclopedia Arctica*, compiled under contract . . . between the Office of Naval Research, U.S. Navy Department, and the Stefansson Library, Dartmouth College); Gustav Smedal, *Acquisition of Sovereignty over Polar Areas* (Oslo: I Kommisjon Dos Jacob Dybwad, 1931); Gordon W. Smith, "The Historical and Legal Background of Canada's Arctic Claims" (Ph.D. diss., Columbia University, 1952).

11. King, *Title of Canada*, p. 8.

12. Ibid.

13. Ibid.

14. Ibid., pp. 26–34.

15. See the following accounts of the various voyages: Canada, Department of Marine and Fisheries, *Report of the Hudson's Bay Expedition of 1884 under the Command of A. R. Gordon, R.N.* (1884); *Report of the Expedition to Hudson's Bay and Cumberland Sound in the Steamship Diana under the Command of William Wakeham in the Year 1897* (1898); *Report of the Dominion Government Expedition to the Arctic Islands and Hudson Strait on Board the D.G.S. Arctic, 1906–07, by Captain J. E. Bernier, Officer in Charge and Fisheries Officer* (Ottawa, 1909); *Report on the Dominion of Canada Expedition to the Arctic Islands and Hudson Strait on Board the D.G.S. Arctic [1908–9]* (Ottawa, 1910); *Report on the Dominion Government Expedition to the Northern Waters and Arctic Archipelago of the D.G.S. Arctic in 1910 under the Command of J. E. Bernier* (Ottawa, 1911[?]); A. P. Low, *The Cruise of the Neptune, 1903–04* (Ottawa, 1906).

16. Canada, North West Mounted Police, *Annual Report*, 1903–4.

17. Low, *Cruise of the Neptune*, pp. 277–78.

18. Zaslow, *Opening of the Canadian North*, p. 260.
19. J. E. Bernier, *Master Mariner and Arctic Explorer: A Narrative of Sixty Years at Sea from the Logs and Yarns of Captain J. E. Bernier* (Ottawa: n.p., 1939), pp. 306–7.
20. Le Bourdais, *Stefansson, Ambassador*, p. 16; Gimli could also mean "Heaven." Stefansson, *Discovery: the Autobiography of Vilhjalmur Stefansson* (New York: McGraw–Hill, 1964), p. 7.
21. Stefansson, *Discovery*, p. 6.
22. For a description of the early years of uncertainty in the fledgling Icelandic communities in Manitoba see W. Kristjanson, *The Icelandic People in Manitoba* (Winnipeg: Willingford Press, 1965), pp. 29–129.
23. Stefansson, *Discovery*, p. 12.
24. Ibid., pp. 9–10.
25. Ibid., pp. 25–47.
26. Dartmouth College, Stefansson Collection (hereafter cited as SC), International Correspondence Schools—1902 file, Stefansson (hereafter VS) to A. J. Hatfield, 15 June 1902; SC, 1897–1903 file, VS to A. C. McLane, 19 September 1902.
27. Stefansson, *Discovery*, p. 32.
28. SC, 1899–1904 file, VS to Mrs. Sara Brinjolfson, ca. fall or early winter of 1898.
29. Ibid.; Myers and Burnett, p. 132.
30. SC, 1899 file, VS to Mrs. S. Bjorfson [Brinjolfson?], 5 February 1899.
31. Stefansson, *Discovery*, p. 29.
32. Quoted in Le Bourdais, *Stefansson, Ambassador*, p. 17.
33. SC, 1903–17 file, V. P. Squires to VS, 5 February 1903.
34. SC, 1897–1903 file, W. Merrifield to VS, 21 September 1901.
35. Stefansson, "A North Dakotan at Harvard," *The Student* [The University of North Dakota] 17 (January 1904): 4–6.
36. SC, 1899–1904 file, VS to Mrs. Bjorfson [Brinjolfson?], 3 October 1898.
37. For example, see the following poems by Stefansson: SC, 1897–1903 file, "To Helen," "Cicilia," also "To Mabel," and "Love Sonnets of a College Man."
38. Richard Hofstadter, *Social Darwinism in American Thought* (Boston: Beacon Press, 1960), pp. 19–20.
39. Ibid., pp. 13–50.
40. SC, random, untitled file, VS memo, n.d.
41. SC, 1897–1903 file, VS to A. E. Morrison, 28 August 1899.
42. SC, Diary/Notebook, 1904.
43. Stefansson, *Discovery*, pp. 32–47.
44. SC, Thorvaldson—1899 file, VS to T. Thorvaldson, 2 October 1899.
45. Stefansson, *Discovery*, pp. 32–47.

46. SC, 1897–1903 file, A. E. Morrison to VS, 7 July 1899.
47. SC, Thorvaldson—1899 file, VS to Thorvaldson, 2 October 1899.
48 SC, uncatalogued. Fragments of an untitled, undated, and unpublished poem by Stefansson.
49. SC, miscellaneous—1903 file, poem entitled "Science."
50. Ibid., poem entitled "A Dream when Dreams are Vanished."
51. SC, uncatalogued. Fragments of an untitled, undated, and unpublished poem by Stefansson.
52. Stefansson Diary, 28 May 1912. Microfilm edition of *The Polar Expedition Diaries of Vilhjalmur Stefansson in the Years 1906–1918* (Ann Arbor: Xerox University Microfilms in collaboration with Dartmouth College Library, 1974). Original for years 1906–12 in SC. Original for years 1913–18 in Public Archives of Canada (hereafter PAC) in Manuscript Group (MG) 30, B81. Microfilm copy of diaries for 1906–12 in PAC, also in MG 24, B81.
53. Ibid.

Chapter 2 Arctic Initiation

1. Stefansson, *Discovery: the Autobiography of Vilhjalmur Stefansson* (New York: McGraw–Hill, 1964), p. 48.
2. Stefansson, "The Icelandic Colony in Greenland," *The American Anthropologist* 8 (June 1906) : 262–70.
3. Stefansson, *Hunters of the Great North* (New York: Harcourt, Brace, 1922), p. 9.
4. R. A. Harris, "Evidence of Land Near the North Pole," *Report of the 8th International Congress* (1904), pp. 397–406.
5. George Washington De Long, *The Voyage of the Jeannette*, 2 vols. (Boston, 1884).
6. F. Nansen, *Farthest North* (New York, 1897).
7. Ejnar Mikkelsen, *Mirage in the Arctic* (London: Rupert Hart–Davis, 1955), p. 9.
8. See A. P. Crary, R. D. Cotell, and T. F. Sexton, "Preliminary Report on Scientific Work on Fletcher's Ice Island, T. 3," *Arctic* 5 (1952) : 211–23; L. S. Loenig, K. R. Greenaway, M. Dunbar, and G. Hattersley-Smith, "Arctic Ice Islands," *Arctic* 5 (1952) : 67–103; N. N. Zubov, "Arctic Ice Islands and How They Drift," *Priroda* no. 2 (1955) : 37–45, trans. E. R. Hope, Defence Research Board of Canada.
9. Archives of the American Geographical Society, New York City (hereafter AGS), C. C. Adams to Mikkelsen, 27 March 1906.
10. AGS, Mikkelsen to Adams, 14 April 1906.

11. Stefansson, *Discovery*, p. 61.
12. Ibid., pp. 57–58.
13. Ibid., pp. 61–62.
14. Mikkelsen, *Mirage*, pp. 36–37.
15. Stefansson, *Discovery*, p. 60.
16. Archives of the Peabody Museum, Cambridge, Massachusetts (hereafter PM), VS to Miss Meade, 20 November 1906.
17. AGS, VS to C. C. Adams, 19 November 1906.
18. Alfred H. Harrison, *In Search of a Polar Continent* (Toronto: Musson, 1908), p. 204; cf. University of Toronto. Thomas Fisher Rare Book Library. Ms. Coll. 119. James Mavor Papers (hereafter MC), VS to Stupart, Director of Canadian Meteorological Service, 29 November 1906.
19. PM, VS to Putnam, 10 August 1906.
20. Ibid., 28 August 1906.
21. Ibid., 20 November 1906.
22. Ibid., 28 August 1906.
23. PAC, Stefansson Diary, 2 October 1906.
24. Ibid., 1 January 1907.
25. Ibid., 31 January 1907.
26. Ibid., 21 December 1906.
27. PM, VS to Miss Meade, 20 November 1906.
28. PAC, Stefansson Diary, 1 [January] 1907.
29. Ibid., 20 November 1906.
30. Ibid., 12 February 1907.
31. PM, VS to Putnam, 29 May 1906.
32. MC, VS to Mavor, 28 April 1907.
33. PM, VS to Putnam, 14 August 1906.
34. T. MacInnes, *Klengenberg of the Arctic* (London and Toronto: Jonathan Cape, 1932), pp. 222–23.
35. Ibid., p. 239.
36. MC, VS to Mavor, 28 April 1907.
37. PM, VS to Putnam, 14 August 1906.
38. AGS, Mikkelsen to Chandler Robins, 20 June 1907; Mikkelsen to American Geographical Society, 19 June 1907.
39. Stefansson, "The Home Life of the Eskimo," *Harper's Monthly Magazine* 117 (October 1908) : 730.
40. PAC, MG 30, B40, Crawford Papers, Mrs. R. M. Anderson to Mrs. Crawford, 20 January 1924; also, PAC, Record Group 45, Geological Survey Branch, file 4078C/57, "V. Stefansson, Personal and Controversies," Rudolph Anderson to Charles Camsell, Deputy Minister, 4 January 1921.

41. Mikkelsen, *Conquering the Arctic Ice* (London: Heinemann, 1909), p. 298.
42. Stefansson, *Hunters*, pp. 191, 207.
43. AGS, Mikkelsen to American Geographical Society, 13 August 1907. Original spelling retained.
44. Archives of the American Museum of Natural History, New York City (hereafter AMNH), file 719A, VS to Herman C. Bumpus, Director, 29 August 1908.
45. PAC, Kenneth G. Chipman Papers (hereafter CP), MG 30, B66, Chipman to Mr. LeRoy, 15 July 1915.
46. AGS, American Geographical Society to Mikkelsen, 13 December 1907.
47. Stefansson, *Discovery*, p. 101.
48. MC, VS to Mavor, 5 November 1907.
49. Inscription by VS to Aileen Larkin, 24 July 1923, in flyleaf of Stefansson's *The Northward Course of Empire* (London: Harrap, 1922). This particular copy is in the possession of the author.
50. Stefansson, "Wintering Among the Eskimos," *Harper's Monthly Magazine* 116 (June 1908): 46.
51. SC, 1903–6 uncatalogued, VS to "Charlie" [Karsten Anderson], 27 May 1907.
52. Stefansson Diary, 10 December 1909.
53. Stefansson, "Wintering Among the Eskimos," p. 43.
54. PM, VS to Putnam, 10 August 1906.
55. Stefansson, "A Preliminary Report of the Ethnological Investigation of the Mackenzie Delta," *Summary Report of the Geological Survey*, pp. 192–93. This report includes some of Stefansson's observations from the 1906–7 trip.
56. Ibid.
57. Stefansson, "Suitability of Eskimo Methods of Winter Travel in Scientific Exploration," *American Geographical Society Bulletin* 40 (April 1908): 211.
58. SC, 1903–6 uncatalogued, VS to "Charlie," 21 May 1907.
59. Stefansson, "Wintering Among the Eskimos," p. [38].
60. Stefansson Diary, 10 September 1906.
61. Stefansson, "The Home Life of the Eskimo," p. 730.
62. Ibid., pp. 721–30; cf. MC, VS to Mavor, 28 April 1907.
63. Stefansson Diary, 22 December 1906.
64. Franz Boas, "Human Faculty as Determined by Race," *Proceedings, American Association for the Advancement of Science* 43 (1894): 301–27.
65. Stefansson, "The Home Life of the Eskimo," p. 721.

Chapter 3 The Gold Mines of Victoria Land

1. Stefansson, "The Suitability of Eskimo Methods of Winter Travel in Scientific Exploration," *American Geographical Society Bulletin* 40 (April 1908) : 211.
2. Ibid., p. 213.
3. Stefansson, *Discovery: the Autobiography of Vilhjalmur Stefansson* (New York: McGraw–Hill, 1964), p. 101.
4. AMNH, file 719A, VS to American Museum of Natural History, 25 February 1908.
5. Ibid.
6. Ibid.
7. AMNH, file 719A, Clark Wissler to VS, 28 February 1908.
8. Ibid.
9. MC, VS to Mavor, 21 January 1911, postscript to a letter written 12 December 1910.
10. PAC, MG 30, B40, Papers of Dr. Rudolph Martin Anderson (hereafter RMA), vol. 1, Bumpus to VS, 13 April 1908.
11. SC, 1903–17 correspondence, VS to Stupart, 28 February 1908.
12. Ibid., VS to Stupart, 2 April 1908.
13. Ibid., VS to Stupart, 10 September 1908.
14. Stefansson Diary, 21 April 1908.
15. AMNH, file 719A, VS to Bumpus, 21 April 1908.
16. R. P. Rohner, *The Ethnography of Franz Boas* (Chicago: University of Chicago Press, 1969), pp. xxiv–xxv.
17. Morris Zaslow, *Reading the Rocks: The Story of the Geological Survey of Canada, 1842–1972* (Ottawa: Macmillan, Department of Energy, Mines and Resources, and Information Canada, 1975), pp. 266–69.
18. Canada, Geological Survey of Canada, *Summary Report*, 1908–9, p. 9.
19. AMNH, file 719A, VS to Bumpus, 21 April 1908.
20. Ibid., Bumpus to VS, 25 April 1908.
21. Ibid., Brock to VS, 16 May 1908.
22. Ibid., VS to Bumpus, 17 April 1908.
23. Ibid., Brock to VS, 16 May 1908.
24. Ibid., Bumpus to VS, 18 April 1908.
25. Stefansson, *Discovery*, p. 101.
26. PAC, RMA/1, Frank M. Chapman, Curator of Birds, to Anderson, 26 February 1908.
27. Stefansson, *Discovery*, p. 101.
28. PAC, RMA/1, VS to Anderson, 8 February 1908.
29. Ibid.
30. Ibid., VS to Anderson, 28 February 1908.

31. Ibid., VS to Anderson, 8 February 1908.

32. Ibid., Chapman to Anderson, 26 February 1908.

33. Ibid., VS to Anderson, 11 March 1908.

34. PAC, RMA/13, Anderson to Miss Mae Belle Allstrand, 3 March 1908.

35. PAC, RMA/1, VS to Anderson, 10 March 1908. This was basically the same proposition Bumpus conveyed to Anderson. AMNH, file 719A, Bumpus to Anderson, 25 April 1908.

36. PAC, RMA/1, VS to Anderson, 28 February 1908.

37. PAC, RMA/13, Anderson to Miss Mae Belle Allstrand, 21 March 1908.

38. Ibid., Anderson to Miss Allstrand, 5 May 1908.

39. Ibid., Anderson to Miss Allstrand, 15 October 1908.

40. PAC, RMA/70, Anderson to Mamie Anderson [his sister], 30 April 1908.

41. PAC, RMA/13, Anderson to Miss Allstrand, 19 April 1908.

42. PAC, RMA, Anderson Diary, 27 July 1908.

43. PAC, RMA/13, Anderson to Miss Allstrand, 29 August 1908.

44. PAC, RMA/70 Anderson to Mamie Anderson, 12 August 1908.

45. Stefansson, *Discovery*, p. 102; *My Life with the Eskimo* (New York: Macmillan, 1913), p. 6.

46. AMNH, file 719A, VS to Bumpus, 9 July 1908.

47. Ibid., VS to Bumpus, 11 August 1908.

48. Ibid., VS to Bumpus, 4 June 1908.

49. PAC, Record Group 18, A–1, Records of the Royal Canadian Mounted Police, vol. 372, report of Sergeant F. J. Fitzgerald, 4 December 1908.

50. Stefansson, *Discovery*, pp. 103–4; see also *My Life with the Eskimo*, pp. 37–41.

51. PAC, RMA/18, VS to Mrs. Anderson, 8 February 1914.

52. PAC, RMA, Anderson Diary, 26 July 1908.

53. PAC, RMA/13, Anderson to G. J. Desbarats, Deputy Minister, Department of Naval Service, 13 May 1914.

54. Stefansson, *My Life with the Eskimo*, pp. 83–86.

55. AMNH, file 719C, VS to Bumpus, 6 December 1910; also PAC, Stefansson Diary, entries for 28 October 1908, 8 January 1910, 29 January 1910, 26 November 1910.

56. Stefansson Diary, 26 November 1910.

57. Ibid., 23 November 1909.

58. AMNH, file 719C, memorandum, unsigned, 15 April 1910.

59. Ibid., file 719B, Wissler to Bumpus, n.d., received 17 November 1909.

60. D. M. Le Bourdais, *Stefansson, Ambassador of the North* (Montreal: Harvest House, 1962), p. 51.

61. PAC, RMA/1, Anderson to Bumpus, 15 November 1909.

62. AMNH, file 719C, Bumpus to Anderson, 13 May 1910.
63. Ibid., file 719D, Osborn, Museum President, to VS, 6 January 1911.
64. Ibid., file 719C, Bumpus to VS, 13 May 1910.
65. Ibid., Anderson to Bumpus, 13 August 1910.
66. Ibid., VS to Bumpus, 6 December 1910.
67. SC, Blond Eskimo file, VS to Mr. Rood, 4 December 1910.
68. AMNH, file 719C, VS to Bumpus, 6 December 1910.
69. SC, Blond Eskimo file, VS to Mr. Rood, 4 December 1910.
70. AMNH, file 719C, Anderson to Bumpus, 13 August 1910.
71. PAC, RMA/1, VS to Anderson, 18 June 1912.
72. AMNH, file 719C, VS to Bumpus, 12 August 1910.
73. Stefansson, *My Life with the Eskimo*, p. 200.
74. Stefansson, *Discovery*, p. 135.
75. PAC, RMA/1, VS to Anderson, 13 October 1912.
76. Ibid., VS to Anderson, 16 June 1912.
77. Ibid.
78. Ibid., VS to Anderson, 13 October 1912.
79. Cited in Stefansson, *Discovery*, pp. 137–38.
80. MC, VS to Mavor, 12 December 1910.
81. AMNH, file 719C, VS to Bumpus, 12 August 1910.
82. MC, Mavor to VS, 23 November 1911.
83. MC, John Scott Keltie, Secretary of the Royal Geographical Society, to Mavor, 27 November 1911.
84. AMNH, Crocker Land file no. 48, W. C. Farrabee to E. O. Hovey, 27 May 1912.
85. Stefansson Diary, 3 November 1909.
86. Ibid , 4 October 1909.
87. See PAC, RMA/18, VS to Mrs. Anderson, 16 February [1915].
88. Ibid.
89. AMNH, file 719D, Wissler to Hovey, 19 September 1911; Wissler to VS, 21 November 1911.
90. *New York Times*, 8 October 1911.
91. AMNH, file 719D, F. A. Lucas to Charles D. Bower, Point Barrow, Alaska, 21 November 1911
92. AMNH, file 719E, Lucas to Osborn, 11 January 1912.
93. Ibid., Lucas to Osborn, 23 January 1912.
94. AMNH, file 719, Memorandum of Expenses of Vilhjalmur Stefansson and R. M. Anderson, n.d.
95. The following represent some of the major contributors to this school: F. Boas, "Ethnological Problems in Canada," *Journal of the Royal Anthropological Institute* 40 (1911) : 529–39; Kaj Birket–Smith, "The Caribou Eskimos," *Report of the Fifth Thule Expedition*, vol. 5 (Copenhagen, 1929).

96. E.g., Diamond Jenness, "Origin of the Copper Eskimo and their Copper Culture," *Geographical Review* 13 (October 1923) : 540–51; Therkel Mathiassen, "Archeology of the Copper Eskimo," *Report of the Fifth Thule Expedition*, part 2 (analytical part), vol. 4.

97. Jenness, "Physical Characteristics of the Copper Eskimos," *Report of the Canadian Arctic Expedition* 13 (Ottawa, 1923) : 3.

98. Robert J. McGhee, "Copper Eskimo Prehistory" (Ph.D. diss., University of Calgary, 1968).

99. Ronald P. Rohner and Evelyn C. Rohner, "The Development of North American Ethnology," in *The Ethnography of Franz Boas*, ed. R. P. Rohner, p. xxx.

100. Ibid., p. xxi.

101. Ibid., p. xxii.

102. Stefansson Diary, 13 June 1912.

103. Ronald and Evelyn Rohner, "North American Ethnology," p. xxii.

104. Stefansson Diary, 5 June 1912.

105. Ibid., 9 June 1912.

106. Ibid., 28 May 1912.

Chapter 4 The Building of the Canadian Arctic Expedition

1. PAC, RMA/18, VS to Mrs. Anderson, 16 February [1915].

2. AMNH, file 719D, VS to Bumpus, 1 July 1911.

3. For example, AMNH, file 719E, Lucas to the Associated Press, 7 October 1912; also, Osborn to Frank Muncie, *New York Press*, 10 October 1912.

4. AMNH, file 1027A, Wissler to Lucas, 11 October 1912.

5. See Donald B. MacMillan, *Four Years in the White North* (New York: Harper, 1918).

6. AMNH, file 1027A, Wissler to Osborn, 13 December 1912.

7. AMNH, Crocker Land file no. 48, Dr. George P. Howe to E. O. Hovey, 26 May 1912; Dr. W. C. Farrabee to Hovey, 27 May 1912; Dr. T. W. Thorndyck [Boston acquaintance of Stefansson] to Hovey, 29 May 1912.

8. AMNH, file 1027A, Wissler to Lucas, 11 October 1912.

9. Ibid., Wissler to Osborn, 13 December 1912.

10. Files of the National Geographic Society, Washington, D.C. (hereafter NGS), statement by Admiral Pilsbury, n.d., probably winter 1912.

11. Ibid.

12. SC, Desbarats—1913 file, E. O. Hovey to VS, 9 January 1913.

13. Ibid.
14. Ibid., Lucas to VS, 7 January 1913.
15. AMNH, file 1027A, Gilbert Grosvenor, President of National Geographic Society, to Osborn, 18 January 1913.
16. Ibid., Memorandum of Agreement between Vilhjalmur Stefansson, leader, and members of the expedition, party of the first part, and the National Geographic Society and the American Museum of Natural History, party of the second part, regarding the Stefansson–Anderson Arctic Expedition, n.d. [January 1913].
17. Ibid.
18. Ibid.
19. PAC, Manuscript Group 30, B81, Stefansson Diary, 1 April 1915.
20. AMNH, Memorandum of Agreement . . . [Jan. 1913].
21. Ibid.
22. AMNH, file 1027A, Memorandum of a Conference between President Osborn and Mr. Grosvenor, 30 January 1913.
23. Ibid.
24. PAC, Manuscript Group 26, H, Papers of Sir Robert Borden (hereafter Borden Papers), R. W. Brock to W. S. Roche, Minister of the Interior, 4 February 1913.
25. SC, Desbarats—1913 file, Osborn to VS, telegrams of 4 and 5 February 1913.
26. PAC, Borden Papers, VS to Borden, 4 February 1913.
27. PAC, Record Group 42, Department of Marine [old Department of Naval Service files], Stefansson Arctic Expedition, 1913—[1918] (hereafter RG42), file 84–2–55, Brock to Roche, 4 February 1913.
28. Canada, Senate, *Debates*, 20 February 1907, p. 271.
29. Ibid., p. 274.
30. J. P. Bernier, *The Cruise of the Arctic, 1908–09* (Ottawa, 1910), pp. 1–2, 195.
31. PAC, RG42, 84–2–55, Memorandum initialled "G. H. P." [G. H. Perley], 7 February 1913; see also, RG42, 84–2–24, Roche to VS, 8 February 1913.
32. PAC, RMA/20, R. M. Anderson, "Preliminary History of the Canadian Arctic Expedition, 1913–16," n.d.
33. PAC, RG42, 84–2–1/vol. 1, Brock to Desbarats, 28 May 1913.
34. PAC, RG42, 84–2–55, Perley Memorandum, 7 February 1913.
35. AMNH, file 1027A, Osborn to VS, 12 February 1913.
36. PAC, RMA/20, Anderson, "Preliminary History. . . ."
37. SC, Desbarats—1913 file, Gilbert H. Grosvenor to VS, 11 February 1913.
38. PAC, RG42, 84–2–29/vol. 5, Report of the Committee of the Privy

Council, 22 February 1913.

39. PAC, RG42, 84–2–1/1, "Memorandum for Instructions, Arctic Expedition," n.d. [late Spring, 1913].

40. PAC, RG42, 84–2–29/5, Report of . . . Privy Council, 22 February 1913.

41. PAC, Record Group 12, vol. 29, no. 1654–1, Colonial Secretary to "The Officer administering the Government of Canada," 10 May 1913.

42. See PAC, RMA/1, 2, and 3.

43. PAC, RMA/1, VS to Brock, 1 March 1913.

44. Ibid.

45. PAC, RG42, 84–2–3/1, VS to Desbarats, 25 February 1913.

46. Ibid., Desbarats to VS, 25 February 1913.

47. Stefansson, *The Friendly Arctic* (New York: Macmillan, 1921), p. 47.

48. PAC, RG42, 84–2–3/1, Memorandum of Engineer Commander, Esquimault, 29 March 1913.

49. Ibid., Engineer Commander to Desbarats, 22 April 1913.

50. Ibid., Engineer Commander to Desbarats, 29 March 1913; also, ibid., Memorandum of Captain R. Bartlett, 1 April 1913.

51. Ibid., Engineer Commander to Desbarats, 26 May 1913.

52. R. A. Bartlett and R. T. Hale, *The Last Voyage of the Karluk* (Toronto: McClelland, Goodchild and Stewart, 1916), pp. 39–47.

53. PAC, RG42, 84–2–3/1, VS to Bartlett, 27 May 1913.

54. Ibid., 84–2–3/2, VS to Desbarats, 23 June 1913.

55. Stefansson, *Discovery: the Autobiography of Vilhjalmur Stefansson* (New York: McGraw–Hill, 1964), p. 212.

56. PAC, RMA/20, Anderson, "Preliminary History. . . ."

57. PAC, RG42, 84–2–29/1, VS to Desbarats, 14 May 1913.

58. Stefansson Diary, 28 May 1912.

59. PAC, RG42, 84–2–29/1, Desbarats to VS [telegram], 17 April 1913. See also, ibid., Desbarats to VS [telegram], 14 May 1913; and, PAC, Manuscript Group 30, E89, Desbarats Diary, 22 May 1913.

60. PAC, RG42, 84–2–29/1, Certificate of the Privy Council, 3 May 1913.

61. Ibid., VS to Desbarats, 23 May 1913.

62. PAC, Desbarats Diary, entries for 27, 28, 29 May 1913.

63. PAC, RMA/20, Anderson, "Preliminary History. . . ."

64. PAC, Desbarats Diary, 29 May 1913.

65. PAC, RG42, 84–2–29/1, VS to Desbarats, 14 May 1913.

66. Ibid., 84–2–1/1, Memorandum for Instructions . . . , n.d., probably late May 1913.

67. PAC, RMA/20, Anderson, "Preliminary History. . . ."

68. *Ottawa Free Press*, 27 May 1913.

69. *Toronto Globe*, 30 May 1913.

Chapter 5 Breakdown

1. PAC, CP, Chipman Diary, 15 June 1913.
2. PAC, RMA/20, LeRoy to Brock, n.d., probably early May 1913.
3. Ibid., Memo by LeRoy, n.d., sent with covering letter from Boyd and LeRoy to McConnell, 29 October 1914.
4. Ibid.
5. Ibid., Boyd and LeRoy to McConnell, 29 October 1914.
6. Ibid., Memo by LeRoy, n.d.
7. PAC, CP, Chipman Diary, 17 June 1913.
8. Ibid., 18 June 1913.
9. Ibid., 28 June 1913.
10. Ibid., [23] and 26 June 1913.
11. PAC, CP, Chipman to Boyd, 18 July 1913.
12. Ibid., Chipman Diary, 2 July 1913.
13. Ibid., 19 June 1913.
14. Ibid.
15. PAC, RMA/20, LeRoy and Boyd to McConnell, 29 October 1914.
16. PAC, CP, Chipman Diary, 17 October 1913.
17. Ibid., Chipman to Boyd, 18 July 1913.
18. Ibid.
19. Ibid., Chipman Diary, 9 July 1913.
20. SC, Canadian Arctic Expedition (hereafter CAE)/Desbarats—1913 file, VS to George Phillips, Naval Store Officer, Esquimault, 30 October 1913.
21. PAC, CP, Chipman to Boyd, 18 July 1913.
22. Stefansson, *The Friendly Arctic* (New York: Macmillan, 1921), pp. 33–34; also, *Discovery: the Autobiography of Vilhjalmur Stefansson* (New York: McGraw–Hill, 1964), pp. 154–55.
23. PAC, RMA/1, Henri Beuchat to C. M. Barbeau, Geological Survey, n.d.
24. PAC, CP, Chipman to Boyd, 18 July 1913.
25. Ibid., Chipman Diary, 10 July 1913.
26. Ibid.
27. PAC, CP, Chipman to Boyd, 18 July 1913.
28. PAC, RMA/1, Beuchat to Barbeau, n.d.
29. PAC, RG42, 82-2-3/1, VS to Desbarats, 23 June 1913.
30. Ibid. Also, PAC, CP, Chipman Diary, 11 July 1913.
31. PAC, CP, Chipman Diary, 11 June 1913.
32. Ibid. Also, PAC, RMA/5, William McKinlay to Anderson, 10 April 1922.
33. Stefansson, *The Friendly Arctic*, pp. 72–73.
34. PAC, RMA/1, Beuchat to Barbeau, n.d.

35. PAC, CP, Chipman Diary, 12 July 1913.

36. Ibid., 10 July 1913.

37. Ibid., Chipman to Boyd, 18 July 1913.

38. Ibid.

39. Ibid., Chipman Diary, 10 July 1913.

40. PAC, RMA/13, Anderson to Mrs. Anderson, 17 October 1913.

41. SC, Diamond Jenness Diary (copy), 20 September 1913.

42. PAC, RG42, 84–2–27, Diary of R. A. Bartlett, 20 September 1913.

43. PAC, RMA/3, Mrs. Anderson to Anderson, 27 June 1915.

44. Archives of the RCMP Headquarters (active files), file G804–8 (1940), Commissioner to E. Blount, Privy Council, 20 March 1914.

45. PAC, Stefansson Diary, 1 August 1914.

46. For an account of the tragedy see R. A. Bartlett and R. T. Hale, *The Last Voyage of the Karluk* (Toronto: McClelland, Goodchild and Stewart, 1916) ; and William Laird McKinlay, *Karluk* (London: Weidenfeld and Nicolson, 1976).

47. Stefansson, *The Friendly Arctic*, p. 47.

48. SC, CAE/General—1914 file, VS to Phillips, 14 February 1914.

49. PAC, RG42, 84–2–21/1, VS to [presumably] Dr. J. Scott Keltie, Secretary, Royal Geographic Society, 29 October 1913.

50. Stefansson, *The Friendly Arctic*, p. 72.

51. PAC, CP, Chipman Diary, 14 December 1913.

52. Ibid., 15 December 1913.

53. Stefansson, *The Friendly Arctic*, pp. 92–93.

54. PAC, CP, Chipman Diary, 15 December 1913.

55. Ibid., 14 February 1914.

56. Ibid., 17 December 1913.

57. Ibid., 26 December 1913.

58. Ibid.

59. Ibid., 16 December 1913.

60. Ibid., 26 December 1913.

61. Ibid., 16 December 1913.

62. Ibid., 11 March 1914.

63. Ibid.

64. Ibid., 14 February 1914.

65. Ibid., 11 March 1914.

66. PAC, RMA/18, VS to Mrs. Anderson, 16 February [1915].

67. SC, CAE/Directives and Orders—1915 file, VS to Anderson, 27 August 1915.

68. PAC, Stefansson Diary, 3 November 1915.

69. PAC, RG42, 84–2–29/2, VS to Desbarats, January 1915. Lengthy narrative covering Stefansson's actions from February 1914 to 22 March 1914.

70. Ibid., 84–2–31/1, L. Foresture, Comptroller, to Desbarats, 28 May 1913.

71. Archives of RCMP (active file), file G804–4 (1940), Report of J. W. Phillips, Officer Commanding "N" Division, Athabaska Landing, 8 February 1914.

72. PAC, CP, Chipman Diary, 4 April 1914.

73. Ibid.

74. PAC, RMA/13, John R. Cox to Mrs. Anderson, 7 July 1914.

75. PAC, CP, Chipman Diary, 10 February 1914.

76. SC, CAE/General—1914 file, Anderson to Storker T. Storkerson, 15 February 1914.

77. PAC, RG42, 84–2–29/2, VS to Desbarats, [narrative of] January 1915.

78. PAC, CP, Chipman Diary, 31 May 1915.

79. PAC, RG42, 84–2–29/2, VS to Desbarats, [narrative of] January 1915.

80. SC, CAE/General—1914 file, VS to George Phillips, 14 February 1914.

81. PAC, RG42, 84–2–29/2, VS to Desbarats, [narrative of] January 1915.

82. D. M. Le Bourdais, *Stefansson, Ambassador of the North* (Montreal: Harvest House, 1962), p. 83.

83. Ibid.

84. Stefansson, *My Life with the Eskimo* (New York: Macmillan, 1913), pp. 370–422, 428.

85. PAC, CP, Chipman Diary translation, 12 March 1914. The indictment was also recorded by Stefansson. PAC, RG42, 84–2–29/2, VS to Desbarats, 13 February 1914.

86. See Georgina Stefansson, "My Grandfather, Dr. Vilhjalmur Stefansson," *North* 8, no. 4 (July–August 1961) : 25.

87. *Toronto Globe*, 12 June 1913.

88. PAC, CP, Chipman Diary, 8 March 1914.

89. SC, CAE/General—1915 file, VS to Phillips, 19 February 1915.

90. PAC, CP, Chipman Diary, 8 March 1914.

91. PAC, RMA/13, Anderson to Brock, 15 May 1914.

92. PAC, CP, Chipman Diary, 8 March 1914.

93. PAC, RMA/13, Anderson to Brock, 15 May 1914.

94. PAC, RG42, 84–2–29/2, VS to Desbarats, [narrative of] January 1915.

95. PAC, CP, Chipman Diary, 8 March 1914.

96. PAC, RG42, 84–2–29/2, VS to Desbarats, [narrative of] January 1915.

97. PAC, RMA/13, Anderson to Brock, 15 May 1914.

98. PAC, RG42, 84–2–29/1, VS to Desbarats, [narrative of] January 1915.

99. Ibid.

100. Ibid.

101. Ibid.

102. Ibid.

103. PAC, RG42, 84–2–29/5, Anderson to Isaiah Bowman (editor of the *Geographical Review* and secretary of Explorers' Club of New York), 6 November 1918.

104. Ibid.

105. PAC, RMA/14, Anderson to Mrs. Anderson, [?] May 1915.

106. AMNH, file 719, Anderson to Lucas, 11 April 1913.

107. PAC, RG42, 84–2–21/1, Brock to Desbarats, 28 May 1913.

108. PAC, RMA/20, Anderson, "Preliminary History. . . ."

109. PAC, RMA/35, Anderson Diary, 8 June 1913.

110. PAC, RMA/20, Anderson, "Preliminary History. . . ."

111. PAC, RMA/20, Agreement entered into between V. Stefansson . . . and R. M. Anderson . . . [12 June 1913].

112. PAC, RMA/13, Anderson to Mrs. Anderson, 16 July 1913.

113. PAC, RMA/3, Mrs. Anderson to Anderson, 8 January 1913; 29 March 1914; 14 November 1915.

114. SC, CAE/General—1914 file, Mrs. Anderson to VS, 5 April 1914.

115. PAC, RMA/18, VS to Mrs. Anderson, 16 February [1915].

116. Ibid.; SC, CAE/General—1914 file, VS to George Phillips, 14 February 1914.

117. PAC, RMA/14, Anderson to Mrs. Anderson, 21 January 1916.

118. PAC, RMA/13, Anderson to Mrs. Anderson, n.d. [1914?].

119. Ibid., Anderson to Mrs. Anderson, 28 June 1914.

120. Cf. *My Life with the Eskimo*, pp. 11–12, 12–13, 10, 13, 15, 16, 19, 34, and 35, respectively, with Anderson's 1908 Diary, PAC, RMA/35, entries for 8 May, 11 May, 3 May, 2 May, 16–18 May, 21–22 May, 1 June, 14 July, and 23 July.

121. PAC, RMA/2, Mrs. Anderson to Anderson, 12 November 1913; RMA/13, Mrs. Anderson to Anderson, 18 January 1914; RMA/3, Mrs. Anderson to Anderson, 11 February 1914.

122. PAC, RMA/13, Anderson to Mrs. Anderson, 28 June 1914.

Chapter 6 The Politics of the Canadian Arctic Expedition

1. PAC, RG42, 84–2–29, VS to Anderson, 10 March 1914.

2. PAC, CP, Chipman Diary, 8 March 1914.

3. Ibid., 11 March 1914.

4. PAC, RG42, 84–3–2 to 84–3–11, "Estimates" [of expenditures for Canadian Arctic Expedition], 1913–25.

5. Ibid., 84–2–20/2, VS to Desbarats, 23 June 1913.

6. Ibid.

7. Ibid.

8. Ibid.

9. Ibid., 84–2–55, Desbarats to Minister of the Naval Service, 27 September 1913.

10. Ibid., Privy Council decision of 8 October 1913.

11. Ibid., 84–2–29/5, Desbarats to VS, 30 April 1914.

12. Ibid., VS to Desbarats, 5 May 1914.

13. Ibid.

14. SC, CAE/Desbarats—1914 file, Desbarats to Anderson, 16 November 1914.

15. PAC, Stefansson Diary, 11 September 1914.

16. SC, CAE/General—1914 file, Brock to VS, 7 May 1914.

17. SC, CAE/General—1915 file, VS to Brock, 10 February 1915.

18. PAC, Stefansson Diary, 23 April 1914; 27 April 1914.

19. Ibid., 11 May 1914.

20. D. M. Le Bourdais, *Stefansson, Ambassador of the North* (Montreal: Harvest House, 1962), p. 83.

21. PAC, Stefansson Diary, 8 May 1914.

22. Ibid., 1 May 1914.

23. Ibid., 8 May 1914. Italics added.

24. Ibid., 31 May 1914.

25. Stefansson, *The Friendly Arctic* (New York: Macmillan, 1921), pp. 126–34.

26. Ibid., p. 184.

27. Ibid., p. 205.

28. For example: PAC, Stefansson Diary, 8, 11, 12, 18, and 30 January 1915; 30 June 1915; 13 July 1915; 20 April 1917; 20 May 1917.

29. PAC, Stefansson Diary, 18 January 1915.

30. Ibid., 29 June 1914.

31. Stefansson, *Discovery: the Autobiography of Vilhjalmur Stefansson* (New York: McGraw–Hill, 1964), pp. 163–213. Also, PAC, Stefansson Diary, 26 November 1914; 27 January 1915.

32. PAC, Stefansson Diary, 21 May 1917. Harold Noice, who contracted scurvy, was probably the most enthusiastic of all of Stefansson's companions, and this disposition naturally impressed Stefansson. Nevertheless, the presence of scurvy on the 1917 trip certainly does not speak well for Stefansson's method.

33. PAC, MG30, B14, Diary of E. L. Knight, 11 November 1916 to 27 July 1917.

34. PAC, RMA/4, Anderson to Mrs. Anderson [?], 17 January 1916.

35. PAC, Stefansson Diary, 21 May 1917.

36. PAC, MG30, B17, Storkerson Diary, 8 March 1915; 15 April 1915.

37. PAC, Stefansson Diary, 20 May 1915, "Agreement between Storker T. Storkerson and Vilhjalmur Stefansson."

38. PAC, Storkerson Diary, 4 May 1915.

39. PAC, CP, Chipman Diary, 8 August 1915.
40. PAC, Stefansson Diary, 29 June 1914.
41. PAC, Storkerson Diary, 23 July 1915.
42. PAC, Stefansson Diary, 13 September 1916; 30 June 1917.
43. Ibid., 13 September 1916.
44. SC, CAE/Dispatches and Orders—1914 file, VS to Anderson, 6 April 1914.
45. PAC, RG42, 84–2–29/2, Anderson to Wilkins, 10 August 1914.
46. Ibid.
47. Stefansson, *The Friendly Arctic*, p. 272.
48. PAC, RG42, 84–2–20/2, VS to Desbarats, n.d.
49. Ibid.
50. Ibid., 84–2–29/2, VS to Desbarats, 16 September 1914.
51. Ibid., 84–2–3/3, Wilkins to Desbarats, 19 August 1914.
52. Stefansson, *The Friendly Arctic*, pp. 271–73.
53. PAC, Stefansson Diary, 1 April 1915.
54. Ibid., 11 April 1915.
55. PAC, CP, Chipman Diary, 31 May 1915.
56. SC, American Museum of Natural History/Blond Eskimo file, VS to "To Whom it may Concern," 6 April 1915.
57. PAC, CP, Chipman Diary, 31 May 1915.
58. PAC, RMA/3, Anderson to VS, 1 June 1915.
59. SC, uncatalogued manilla envelope, Wilkins to VS, 6 January 1916. Also, PAC, CP, Chipman Diary, 31 May 1915.
60. PAC, RMA/3, Anderson to VS, 1 June 1915.
61. Ibid.
62. Ibid.
63. SC, Wilkins Diary, 1 June 1915.
64. PAC, CP, Chipman Diary, 31 May 1915.
65. PAC, RG42, 84–2–29/3, VS to Desbarats, 9 January 1916.
66. SC, uncatalogued manilla envelope, Wilkins to VS, 6 January 1916.
67. PAC, CP, Chipman Diary, 31 May 1915.
68. Ibid.
69. Ibid.
70. SC, uncatalogued manilla envelope, Wilkins to VS, 6 January 1916.
71. SC, Wilkins Diary, 30 December 1915.
72. PAC, RG42, 84–2–29/3, VS to Desbarats, 9 January 1916.
73. Le Bourdais, *Stefansson, Ambassador*, p. 117.
74. SC, Wilkins Diary, 16 June 1916.
75. PAC, MG30, B40, Crawford Papers (now incorporated into RMA), Mrs. Anderson to Mrs. J. T. Crawford, 4 February 1925.
76. Le Bourdais, *Stefansson, Ambassador*, p. 118.
77. Stefansson, *The Friendly Arctic*, p. 394.

78. SC, Wilkins Diary, 12 February 1916.

79. Ibid., 24–26 April 1916.

80. Ibid., 30 December 1915.

81. Ibid.

82. Ibid., 16 August 1915.

83. Ibid., 24–26 April 1916.

84. Ibid., 10 February 1916.

85. PAC, RG42, 84–2–55, copy of the Report of the Committee of the Privy Council, 14 January 1916.

86. Ibid., 84–2–1/1, copy of the Report of the Committee of the Privy Council, 19 January 1916.

87. Ibid., 84–2–39, copy of the Report of the Committee of the Privy Council, 20 January 1916.

88. Canada, House of Commons, *Debates*, 2 June 1914, pp. 4557, 4629; 22 February 1915, p. 310; 27 March 1915, p. 1630; 9 April 1915, p. 2298.

89. *Ottawa Citizen*, 25 November 1916. Inspector J. W. Phillips, when queried by his superiors about such statements, denied "emphatically" having written the statement attributed to him. Archives of the RCMP (active files), file G804–4 (1940), Phillips to Commissioner A. B. Perry, 29 November 1916.

90. PAC, RG42, 84–2–29/2, VS to Borden, 21 June 1915.

91. SC, CAE/Desbarats—1915 file, VS to Desbarats, 17 November 1915.

92. PAC, RG42, 84–2–24/2, Desbarats to VS, 17 November 1915.

93. Ibid.

94. SC, Demming—1914–18 file, VS to Miss Demming, 14 January 1916.

95. NGS, VS to Gilbert Grosvenor, 14 January 1916.

96. PAC, Stefansson Diary, 6 June 1916.

97. Ibid., 20 October 1917.

98. Ibid.

99. PAC, RG42, 84–2–31/1, J. M. Tupper to Commissioner A. B. Perry, 30 November 1917.

100. PAC, Stefansson Diary, 18 December 1917.

101. SC, CAE/General—1917 file, VS to Inspector Phillips, 24 December 1917.

102. Ibid.

103. SC, CAE/Desbarats—1918 file, VS to the *Toronto Globe* [telegram], 21 January 1918.

104. PAC, RG42, 82–2–31/1, Desbarats to Comptroller, Royal North West Police, 9 April 1918.

105. Ibid., 84–2–29/4, Desbarats to VS, 3 April 1918.

106. Ibid.

107. Canada, House of Commons, *Debates*, 14 April 1916, pp. 2915–16;

6 August 1917, pp. 4173–74.
108. SC, CAE/Desbarats—1918 file, Desbarats to VS, 29 June 1918.

Chapter 7 The Arctic Empire of Vilhjalmur Stefansson

1. SC, uncatalogued 1903–7 file, VS to E. H. Perreth, editorial department, *London Daily Chronicle*, 13 February 1916.
2. *New York Times*, 8 November 1916.
3. In 1921, for example, Stefansson claimed he had earned between $20,000 and $30,000 in the previous year. He stated that he had not received pay while in the north, but that it was his years in the Arctic which enabled him to work as a lecturer. SC, 1920–26 file, VS to Deputy Minister of Finance, 6 January 1921.
4. PAC, RMA/18, VS to Mrs. Anderson, 16 February [1915].
5. SC, National Geographic—1922 file, VS to Gilbert Grosvenor, 29 May 1922.
6. Inscription by VS to Aileen Larkin, 24 July 1923, in flyleaf of Stefansson's *The Northward Course of Empire* (London: Harrap, 1922).
7. Stefansson, *Northward*, p. v.
8. S. Columb GilFillan, "The Coldward Course of Progress," *Political Science Quarterly* 35 (September 1920) : 395–410.
9. Stefansson, *Northward*, p. 19.
10. Ibid., p. 21.
11. Ibid.
12. W. H. Hobbs, *Peary* (New York: Macmillan, 1936), pp. 429–43.
13. *Toronto Globe*, 11 November 1918.
14. Simon Lake, *The Submarine in War and Peace* (Philadelphia: Lippincott, 1918) ; also, SC, Submarine—1919 file, Simon Lake to VS, 25 March 1919.
15. SC, Submarine—1919 file, VS to Gilbert Grosvenor, 10 February 1919; NGS, VS to Grosvenor, 22 February 1919.
16. Stefansson, *Northward*, pp. 192–93, 195–97.
17. Ibid., p. 199.
18. Stefansson, *Discovery: the Autobiography of Vilhjalmur Stefansson* (New York: McGraw–Hill, 1964), pp. 300–2.
19. PAC, Borden Papers, VS to Sir Clifford Sifton, 8 February 1914.
20. Ibid., VS to Borden, 8 January 1914.
21. Ibid.
22. PAC, Borden Papers, VS to Sifton, 8 February 1914.
23. Ibid., VS to Borden, 8 January 1914.
24. PAC, RG42, 84–2–38, VS to Sir Richard McBride, 9 February 1917.
25. Ibid.

26. Ibid.
27. SC, Desbarats—1919 file, VS to Borden, 15 March 1917.
28. Ibid.
29. SC, W/General—1919 file, Walker to VS, 6 May 1918.
30. Harvard University College Library, Houghton Reading Room, Cambridge, Massachusetts, Theodore Roosevelt Papers, Theodore Roosevelt to VS, 23 March 1918.
31. Ibid., T. Roosevelt to VS, 28 October 1918.
32. From, "Review of the Alaskan Reindeer Service of the United States Department of the Interior as compiled from the Official Reports of the United States Government," in Canada, *Report of the Royal Commission to Investigate the Possibilities of the Reindeer and Musk-Ox Industries in the Arctic and Sub-Arctic Regions of Canada* (hereafter *Reindeer Commission*) (Ottawa, 1922), Appendix II, pp. 48–49.
33. PAC, RG42, 84–2–38, Address to the Empire Club, Toronto, 11 November 1918.
34. Ibid., Address of Sir Edmund Walker, 11 November 1918.
35. SC, General Considerations—1918 file, VS to Keedick, 14 November 1918.
36. SC, Wrangel Island Main File (hereafter WIMF), Report of the Privy Council, 25 July 1918.
37. SC, CAE/Desbarats—1918 file, Lindeberg to VS, 13 August 1918.
38. Ibid., VS to Lindeberg, 13 August 1918.
39. Ibid., VS to Lindeberg, 16 November 1918.
40. Ibid.
41. SC, General Considerations—1918 file, VS to Keedick, 14 November 1918.
42. SC, Lindeberg—1919 file, VS to Lindeberg, 25 January 1919.
43. SC, Stefansson Diary, 10 January 1919.
44. SC, "Notes," n.d., probably January 1919.
45. PAC, RG42, 84–2–38, Report of the Advisory Board on Wild Life Protection, 20 February 1919.
46. SC, Lindeberg—1919 file, VS to Lindeberg, 25 January 1919; Ibid., VS to Lindeberg, 27 February 1919.
47. Ibid., VS to Lindeberg, 4 March 1919.
48. Ibid., Lindeberg to D. C. Scott, 11 February 1919.
49. PAC, RG42, 84–2–38, Meighen to C. C. Ballyntyne, Minister of Marine and Fisheries, 22 March 1919.
50. Ibid., VS to Meighen [?], March 1919.
51. Ibid.
52. SC, WIMF, Address to the House of Commons and Senate, 6 May 1919.
53. SC, Lindeberg—1919 file, VS to Lindeberg, 14 May 1919.

54. PAC, MG26, I, Meighen Papers, Meighen to J. S. McLean, Harris Abattoir Co. of Toronto, 9 May 1919; PAC, Desbarats Diary, 10 May 1919.

55. PAC, Meighen Papers, Meighen to McLean, 9 May 1919.

56. Ibid., McLean to Meighen, 14 May 1919.

57. SC, WIMF, VS to Reverend W. Henry Fry, Brantford, Ontario, 30 January 1920.

58. Ibid., Report of the Privy Council, 20 May 1919.

59. SC, Lindeberg—1919 file, VS to D. C. Scott, 25 May 1919.

60. Ibid., VS to Meighen, 26 May 1919.

61. Stefansson, *Discovery*, pp. 219–20. Also, SC, WIMF, VS to A. Ford, House of Commons Press Gallery, 26 May 1919; VS to J. J. Mitchell (Meighen's private secretary), 26 May 1919; VS to Colonel J. S. Dennis, 24 May 1919.

62. *Reindeer Commission*, p. 9.

63. Ibid., p. 40.

64. Ibid., p. 16.

65. Ibid., p. 17.

66. Ibid., p. 15.

67. Ibid., pp. 21–22.

68. SC, Lindeberg—1919 file, VS to Lindeberg, 15 June 1919; VS to Lindeberg, 16 June 1919.

69. SC, WIMF, VS to Meighen, 8 March 1920. See also SC, Hudson's Bay Reindeer Company file (hereafter HBRC), Stefansson's "Memorandum re Reindeer Syndicate," n.d., probably winter of 1919–20.

70. SC, Hudson's Bay/Baffin Island Reindeer Project—1920 file, VS to J. B. Harkin, 29 March 1920.

71. SC, Lindeberg—1919 file, Lindeberg to VS, 16 June 1919.

72. SC, WIMF, VS to Rutherford, 14 August 1919.

73. SC, Lindeberg—1919 file, Lindeberg to Scott, 11 February 1919.

74. SC, HBRC, Charles Sale, for the Governor and Committee of the Hudson's Bay Company, London, to Hudson's Bay Company "agent," New York City, 21 January 1920.

75. SC, HBRC, Indenture between the Government of Canada and Vilhjalmur Stefansson, 1 June 1920.

76. SC, Stefansson Diary, 25 March 1920. Sir Edmund Walker had provided him with a letter of introduction to Kindersley, University of Toronto. Sir Edmund Walker Papers, VS to Walker, 1 May 1920.

77. SC, Stefansson Diary, 26 March 1920.

78. Ibid., 8 April 1920.

79. SC, Northern Development—1920 file, VS to Rutherford, 12 April 1920.

80. SC, HBRC, VS to Storkerson, 12 April 1920.

81. Ibid., Sale to VS, 14 April 1920.
82. SC, Hudson's Bay/Baffin Island Reindeer Project—1920 file, Sale to New York "agent" of Hudson's Bay Company, 26 May 1920.
83. SC, HBRC, Sale to Stefansson, 16 April 1920.
84. SC, Doyle—1920 file, VS to Sir Arthur Conan Doyle, 4 May 1920.
85. SC, "M" General—1920 file, VS to Meighen, 26 April 1920.
86. SC, Lindeberg—1920 file, VS to McLean, 27 April 1920.
87. SC, HBRC, Indenture between Government of Canada and Vilhjalmur Stefansson, 1 June 1920.
88. SC, Hudson's Bay/Baffin Island Reindeer Project—1920 file, W. W. Cory, Deputy Minister, Department of the Interior, to VS, 19 June 1920.
89. SC, HBRC, Agreement between Vilhjalmur Stefansson . . . and Sir Augustus Nanton and Edward Fitzgerald . . . who are trustees on behalf of the . . . Hudson's Bay Reindeer Company, 30 June 1920.
90. SC, Stefansson Diary, 6 November 1920.
91. Stefansson, *Discovery*, p. 266.
92. SC, HBRC, VS to Fitzgerald, 23 June 1920.
93. SC, Lindeberg—1920 file, Lindeberg to VS, 22 December 1920.
94. Ibid.
95. SC, Stefansson Diary, 5 November 1920.
96. SC, HBRC, John Hughes, secretary-treasurer of the Hudson's Bay Reindeer Company, 6 January 1921.
97. SC, 1920–26 file, O. S. Finnie to VS, 21 December 1920.
98. SC, HBRC, VS to H. Mercier, 20 July 1920.
99. SC, Stefansson Diary [27 December 1920].
100. SC, HBRC, VS to Fitzgerald, Deputy Chairman, Hudson's Bay Company, Montreal, 27 December 1920; see also SC, HBRC, [Firm of] Meredith, Holden, Haag, Shawnessay and Hewert to Fitzgerald, 21 April 1921.
101. Ibid.
102. SC, HBRC, Fitzgerald to Holden, 27 December 1920.
103. Ibid., VS to Fitzgerald, 29 August 1921.
104. Ibid., Storkerson to the Director of the Hudson's Bay Company, 9 November 1920.
105. SC, HBRC, Fitzgerald to VS, 21 May 1921.
106. Ibid., Storkerson to Governor and Committee of the Hudson's Bay Company, 7 May 1921.
107. Ibid.
108. SC, HBRC, VS to Fitzgerald, 22 June 1921.
109. Ibid., Fitzgerald to VS, telegram, 17 May 1921.
110. Ibid., VS to Fitzgerald, telegram, 18 May 1921.
111. Ibid., Fitzgerald to VS, telegram, 21 May 1921.

112. Stefansson, *Discovery*, p. 124.

113. SC, HBRC, VS to Fitzgerald, telegram, 7 June 1921.

114. Ibid., VS to Fitzgerald, 1 June 1921.

115. SC, HBRC, Report of the Hudson's Bay Reindeer Company, n.d.

116. Ibid.

117. Ibid.

118. Ibid.

119. Ibid.

120. Ibid., Report of Neilson Thuri.

121. SC, HBRC, Frank Melton to Governor and Committee of the Hudson's Bay Reindeer Company, 13 July 1924.

122. Ibid., VS to Fitzgerald, 29 December 1922.

123. Ibid., VS to Sale, 4 May 1923.

124. Diamond Jenness, *Eskimo Administration: Canada*, Arctic Institute of North America, Technical Paper no. 14 (Montreal: Arctic Institute of North America, 1964), p. 27. This same observation was made by J. Mikkelborg, "Reindeer from Lapland," *The Bay* (1949–50), pp. 22–27, 37–39, 16–18, 25, 28, 30, 12–16, from consecutive issues.

125. R. M. Hill, *Mackenzie Reindeer Operations*, Northern Co-ordination and Research Centre, no. 67–1 (Ottawa, 1967), pp. 53–56.

126. Ibid., pp. 115–17.

127. SC, HBRC, J. Chadwick Brooks (for the Hudson's Bay Company) to VS, 30 October 1923.

128. Ibid., Sale to VS, 5 November 1925.

129. Ibid., Sale to VS, 30 November 1926.

130. Ibid., VS to Sale, 12 March 1927.

131. Stefansson, *Discovery*, p. 268.

132. Ibid.

133. SC, HBRC, Sale to VS, 30 November 1926.

134. Files of the Department of Indian Affairs and Northern Development, Ottawa (hereafter DIAND), 20—Stefansson file, vol. 2, T. Clifford to Mr. Cumming, Bureau of the Northwest Territories and Yukon Affairs, 28 May 1947.

Chapter 8 The Misadventure of Wrangel Island

1. Diamond Jenness, *Eskimo Administration: Canada*, Arctic Institute of North America, Technical Paper no. 14 (Montreal: Arctic Institute of North America, 1964), p. 28.

2. Stefansson, *The Adventure of Wrangel Island* (New York: Macmillan, 1925), pp. 15–26.

3. E.g., ibid., pp. 25, 60.

4. PAC, RG42, 84–2–54, photograph packet.

5. PAC, MG30, B25, McKinlay Diary, 1 July 1914.

6. PAC, RG42, 84–2–21/1, E. Hawkin, Assistant Deputy Minister of the Department of the Interior, to Bartlett, 25 March 1925.

7. E.g., PAC, RG42, 84–2–46, Hadley Diary, entries for 13, 14, 16, 17 July 1914; 25 August 1914.

8. Compare with Hadley Diary, 12 March 1914 and 7 September 1914.

9. PAC, RG42, 84–2–46, J. T. Crawford to A. Johnston, Deputy Minister of Marine and Fisheries, 10 December 1925.

10. Ibid., William McKinlay to Mrs. Crawford, 3 November 1925; PAC, RMA/5, Bartlett to Anderson, 6 February 1922.

11. Stefansson, *The Northward Course of Empire* (London: Harrap, 1922).

12. Stefansson, *Discovery: the Autobiography of Vilhjalmur Stefansson* (New York: McGraw–Hill, 1964), p. 231. See also, PAC, Meighen Papers, Borden to Meighen, 3 November 1920, 11 January 1921.

13. Canada, Senate, *Debates*, 20 February 1907, pp. 266–73.

14. SC, Harold Noice correspondence, 1923–26, VS to L. C. Christie, 25 September 1920.

15. PAC, RG15, A2, vol. 2, Department of the Interior, Northwest Territories and Yukon Branch, miscellaneous records, VS to J. B. Harkin, 7 February 1921. (Transferred recently to MG30, E169.)

16. SC, Wrangel Island—1920 file, VS to W. W. Cory, 30 October 1920.

17. PAC, MG26, J1, William Lyon Mackenzie King Papers, vol. 86, fol. 69271, VS to King, 11 March 1922.

18. PAC, MG30, E169, "Memo Re: Northern Islands Prepared for Information Technical Advisory Board Meeting, November 10, 1920."

19. SC, Noice correspondence, 1923–26, VS to Christie, 25 September 1920.

20. SC, Wrangel Island—1920 file, VS to Cory, 30 October 1920.

21. PAC, Meighen Papers, VS to Meighen, 30 October 1920.

22. Ibid., Pope to Meighen, 25 November 1920.

23. PAC, RG12, 1654–1, vol. 29, copy of Report of Privy Council, 2 June 1913.

24. PAC, Meighen Papers, Pope to Meighen, 25 November 1920.

25. Ibid., Meighen to VS, 19 February 1921.

26. SC, WIMF, VS to C. V. Sale, 23 February 1921.

27. Ibid.

28. D. M. Le Bourdais, *Stefansson, Ambassador of the North* (Montreal: Harvest House, 1962), p. 160. The Hudson's Bay Company decided at this point that it would establish a post on Wrangel Island. SC, 1920–26 file, Sale to VS, 11 April 1921. Their enthusiasm cooled, however, when they lost confidence in Stefansson and his Baffin Island venture.

First the company postponed any action regarding Wrangel Island and eventually they abandoned the idea. SC, WIMF, T. W. Sterling, for the Hudson's Bay Company, to VS, 23 July 1923.

29. PAC, Meighen Papers, Meighen to VS, 1 March 1921.
30. Ibid., Christie to Meighen, 28 February 1921.
31. Stefansson, *Adventure*, p. 78.
32. PAC, MG30, E169, J. B. Harkin to W. W. Cory, 2 March 1921.
33. Ibid.
34. Stefansson, *Discovery*, pp. 237–40.
35. PAC, Meighen Papers, Shackleton to Meighen, 6 May 1921.
36. Ibid., Meighen to Shackleton, 9 May 1921.
37. Ibid., Shackleton to Meighen, 12 May 1921.
38. Stefansson, *Adventure*, p. 77.
39. SC, WIMF, "Statement by Vilhjalmur Stefansson Regarding Men Now in Danger on Wrangel Island," 8 August 1922.
40. Stefansson, *Adventure*, p. 88. Cf., SC, WIMF, VS to O. S. Finnie, 16 March 1923.
41. SC, Katherine Wright—1925 file, VS to Orville Wright, 24 August 1922.
42. SC, WIMF, VS to F. Paysant, 31 August 1921.
43. Ibid., VS to Dr. George Jennings, 30 August 1921.
44. Ibid., VS to Crawford, 15 August 1921. Italics added.
45. Stefansson, *Adventure*, pp. 118–23.
46. PAC, King Papers, J1, vol. 86, fol. 69270, VS to King, 11 March 1922.
47. Ibid., fol. 69271.
48. Ibid., fol. 69274.
49. PAC, King Papers, J4 [Wrangel Island File], Pope to King, 21 March 1922.
50. DIAND, file 1005–5–1, Wrangel Island, U.S.S.R., General File, VS to Finnie, 3 May 1922.
51. SC, WIMF, Alfred J. T. Taylor to VS, 26 June 1922.
52. DIAND, J. D. Craig to Hensley R. Holmden, 5 April 1923.
53. Ibid., Craig to Finnie, 10 May 1922; 9 April 1923.
54. Canada, House of Commons, *Debates*, 12 May 1922, p. 1751.
55. Ibid.
56. PAC, King Papers, Wrangel Island File, Pope to King, 5 April 1923.
57. Ibid., Christie to King, 9 August 1922.
58. DIAND, T. L. Cory to W. W. Cory, 15 June 1922, cited from W. E. Hall, *International Law*, pp. 102 ff.
59. Ibid., W. W. Cory to VS, telegram, 12 August 1922.
60. SC, WIMF, "Statement . . . regarding Men in Danger. . . . ," 8 August 1922.

61. DIAND, memorandum by VS, 16 March 1923.

62. Ibid., VS to Finnie, 14 March 1923.

63. PAC, King Papers, vol. 85, fol. 68853–54, U.S. Memorandum, 27 September 1922, enclosed in a dispatch from Devonshire to Byng, 4 November 1922.

64. Ibid., fol. 63352, Devonshire to Byng, 4 November 1922.

65. Ibid., vol. 103, fol. 80358, O. D. Skelton, Acting Under-Secretary of State for External Affairs, to A. F. Sladen, Governor General's Secretary, 9 April 1923.

66. PAC, King Papers, Wrangel Island File, Pope to King, 22 March 1923.

67. PAC, King Papers, vol. 103, fol. 80358, Skelton to Sladen, 9 April 1923.

68. PAC, RG7, Governor General's Office, G21, vol. 411, no. 10045, Devonshire to Byng, 11 May 1923.

69. SC, Katherine Wright—1923 file, VS to Orville Wright, 18 April 1923.

70. SC, Wrangel Island—1925 file, VS to Sir Samuel Hoare, 28 June 1923.

71. Cited in ibid.

72. SC, Katherine Wright—1923 file, VS to Orville Wright, 18 April 1923.

73. Ibid.

74. SC, Canadian government—1923 file, "Substance of Remarks Made Before the General Board of the U.S. Navy by Vilhjalmur Stefansson," 7 May 1923.

75. SC, Katherine Wright—1925 file, VS to Katherine Wright, 9 May 1923.

76. SC, "D" General—1923 file, VS to Devonshire, 9 June 1923.

77. Stefansson, *Adventure*, pp. 144–49.

78. PAC, King Papers, vol. 100, fol. 78267, cited in a Foreign Office Memorandum on the History, Value and Ownership of Wrangel Island, 2 June 1923.

79. SC, Air Ministry, British—1923 file, secret Air Staff memorandum on the incorporation of Wrangel Island within the British Empire, 1 June 1923.

80. PAC, King Papers, vol. 103, fol. 79827, Russian note of 25 May 1923, enclosed in a dispatch from Devonshire to Byng, 20 August 1923.

81. Ibid., fol. 79828, American note, 4 June 1923, enclosed in a dispatch from Devonshire to Byng, 20 August 1923.

82. SC, Wrangel Island—1925 file, VS to Hoare, 28 June 1923.

83. SC, WIMF, VS to Taylor, 15 August 1923; cf. SC, Stefansson Diary, 1 August 1923.

84. SC, Stefansson Diary, 25 July 1923.
85. PAC, King Papers, vol. 103, fol. 79834, Curzon to Chilton, 10 August 1923, enclosed in a dispatch from Devonshire to Byng, 25 August 1923.
86. Ibid., fol. 79840, Chilton to Curzon, 15 August 1923, enclosed in a dispatch from Devonshire to Byng, 25 August 1923.
87. Ibid., fol. 80047–48, Christie to Chilton, 21 September 1923, enclosed in a dispatch from Devonshire to Byng, 12 October 1923.
88. DIAND, Foreign Office note to its agent in Moscow, 1 September 1923, enclosed in a dispatch from Devonshire to Byng, 17 September 1923.
89. E.g., SC, WIMF, Crawford to VS, 7 January 1923; PAC, RMA/15, Fred Maurer to Mrs. Fred Maurer, 29 January 1923.
90. Stefansson, *Discovery*, p. 262.
91. SC, WIMF, Crawford to VS, 7 January 1923.
92. PAC, RMA/15, Fred Maurer to Mrs. Fred Maurer, 29 January 1923.
93. SC, WIMF, VS to A. J. Taylor, 4 November 1923. See also, SC, WIMF, VS to Mrs. Crawford, 5 November 1923.
94. *Saturday Night*, 15 September 1923.
95. SC, British Admiralty—1923 file, VS to Amery, 5 September 1923.
96. SC, WIMF, VS to Taylor, 3 June 1924.
97. Stefansson, *Discovery*, p. 267.
98. SC, Lomen—1924 file, VS to Carl Lomen, 29 April 1924.
99. Stefansson, *Adventure*, p. 300.
100. National Archives, Washington, D.C., Records of the Department of State relating to the Internal Affairs of Russia and the Soviet Union, 1910–29, Microcopy no. 316, Roll no. 77, Charles Hughes to the Secretary of the Navy, 31 May 1923.
101. Ibid., memo of conversation with Helmer H. Bryn, Minister of Norway, 12 June 1926.
102. Ralph Brown, "Wrangel Island Has Had Fantastic History," *Anchorage Daily Times*, 10 and 11 February 1960.
103. PAC, King Papers, vol. 121, fol. 91841–43, J. H. Thomas, Colonial Secretary, to Byng, 18 June 1924.
104. Ibid., fol. 92015, Byng to Thomas, 18 July 1924.
105. Ibid., vol. 122, fol. 92334, declaration made on behalf of the British Delegation at the Anglo-Soviet Conference, 6 August 1924, enclosed in a dispatch, Arnold to Byng, 10 September 1924.
106. *Toronto Daily Star*, 22 January 1925.
107. *New York Times*, 18 October 1924.
108. *Toronto Daily Star*, 22 January 1925.
109. *Indianapolis Star*, 14 February 1925.
110. Ralph Brown, "Wrangel Island . . . ," *Anchorage Daily Times*, 10 and 11 February 1960.

111. From T. A. Taracouzio, *Soviets in the Arctic: An Historical, Economic and Political Study of the Soviet Advance into the Arctic* (New York: Macmillan, 1938), p. 320.
112. M. Velichko, "On Wrangel Island," *Soviet Woman* (1948), pp. 26–28.
113. Translation from the "Introduction" by Dr. G. A. Agranat, ed., in E. A. Ol'khina, *Vilhjalmur Stefansson* (Moscow: Academy of Sciences of the U.S.S.R., 1970), pp. 5–7.

Chapter 9   Exit Stefansson

1. PAC, RG42, 84–2–29/4, Desbarats to VS, 8 May 1918.
2. Ibid., Desbarats to VS, 29 June 1918.
3. Ibid.
4. PAC, RG42, 84–2–29/4, VS to John Greenough, 17 July 1918.
5. Ibid. Also AMNH, file 545H, VS to Osborn, 17 July 1918.
6. PAC, RG42, 84–2–29/4, VS to Desbarats, 26 July 1918.
7. SC, CAE/Desbarats—1918 file, VS to Desbarats, 4 August 1918.
8. Ibid.
9. PAC, RMA/4, Ralph Wolf, legal adviser, American Red Cross, to Anderson, 10 September 1918.
10. Ibid.
11. PAC, RG42, 84–2–5, Desbarats to VS, 13 September 1918.
12. Ibid.
13. PAC, RG42, 84–2–29/5, VS to Desbarats, 19 September 1918.
14. Ibid.
15. PAC, Desbarats Diary, 2 October 1918.
16. PAC, RG42, 84–2–5, Desbarats to VS, 3 October 1918.
17. SC, General Considerations—1918 file, VS to Keedick, 14 November 1918.
18. Ibid.
19. Stefansson, *Discovery: the Autobiography of Vilhjalmur Stefansson* (New York: McGraw–Hill, 1964), p. 212.
20. SC, WIMF, VS to Rutherford, 5 January 1920.
21. SC, 1920 file, VS to Professor William H. Hobbs, Department of Geology, University of Michigan, 31 January 1920.
22. SC, "Safe" file, Report of Frank D. Miller, M.D., to Dr. Milhau (Stefansson's attorney), 23 June 1920.
23. *New York Tribune*, 18 January 1922.
24. SC, "Safe" file, Lee Keedick vs. V. Stefansson, New York Supreme Court, New York County, n.d.
25. Stefansson, *Discovery*, pp. 218–19.
26. SC, CAE/Desbarats—1919 file, VS to Desbarats, 13 June 1919.

27. PAC, RG42, 84–2–29/5, VS to Desbarats, 10 July 1919.
28. Ibid.
29. Ibid., Desbarats to Borden, 12 July 1919.
30. PAC, RG45, Geological Survey Branch file 4078C/57, "V. Stefansson, Personal and Controversies," Report of the Minutes of the Arctic Biological Committee, 12 November 1919. Members of this committee were E. E. Prince, Dr. A. B. Macullum, C. Gordon Hewitt, Rudolph Anderson, and James M. Macoun.
31. Ibid.
32. R. M. Anderson, "Recent Explorations on the Canadian Arctic Coast," *Geographical Review* 4 (October 1917) : 241–66.
33. SC, CAE/Desbarats—1919 file, VS to Desbarats, 20 August 1919.
34. SC, Correspondence—1922 file, VS to Grosvenor, 29 May 1922.
35. PAC, RG45, file 4078C/57, Anderson to Charles Camsell, Deputy Minister of Mines, 30 December 1921.
36. Ibid.
37. PAC, RMA/15, Mrs. Anderson to Captain R. Bartlett, 2 January 1922.
38. Ibid., Mrs. Anderson to Mrs. A. Allstrand, 5 January 1922.
39. For Jenness's initial views, which are very similar to Anderson's, see "Declares Stefansson Acted Aggressively," *Toronto Star*, 14 January 1922.
40. "Charges against Stefansson True. . . . ," *Montreal Daily Star*, 16 January 1922.
41. *Montreal Gazette*, 14 January 1922.
42. PAC, RG42, 84–2–29/5, Anderson to Bowman, 6 November 1918.
43. SC, CAE/unmarked file, VS to Desbarats, 24 August 1920.
44. Ibid., VS to Desbarats, 17 September 1920.
45. PAC, RG45, file 4078C/57, Borden to Anderson, 11 May 1923.
46. SC, 1920–26 file, VS to Borden, 13 October 1921.
47. PAC, RMA/4, Anderson to William F. Riley, Lawyer in Des Moines, Iowa [27 January 1922].
48. PAC, RG45, file 4078C/57, Camsell to Mr. L. L. Bolton, 15 January 1922.
49. PAC, MG30, B38, Camsell Papers, vol. 3, "N-O" file, no. 6, J. J. O'Neill to Camsell, 24 January 1923.
50. PAC, RG45, file 4078C/57, Anderson, Chipman, O'Neill, and Jenness to Charles Stewart, 25 February 1922.
51. *Ottawa Morning Journal*, 8 March 1922.
52. E.g., PAC, RG42, 84–2–29/5, Desbarats to VS, telegram, 20 January 1922. SC, WIMF, Camsell to VS, 23 January 1922; Mr. McGregor (private secretary to Mackenzie King) to VS, 18 February 1922.

53. PAC, RG45, file 4078C/57, memorandum of interview of 16 March 1922, between Charles Stewart, Charles Camsell, Rudolph Anderson, K. G. Chipman, D. Jenness, 21 March 1922.

54. PAC, Crawford Papers (now in RMA), Mrs. Anderson to Mrs. Crawford, 4 June 1925.

55. PAC, RG45, file 4078C/57, Camsell to Brock, 16 April 1923.

56. D. Jenness, "The Friendly Arctic," *Science* 56 (7 July 1922): 8–12. Published by permission of the Deputy Minister of Mines.

57. Stefansson's explorations, discoveries, and techniques of observation were lauded by F. A. McDiarmid of Canada's Geodetic Survey in "Geographical Determinations of the Canadian Arctic Expedition," *Geographical Journal* [Royal Geographical Society] 62 (October 1923): 293–302. McDiarmid's contentions were questioned by James White, formerly chief geographer to the Canadian government, in the June 1924 issue of the *Geographical Journal*. White followed this attack with a longer memorandum in April 1925. Essentially, White contended that some of Stefansson's "discoveries" had been on older charts and that Stefansson's statements concerning the charting of Banks Land were incorrect. The editors of the *Journal*, however, were disinclined to accept White's arguments and gave the benefit of the doubt to Stefansson. J. H. White, "The Geographical Work of the Canadian Arctic Expedition," *Geographical Journal* 62 (June 1924): 508–11. "The Geographical Work of the Canadian Arctic Expedition," *Geographical Journal* 65 (April 1925): 340–42. It was not until 1946, however, that Stefansson's discoveries were corroborated by aerial surveys. M. Dunbar and K. R. Greenaway, *Arctic Canada From the Air* (Ottawa, 1956), pp. 8, 27, 195–96, 221, 236, 238, 244, 357, 362, 383, 384, 400, 401, 436, 437, 482. For many years, however, Stefansson's discoveries were allegedly called the "Tory Archipelago" during the Liberal administrations, because of the name he gave to his discoveries. D. M. Le Bourdais, *Stefansson, Ambassador of the North* (Montreal: Harvest House, 1962), p. 185.

58. PAC, RMA/15, Mrs. Anderson to William L. McKinlay, 21 September 1922.

59. Ibid.

60. W. H. Hobbs, "The Friendly Arctic," *The Journal of Geology* 31 (February–March 1923): 154–58.

61. PAC, Camsell Papers, VS to Camsell, 20 November 1922.

62. SC, General—1922 file, VS to Stephen Leacock, 19 December 1922.

63. Diamond Jenness, "The Physical Characteristics of the Copper Eskimo," *Report of the Canadian Arctic Expedition, 1913–18*, vol. 12, 46Bff.

64. PAC, RG45, file 4078C/57, Camsell to E. E. Prince, 26 April 1926.
65. Ibid., memo of "[Telephone] Call from V. Stefansson and Dr. Prince" to Camsell, 7 April 1923.
66. Ibid.
67. PAC, RG45, file 4078C/57, VS to Camsell, 18 April 1923.
68. Ibid., "[Telephone] Call from Stefansson and Prince" to Camsell, 7 April 1923.
69. PAC, RG45, file 4078C/57, memo by Jenness, "Account of Call from Mr. V. Stefansson and Dr. Prince," 7 April 1923.
70. Ibid., Prince to Camsell, 19 April 1923.
71. Ibid., Anderson to Camsell, 24 April 1923.
72. Ibid., Camsell to Prince, 26 April 1923.
73. Ibid., VS to Camsell, 5 May 1923.
74. PAC, RG42, 84–2–29/6, VS to McVeigh, 3 January 1924.
75. Ibid., VS to McVeigh, 3 February 1924.
76. PAC, RG42, 84–2–8, McVeigh to William L. McKinlay, 22 April 1925.
77. Ibid., 84–2–11/2, VS to McVeigh, 4 February 1931.
78. Ibid., VS to McVeigh, 10 February 1931.
79. SC, 1920–26 file, VS to Deputy Minister of Finance, 6 January 1921.
80. Notice in vol. 12 of the *Report of the Canadian Arctic Expedition, 1913–18* (Ottawa, 1923).
81. PAC, RG45, file 4078C/57, Brock to Camsell, 24 April 1923.
82. Ibid., Camsell to Prince, 26 April 1923.
83. See, PAC, Crawford Papers, 1923–24.
84. E.g., PAC, Crawford Papers, Mrs. Anderson to Mrs. Crawford, 19 March 1924; 21 March 1924. See, Georgina Stefansson, "My Grandfather, Dr. Vilhjalmur Stefansson," *North* 8, no. 4 (July–August 1961): 25.
85. E.g., PAC, RMA/5, Anderson to Mrs. Crawford, 2 April 1924.
86. PAC, RMA/19, Mrs. Crawford to Mrs. Anderson, 9 March 1952.
87. Le Bourdais, *Stefansson, Ambassador*, pp. 9–15, 173–81.
88. PAC, CP, *The Bulletin*, Sydney, Australia, 16 April 1925.

Chapter 10   Conclusion

1. Stefansson, *Discovery: the Autobiography of Vilhjalmur Stefansson* (New York: McGraw–Hill, 1964), pp. 296–97.
2. Ibid., p. 297.
3. DIAND, 20—Stefansson file, vol. 1, VS to MacBrien, 20 February 1933.

4. Ibid., Questionnaire of Major General J. H. MacBrien, 25 February 1933.
5. Ibid., H. H. Rowatt (on behalf of the Reindeer Committee) to Mac-Brien, 3 August 1933.
6. Ibid., Director [illegible] to Mr. Cumming [1938].
7. Ibid., vol. 2, Deputy Commissioner of Lands and Forest Branch (Bureau of the Northwest Territories and Yukon) to the Deputy Minister of the Interior, 1 May 1943.
8. Ibid.
9. Ibid., vol. 3, ——— to Mr. Wright, 9 February 1948.

BIBLIOGRAPHY

Below can be found a fairly comprehensive list of the archival material examined. A host of published accounts exist, particularly Stefansson's own voluminous writings, a score of books and some 350 articles. A select Stefansson bibliography follows the manuscript sources. Stefansson's final work, *Discovery*, his autobiography, has merit. Compared with some of his earlier writings dealing with his Canadian career, *Discovery* is relatively free of the exaggerations that detracted from earlier works. Nevertheless, as with most autobiographies—especially when written at a distance of more than forty years removed from the events—Stefansson's assertions do not always square with the contemporary records. For a complete list, see the chronological and subject bibliographies published by the Stefansson Collection, January and July 1960. Most works which deal with Stefansson came from the pens of admirers, who are less than objective in their applause for the man. All, in one fashion or another, have drawn heavily on Stefansson's own accounts of his exploits or have used D. M. Le Bourdais's study, written in 1930, but not published until shortly after Stefansson's death in 1962. Le Bourdais's *Stefansson, Ambassador of the North* has incorporated some archival material and has more balance, but he was a long-time friend and travelling companion of Stefansson's in the 1920s and shared the latter's sentiments.

PRIMARY SOURCES

ARCHIVAL SOURCES

American Geographical Society, New York City:
> Anglo-American Polar Expedition files.

American Museum of Natural History, New York City:
> Files pertaining to Vilhjalmur Stefansson; Crocker Land Files.

Baker Library, Dartmouth College, Hanover, New Hampshire, Stefansson Collection:
> Vilhjalmur Stefansson Correspondence and Diaries.
> Other Diaries: Ada Blackjack; Diamond Jenness; Lorne Knight; and Sir Hubert Wilkins.

Department of Indian Affairs and Northern Development, Ottawa:
    Stefansson Files.
Fletcher Library, Harvard University, Cambridge, Massachusetts:
    Theodore Roosevelt Papers.
National Archives, Washington, D.C.:
    Records of the Department of State relating to internal affairs of
    Russia and the Soviet Union, 1910–29.
National Geographic Society, Washington, D.C.:
    Correspondence pertaining to Stefansson.
Public Archives of Canada, Ottawa:
    Diaries: Karsten Anderson; William J. Baur; Peter Bernard;
               Aarnout Castel; George J. Desbarats; Adelbert G. Gumaer;
               John Hadley; Herman Kilian; Martin Kilian; Lorne
               Knight; Charles A. Lewin; Bjarne Memen; August Masik;
               Bert M.McConnell; William L. McKinlay; Harold Noice;
               Vilhjalmur Stefansson; Storker T. Storkerson; and Robert
               J. Williamson.
    Rudolph Martin Anderson Papers; Sir Robert Borden Papers; Charles
    Camsell Papers; Kenneth G. Chipman Papers; Papers of Mrs. J. T.
    Crawford; Governor General's Office; J. B. Harkin Papers; William
    Lyon Mackenzie King Papers and Diaries; Arthur Meighen Papers;
    Privy Council Records; Records of the Department of the Interior;
    Records of the Departments of Transport and Marine; and Records
    of the Geological Survey of Canada.
Royal Canadian Mounted Police. Ottawa Headquarters:
    Canadian Arctic Expedition files (active).
University of Toronto Library, Rare Books and Special Collections:
    James Mavor Papers; and Sir Edmund Walker Papers.

INTERVIEWS

Dr. Diamond Jenness; and Mr. Kenneth G. Chipman.

FILMED INTERVIEWS

The National Film Board of Canada. Arctic Circle Series (1962).
(Three of the four films pertain to Stefansson; the other is an inter-
view with Henry Larson, retired superintendent of the RCMP, and
commander of the St. Roch.) Interviewer-moderator, Trevor Lloyd,
Department of Geography, McGill University:
*The Early Journeys of Vilhjalmur Stefansson; The Later Journeys of
Vilhjalmur Stefansson;* and *Memories and Predictions.*

PRINTED SOURCES AND GOVERNMENT PUBLICATIONS

Canada. Department of Marine and Fisheries. *Report of the Hudson's Bay Expedition of 1884 under the Command of A. R. Gordon, R.N.* Ottawa, 1884.

———. Department of Marine and Fisheries. *Report of the Expedition to Hudson's Bay and Cumberland Sound in the Steamship Diana under the command of William Wakeham in the year 1897.* Ottawa, 1898.

———. Department of Marine and Fisheries. *Report of the Dominion Government Expedition to the Arctic Islands and Hudson Strait on Board the D.G.S. Arctic, 1906–07, by Captain J. E. Bernier in Charge and Fisheries Officer.* Ottawa, 1909.

———. Department of Marine and Fisheries. *Report of the Dominion of Canada Expedition to the Arctic Islands and Hudson Strait on Board the D.G.S. Arctic 1908–09.* Ottawa, 1910.

———. Department of Marine and Fisheries. *Report of the Dominion Government Expedition to the Northern Waters and Arctic Archipelago of the D.G.S. Arctic in 1910 under the Command of J. E. Bernier.* Ottawa, [1911?].

———. Department of Mines, Geological Survey Branch. *Annual Reports.*

———. Department of Mines and Resources. *Canada's Reindeer Herd.* Ottawa, 1938.

———. Northwest Mounted Police. *Annual Reports.*

———. *Report of the Royal Commission to Investigate the Possibilities of the Reindeer and Musk-Ox Industries in the Arctic and Sub-Arctic Regions of Canada.* Ottawa, 1922.

———. Department of the Interior. *Annual Reports.*

———. Department of the Naval Service. *Annual Reports.*

———. Department of the Naval Service. *Reports of the Canadian Arctic Expedition, 1913–18.* 14 vols. Ottawa, 1920–46. [Not published: vols. 1; 2; 6, Pt. A; 7, Pt. M; 8, Pt. F; 9, Pts. F, I, K; 10, Pts. A, B.]

———. House of Commons. *Debates.* 1906–26.

———. Senate. *Debates.* 1906–26.

Denmark. Ministry of Education. *Report of the Fifth Thule Expedition. The Danish Expedition to arctic North America in charge of Knud Rasmussen.* 12 vols. Copenhagen, 1927–19—. [Not published: vols. 3, 4, 5, 11, 12.]

Dunbar, M., and Greenaway, K. R. *Arctic Canada from the Air.* Ottawa, 1956.

Hill, R. M. *Mackenzie Reindeer Operations.* Ottawa, 1967.

Kelsall, John P. *The Migratory Barren-Ground Caribou of Canada.* Ottawa, n.d.

King, W. F. *Report upon the Title of Canada to the Islands North of the Mainland of Canada*. Ottawa, 1905.

Low, A. P. *The Cruise of the Neptune, 1903–04*. Ottawa, 1906.

United States of America. Naval War College. "Jurisdiction and Polar Areas," *International Law Situations: With Solutions and Notes*. Situation 3:69–131. Washington, D.C., 1937.

NEWSPAPERS (1906–26)

London Daily Chronicle; *Montreal Gazette*; *Montreal Daily Star*; *New York Times*; *New York Tribune*; *Ottawa Citizen*; *Ottawa Evening Journal*; *Ottawa Free Press*; *Ottawa Morning Journal*; *Seattle Daily Times*; *Toronto Daily Star*; and *Toronto Globe*.

Also *Anchorage Daily Times*, February 1960; *Indianapolis Star*, February 1925; and *The Bulletin*, Sydney, Australia, April 1925.

SELECT LIST OF WORKS BY VILHJALMUR STEFANSSON

BOOKS

My Life With the Eskimo. New York: Macmillan, 1913.

The Friendly Arctic. New York: Macmillan, 1921.

Hunters of the Great North. New York: Harcourt, Brace, 1922.

The Northward Course of Empire. London: Harrap, 1922.

The Adventure of Wrangel Island. New York: Macmillan, 1925.

Northward ho! New York: Macmillan, 1927.

The Standardization of Error. London: Paul, Trench, Trubner, 1928.

Greenland. Garden City, New York: Doubleday, Doran and Co., 1942.

Ultima Thule: Further Mysteries of the Arctic. New York: Macmillan, 1944.

Not by Bread Alone. New York: Macmillan, 1946.

Iceland, the First American Republic. New York: Doubleday, Doran and Co., 1947.

Unsolved Mysteries of the Arctic. New York: Macmillan, 1951.

The Fat of the Land. New York: Macmillan, 1957.

Northwest to Fortune; the Search of Western Man for a Commercially Practical Route to the Far East. New York: Duell, Sloan and Pearce, 1958.

Cancer: Disease of Civilization? An Anthropological and Historical Study. New York: Hill and Wang, 1960.

Discovery: the Autobiography of Vilhjalmur Stefansson. New York: McGraw–Hill, 1964.

ARTICLES

"A North Dakotan at Harvard," *The Student* [The University of North Dakota] 17 (January 1904) : 4–6.

"The Newer Literature of Iceland," *Poet Lore* (Spring 1904), pp. 62–76.

"The Icelandic Colony in Greenland," *The American Anthropologist* 13 (June 1906) : 262–70.

"Icelandic Beast and Bird Lore," *Journal of American Folklore* 19 (October–December 1906) : 300–308.

"The Theory and Treatment of Disease among Mackenzie River Eskimos," *Journal of American Folklore* 21 (January 1908) : 43–45.

"The Anglo-American Polar Expedition," *Harper's Monthly Magazine* 116 (February 1908) : 327–42.

"On the Mackenzie River," *Bulletin of the American Geographical Society* 40 (March 1908) : 157–58.

"Suitability of Eskimo Methods of Winter Travel in Scientific Exploration," *Bulletin of the American Geographical Society* 40 (April 1908) : 210–13.

"Wintering among the Eskimos," *Harper's* 116 (June 1908) : 38–48.

"The Home Life of the Eskimo," *Harper's* 117 (October 1908) : 721–30.

"A Preliminary Report of an Ethnological Investigation of the Mackenzie Delta," Canada, Department of Mines, Geological Survey *Annual Report* (1908), pp. 190–202.

"The Eskimo Trade Jargon of Herschel Island," *American Anthropologist* 2 (April–June 1909) : 217–32.

"Northern Alaska in Winter," *Bulletin of the American Geographical Society* 41 (October 1909) : 601–10.

"Underground Ice in Northern Alaska," *Bulletin of the American Geographical Society* 42 (May 1910) : 337–45.

"Turning Kogmolli for Science," *The American Museum Journal* 10 (November 1910) : 212–20.

"Stefansson and Anderson in the Canadian Arctic," *Bulletin of the American Geographical Society* 43 (October 1911) : 771–75.

"The Technique of Arctic Winter Travel," *Bulletin of the American Geographical Society* 45 (May 1912) : 340–47.

"The Eskimo and Civilization," *The American Museum Journal* 12 (October 1912) : 195–204.

"Distribution of Human and Animal Life in the Western Arctic America," *Geographical Journal* 43 (May 1913) : 449–60.

"Canadian Arctic Expedition," *Geographical Journal* 44 (July 1913): 49–54.

"The Stefansson-Anderson Arctic Expedition of the American Museum; Preliminary Report," *Anthropological Papers of the American Museum of Natural History* 14, part 1 (1914).

"Original Observations on Scurvy and my Opinion of the Medical Profession," *Medical Review of Reviews* 24 (May 1918): 257–64.

"Polar Regions. Mr. Rasmussen's Expedition to Northern Greenland," *Geographical Journal* 52 (July 1918): 63.

"Observations on Three Cases of Scurvy, Meat Diet in Health and Disease," *Journal of the American Medical Association* 71 (23 November 1918): 1715–18.

" 'Living off the Country' as a Method of Arctic Exploration," *The Geographical Review* 7 (May 1919): 291–310.

"Man Can Live on Meat Alone" (Interview), *Physical Culture* (August 1919), pp. 23–24, 64–66.

"Health, Wealth and Enjoyment in the Far, Far North," *The Maple Leaf* 2 (July 1920): 7–10.

"Temperature Factor in Determining the Age of Maturity Among the Eskimos," *Journal of the American Medical Association* 75 (4 September 1920): 665–70.

"The Region of Maximum Inaccessibility in the Arctic," *The Geographical Review* 9 (September 1920): 167–72.

"Ploverland and Borden Land," *The Geographical Review* 11 (April 1921): 283–91.

"The North that Never Was," *The World's Work* 43 (December 1921): 188–200.

"Canada's Caribou Crop," *Maclean's Magazine* (15 January 1922), pp. 27, 35–36.

"Some Erroneous Ideas of Arctic Geography," *The Geographical Review* 20 (April 1922): 264–77.

"The Arctic as an Air Route of the Future," *National Geographic* 42 (August 1922): 205–18.

"Every Science an Exact Science," *The American Mercury* 1 (March 1924): 455–63.

"Arctic Air Routes to the Orient," *The Forum* 72 (December 1924): 721–32.

"Spend your Vacation at the North Pole," *Collier's* 26 (November 1925).

"The Arctic: Its Changing Phases," *Current History* 23 (November 1925): 155–70.

"Polar Pastures," *The Forum* 75 (January 1926): 9–20.

"Living by Forage in Arctic Exploration," *The Geographical Review* 16 (April 1926): 9–15.

"New Polar Trails," *The Forum* 77 (January 1927) : 54–64.

"Are Explorers to Join the Dodo?" *The American Mercury* 11 (May 1927) : 13–18.

"By Air to the Ends of the Earth," *Natural History* 28 (September–October 1928) : 451–62.

"Defense of Nobile," *World's Work* 58 (May 1929) : 70–73, 138, 140, 142, 148.

"The Theoretical Continent," *Natural History* 29 (September–October 1929) : 465–80.

"The Eskimo Word 'Iglu'," *Science* 73 (13 March 1931) : 285–86.

"Blue Eyes for Brown," *Science* 77 (17 February 1933) : 191–92.

"Adventures in Diet," *Harper's Magazine*, part 1 (November 1935), pp. 668–75; part 2 (December 1935), pp. 46–54; part 3 (January 1936), pp. 178–79.

"Food of Ancient and Modern Stone Age Man," *Journal of the American Dietetic Association* 13 (July 1937) : 102–19.

"Background of the Trans-Polar Flights," *Research Bulletin on the Soviet Union* 2 (30 August 1937) : 83–84.

"Disappearance of the Greenland Colony," *Natural History* 43 (January 1939) : 7–12.

"Routes to Alaska," *Foreign Affairs* 19 (July 1941) : 861–69.

"Pemmican," *The Military Surgeon* 95 (August 1944) : 89–98.

"See Your Dentist Twice a Year," *The Atlantic* 176 (November 1945) : 61–66.

"Our Neglected Arctic," *Science Illustrated* 2 (November 1947) : 17–21, 112–15.

"The Arctic," *Air Affairs* 3 (Spring 1950) : 391–402.

"From the Pioneer West to the Arctic" (Interview), *The Westerner's Brand Book* 13 (October 1956) : 57–58.

"Causes of Eskimo Birth-Rate Increase," *Nature* 177 (17 November 1956) : 1132.

SECONDARY SOURCES

BOOKS

Amundsen, Roald Engelbregt Gravning. *Roald Amundsen—my life as an explorer*. Garden City, New York: Doubleday, Page and Co., 1927.

———. *The Northwest Passage; being the record of the voyage of exploration of the ship 'Gjoa', 1903–07*. New York: Dutton, 1908.

Bartlett, R. A., and Hale, R. T. *The Last Voyage of the Karluk*. Toronto: McClelland, Goodchild and Stewart, 1916.

Bériault, Yvon. *Les Problèmes Politiques du Nord Canadien*. Ottawa: Université d'Ottawa, 1942.

Bernier, J. *Master Mariner and Arctic Explorer*. Ottawa: n.p., 1939.

Berry, Erick. *Mr. Arctic; an account of Vilhjalmur Stefansson*. New York: David McKay, 1966.

Billington, R. A. *America's Frontier Heritage*. New York: Holt, Rinehart and Winston, 1966.

Birket-Smith, K. *The Eskimos*. London: Methuen, 1959.

Borden, H., ed. *Robert Laird Borden: His Memoirs*. 2 vols. Toronto: Macmillan, 1938.

Brebner, J. B. *The Explorers of North America*. London: A. & C. Black, 1933.

Cameron, A. D. *The new North; being some account of a woman's journey through Canada to the Arctic*. New York and London: D. Appleton and Co., 1910.

Caswell, John Edwards. *Arctic Frontiers: United States explorations in the Far North*. Norman, Okla.: University of Oklahoma Press, 1956.

Clark, S. D. *The Social Development of Canada*. Toronto: University of Toronto Press, 1942.

Croft, Andrew. *Polar Exploration*. London: A. & C. Black, 1939.

Cross, M. S. *The Frontier Thesis and the Canadas: The Debate on the impact of the Canadian Environment*. "Issues in Canadian History" series, J. L. Granatstein, ed. Toronto: Copp Clark, 1970.

Dawson, R. MacGregor. *William Lyon Mackenzie King. A Political Biography, 1874–1923*. Toronto: University of Toronto Press, 1958.

Debenham, Frank. *The Polar Regions*. London: Ernest Benn Ltd., 1930.

De Long, George Washington. *The Voyage of the Jeannette*. 2 vols. Boston, 1884.

Easterbrook, W. T., and Aitken, A. G. J. *Canadian Economic History*. Toronto: Macmillan, 1956.

Evans, A. R. *Meat: a tale of the reindeer trek (1929–1935)*. London: Hurst & Blackett, [1935].

Glazebrook, G. P. deT. *A History of Canadian External Relations*. 2 vols. Toronto: McClelland and Stewart, 1966.

————. *A History of Transportation in Canada*. 2 vols. Toronto: McClelland and Stewart, 1964.

————. *Sir Edmund Walker*. Toronto: Oxford University Press, 1933.

Glines, Lt. Col. C. V. *Polar Aviation*. New York: Franklin Watts, 1964.

Graham, Roger. *Arthur Meighen, a Biography*. Vols. 1 and 2. Toronto: Clarke, Irwin and Co., 1960–63.

Grierson, J. *Sir Hubert Wilkins*. London: Robert Hale, 1960.

Hanson, Earl P. *Stefansson, Prophet of the North*. New York: Harper, 1941.

Harrison, Alfred H. *In Search of a Polar Continent*. Toronto: Musson, 1908.

Hobbs, W. H. *Peary*. New York: Macmillan, 1936.

Hofstadter, Richard. *Social Darwinism in American Thought*. Boston: Beacon Press, 1960.

————. *The Progressive Historians, Turner, Beard, Parrington*. New York: Knopf, 1968.

Horwood, Harold. *Bartlett, The Great Canadian Explorer*. New York and Toronto: Doubleday, 1977.

Huntington, E. *Civilization and Climate*. New Haven: Yale University Press, 1915.

Innis, H. A. *The Fur Trade in Canada*. Toronto: University of Toronto Press, 1956.

Jenness, D. *Eskimo Administration: Canada*. Arctic Institute of North America, Technical Paper no. 14. [Montreal: The Arctic Institute of North America], 1964.

Joerg, W. L. G. ed. *Problems of Polar Research*. American Geographical Society Special Publication no. 7. New York: American Geographical Society, 1928.

Jones, Stephen B. *The Arctic: Problems and Possibilities*. New Haven: Yale Institute of International Studies, 1948.

Keller, Arthur S., Lissitzyn, Oliver J., and Mann, Fred J. *Creation of Rights of Sovereignty Through Symbolic Acts, 1400–1800*. New York: Columbia University Press, 1938.

Kristjanson, W. *The Icelandic People in Manitoba*. Winnipeg: Willingford Press, 1965.

Lake, Simon. *The Submarine in War and Peace*. Philadelphia: Lippincott, 1918.

Le Bourdais, D. M. *Stefansson, Ambassador of the North*. Montreal: Harvest House, 1963.

Lindley, Mark Frank. *The Acquisition and Government of Backward Territory in International Law; Being a Treatise on the Law and Practice Relating to Colonial Expansion*. London: Longmans, Green and Co., 1926.

Lomen, Carl J. *Fifty Years in Alaska*. New York: David McKay, 1954.

MacInnes, T., ed. *Klengenberg of the Arctic*. London and Toronto: Jonathon Cape, 1932.

MacMillan, Donald B. *Four Years in the White North*. New York: Harper, 1918.

Martin, Chester. *Empire and Commonwealth*. Toronto: Oxford University Press, 1929.

McKinlay, William Laird. *Karluk: The great untold story of Arctic exploration*. London: Weidenfeld and Nicolson, 1976.

Mikkelsen, E. *Conquering the Arctic Ice*. London: Heinemann, 1909.
————. *Mirage in the Arctic*. London: Rupert Hart–Davis, 1955.
Mill, Hugh Robert. *The Life of Sir Ernest Shackleton*. London: Heinemann, 1923.
Miller, M. *The Great Trek; the story of the five-year drive of a reindeer herd through the icy wastes of Alaska and northwestern Canada*. Garden City, New York: Doubleday, Doran, 1935.
Mirsky, Jeannette. *To the Arctic!* New York: A. Wingate, 1948.
Myers, Hortense. *Vilhjalmur Stefansson, young Arctic Explorer*. Indianapolis: Bobbs–Merrill, 1966.
Nansen, F. *Farthest North*. New York, 1897.
Neatby, H. Blair. *William Lyon Mackenzie King*, vol. 2, *1924–1932: The Lonely Heights*. Toronto: University of Toronto Press, 1963.
Noice, Harold. *With Stefansson in the Arctic*. New York: Dodd, Mead, [1924].
Ol'Khina, E. A. *Vilhjalmur Stefansson*. Moscow: Academy of Sciences of the U.S.S.R., 1970.
Peary, R. E. *The North Pole*. London: Hodder and Stoughton, 1910.
Phillips, R. A. J. *Canada's North*. Toronto: Macmillan, 1967.
Rasmussen, Knud. *Across Arctic America; narrative of the fifth Thule Expedition*. New York: Putnam, 1927.
Russell, Frank. *Explorations in the Far North*. University of Iowa, 1898.
Skelton, O. D. *The Life and Letters of Sir Wilfrid Laurier*. 2 vols. London: Oxford University Press, 1922.
Smedal, Gustav. *Acquisition of Sovereignty over Polar Areas*. Oslo: I Kommisjon Hos Jacob Dybwad, 1931.
Smith, O. M. *Le Statut Juridique des Terres Polaires*. Paris: Rousseau, 1934.
Smolka, Harry Peter. *Forty Thousand Against the Arctic: Russia's Polar Empire*. London: Hutchinson, 1937.
Sverdrup, O. *The New Land*. London: Longmans, Green & Co., 1904.
Swayze, N. *Canadian Portraits: Jenness, Barbeau, Wintemberg*. Toronto: Clarke, Irwin, 1960.
Taracouzio, T. A. *Soviets in the Arctic: An Historical, Economic, and Political Study of the Soviet Advance into the Arctic*. New York: Macmillan, 1938.
Thomas, Lowell. *Sir Hubert Wilkins*. New York: McGraw–Hill, 1961.
Vyvyan, C. C. *Arctic Adventure*. London: P. Owen, 1961.
Whalley, George. *The Legend of John Hornby*. Toronto: Macmillan, 1962.
Whittaker, C. E. *Arctic Eskimo: a record of fifty years' experience and observation among the Eskimo*. London: Seeley Service, 1937.

Wilkins, Sir George Hubert. *Flying the Arctic*. New York: Grosset & Dunlop, 1928.

————. *Under the North Pole; the Wilkins–Ellsworth submarine expedition*. New York: Brewer, Warren & Putnam, 1931.

Zaslow, Morris. *The Opening of the Canadian North, 1870–1914*. Toronto: McClelland and Stewart, 1971.

————. *Reading the Rocks: The Story of the Geological Survey of Canada, 1842–1972*. Ottawa: Macmillan, in association with the Department of Energy, Mines, and Resources and Information Canada, 1975.

ARTICLES

Abrahamson, G. "Canada's Reindeer," *Canadian Geographical Journal* 65 (June 1963): 188–93.

Anderson, R. M. "Range of the Moose Extending Northward," *Canadian Field Naturalist* 38 (February 1924): 27–29.

————. "Recent Explorations on the Canadian Arctic Coast," *The Geographical Review* 4 (October 1917): 241–66.

Baird, P. D., and Robinson, J. L. "A Brief History of Exploration and Research in the Canadian Eastern Arctic," *Canadian Geographical Journal* 30 (March 1945), 136–57.

————. "Expeditions to the Canadian Arctic," *Beaver* Outfit 279 (1949): 44–47; Outfit 280 (1949): 41–47.

Balch, Thomas W. "The Arctic and Antarctic Regions and the Law of Nations," *The American Journal of International Law* 4 (April 1910): 265–75.

————. "The Hudson Sea is a Great Open Sea," *The American Journal of International Law* 7 (July 1913): 546–65.

————. "Is Hudson Bay a Closed or an Open Sea?" *The American Journal of International Law* 6 (April 1912): 409–59.

Berger, Carl. "The True North Strong and Free," in P. Russell, ed. *Nationalism in Canada*. Toronto: McGraw–Hill, 1966.

Birket-Smith, K. "The Question of the Origin of Eskimo Culture: A Rejoinder," *American Anthropologist* 42 (October 1930): 608–24.

Boas, Franz. "Human Faculty as Determined by Race," *Proceedings, American Association For the Advancement of Science* 43 (1894): 301–27.

Borden, Ethel. "Northward, 1903–04," *Canadian Geographical Journal* 50 (January 1961): 32–39.

Brown, R., and Rudmose, N. "The Sovereignty of Polar Lands," *Discovery* 5 (June 1924): 77–81.

Calvert, James. "Drift Stations and Submarines," *Polar Notes* no. 4 (November 1962): 13–19.

Careless, J. M. S. "Frontierism, Metropolitanism and Canadian History," *Canadian Historical Review* 35 (March 1954) : 1–21.

Chown, B., and Lewis, M. "The Blood Group Genes of the Cree Indians and Eskimos of the Ungava District," *American Journal of Physical Anthropology* 14, no. 2 (1956) : 215–24.

―――. "The Blood Group Genes of the Copper Eskimos," *American Journal of Physical Anthropology* 17, no. 1 (1959) : 13–18.

Cleminson, H. M. "Laws of Maritime Jurisdiction in Time of Peace, with Special Reference to Territorial Waters," *The British Year Book of International Law* 6 (1925) : 144–58.

Collins, H. B. "Stefansson as an Anthropologist," *Polar Notes* no. 4 (November 1962) : 8–13.

Cooper, John C. "Airspace Rights over the Arctic," *Air Affairs* 3 (December 1950) : 517–40.

Corcoran, P. A., Allen, E. H., Allison, A. C., Blumberg, B. S. "Blood Groups of Alaskan Eskimos and Indians," *American Journal of Physical Anthropology* 17, no. 2 (1959) : 187–93.

Crary, A. P., Cotrell, R. D., Sexton, T. F. "Preliminary Report on Scientific Work on Fletcher's Ice Island, T 3," *Arctic* 5 (December 1952) : 211–23.

Dexter, G. "Who Owns the Arctic?" *Canadian Magazine* 73 (March 1930) : 14, 31.

Diubaldo, Richard J. "Wrangling over Wrangel Island," *Canadian Historical Review* 48 (September 1967) : 201–26.

Dubos, R. "The Medical Anthropologist," *Polar Notes* no. 4 (November 1962) : 29–33.

Elder, Robert E. "Decision on Polar Sovereignty by Student Moot Court," *The American Journal of International Law* 41 (July 1947) : 656–59.

Ellis, F. H. "First Flight in the Canadian Arctic," *Beaver* Outfit 281 (1950) : 16–17.

Finnie, O. S. "Reindeer for the Canadian Eskimo," *Natural History* 31 (July–August 1931) : 409–16.

GilFillan, S. C. "The Coldward Course of Progress," *Political Science Quarterly* 35 (September 1920) : 395–410.

Godsell, P. H. "The Passing of Herschel Island," *Royal Canadian Mounted Police Quarterly* 9 (April 1942) : 380–92.

Gould, L. M. "Vilhjalmur Stefansson: A Subjective View," *Polar Notes* no. 4 (November 1962) : 1–3.

Harris, R. A. "Evidence of Land Near the North Pole," *Report of the 8th International Geographical Congress* (1904), pp. 397–406.

Harrison, A. H. "In Search of an Arctic Continent," *Geographical Journal* 20 (March 1908) : 277–87.

Hayes, C. "The American Frontier—Frontier of What?" *American Historical Review* 51 (January 1946) : 199–216.

Hayton, R. "Polar Problems and International Law," *American Journal of International Law* 52 (October 1958) : 746–65.

Hobbs, William H. "The Friendly Arctic," *The Journal of Geology* 31 (February–March 1923) : 154–58.

Holden, Raymond P. "Explorer and Man of Letters," *Polar Notes* no. 4 (November 1962) : 29–33.

Hopper, Bruce. "Sovereignty in the Arctic," *Research Bulletin on the Soviet Union* 2 (30 August 1937) : 81–83.

———. "The Soviet Conquest of the Far North," *Foreign Affairs* 14 (April 1936) : 499–505.

Howard, Robert West. "He eats fat . . . to stay lean," *National Live Stock Producer* 34 (October 1956) : 9, 18.

Hyde, Charles C. "Case concerning the Legal Status of Eastern Greenland," *American Journal of International Law* 27 (October 1933) : 732–38.

Jenness, D. "The Friendly Arctic," *Science* 65 (7 July 1922) : 8–12.

Johnston, V. Kenneth. "Canada's Title to the Arctic Islands," *Canadian Historical Review* 14 (March 1933) : 24–41.

———. "Canada's Title to Hudson Bay and Hudson Strait," *The British Year Book of International Law* 15 (1934) : 1–20.

Lakhtine, Vladimir L. "Rights over the Arctic," *American Journal of International Law* 24 (1930) : 703–17.

Lieb, Clarence. "A Year's Exclusive Meat Diet and Seven Years Later," *The American Journal of Digestion and Nutrition* 11, no. 8 (1935–36) : 473–75.

———. "The Effects of an Exclusive Long-continued Meat Diet, Based on the History, Experience and Clinical Survey of Vilhjalmur Stefansson, Arctic Explorer," *Journal of the American Medical Association* 87 (3 July 1926) : 25–26.

Lister, Althea. "Aviation Pioneer," *Polar Notes* no. 4 (November 1962) : 19–25.

Lloyd, Trevor. "Vilhjalmur Stefansson," *Polar Notes* no. 4 (November 1962) : 3–8.

Loenig, L. S., Greenaway, K. R., Dunbar, M., Hattersley-Smith, G. "Arctic Ice Islands," *Arctic* 5 (July 1952) : 67–103.

McConnell, B. "The Airplane in Exploration," *Scientific American* 115 (30 September 1916) : 295–96.

McConnell, B., and Noice, H. "The Friendly Arctic," *Science* 57 (30 March 1923) : 368–73.

McDiarmid, F. A. "Geographical Determination of the Canadian Arctic Expedition," *Geographical Journal* 62 (October 1923) : 293–302.

McKitterick, T. E. M. "The Validity of Territorial and other claims in the Polar Regions," *Journal of Comparative Legislation* 21, pt. 1 (1939) : 89–97.

Miller, David Hunter. "Political Rights in the Arctic," *Foreign Affairs* 4 (October 1925) : 47–60.

———. "Political Rights in the Polar Regions," in W. L. G. Joerg, ed. *Problems of Polar Research*. New York: American Geographical Society, 1928, pp. 235–50.

Mikkelborg, J. "Reindeer from Lapland," *The Bay* (1949–50), pp. 22–27, 37–39, 16–18, 25, 28, 30, 12–16, from consecutive issues.

Montague, James. "Canada Occupies the Arctic: Services Rendered by the Government," *Canadian Magazine* 76 (December 1931) : 10, 11, 41.

Morton, W. L. "The North in Canadian History," *Northern Affairs Bulletin* 7 (January–February 1960) : 26–29.

Pearl, Raymond. "The Friendly Arctic," *Science* 55 (24 March 1922) : 320–21.

Phillips, R. A. J. "The Eastern Arctic Patrol," *Canadian Geographical Journal* 54 (May 1957) : 214–25.

Plischke, Elmer. "Sovereignty and Imperialism in Polar Regions," in D. E. Lee and G. M. McReynolds, eds. *Essays in History and International Relations in Honor of George Hubbard Blakeslee*. Worcester: Clark University, 1949.

Preuss, L. "The Dispute Between Denmark and Norway Over the Sovereignty of East Greenland," *American Journal of International Law* 26 (July 1932) : 469–87.

Ralston, Jackson H., "Prescription," *American Journal of International Law* 4 (January 1910) : 133–44.

Reeves, Jesse S. "George V Land," *American Journal of International Law* 28 (January 1934) : 117–19.

Robinson, J. Lewis. "Canada's Western Arctic," *Canadian Geographical Journal* 37 (December 1948) : 242–60.

Rowley, Diana. "Stefansson Island," *Arctic Circular* 5 (1952) : 46–53.

Rohner, Ronald P., and Rohner, Evelyn C. "The Development of North American Ethnology," in R. P. Rohner, ed. *The Ethnography of Franz Boas*. Chicago: University of Chicago Press, 1969.

Scott, James Brown. "Arctic Exploration and International Law," *American Journal of International Law* 3 (October 1909) : 928–41.

Seltzer, Carl C. "The Anthropometry of the Western and Copper Eskimos Based on the Data of Vilhjalmur Stefansson," *Human Biology* 5 (September 1933) : 413–70.

Simsarian, James. "The Acquisition of Legal Title to Terra Nullius," *Political Science Quarterly* 53 (March 1938) : 111–28.

Smith, Gordon W. "The Transfer of Arctic Territories from Great Britain to Canada in 1880, and Some Related Matters, As Seen in the Official Correspondence," *Arctic* 14 (March 1961) : 53–73.

———. "Sovereignty in the North: The Canadian Aspect of an International Problem," in R. St. J. Macdonald, ed. *The Arctic Frontier.* Toronto: University of Toronto Press, 1966, pp. 194–255.

Smolka, Harry Peter. "Soviet Strategy in the Arctic," *Foreign Affairs* 16 (January 1938) : 272–78.

Stefansson, Georgina. "My Grandfather, Dr. Vilhjalmur Stefansson," *North* 8 (July–August 1961) : 25.

Stevenson, A. "Herschel Haven," *North* 15 (November–December 1968) : 24–32.

Sutherland, R. J. "The Strategic Significance of the Canadian Arctic," in R. St. J. Macdonald, ed. *The Arctic Frontier.* Toronto: University of Toronto Press, 1966, pp. 256–78.

Svarlien, Oscar. "The Sector Principle in Law and Practice," *Polar Record* 8 (September 1960) : 41–57.

Taylor, W. E. "Hypothesis on the Origin of the Canadian Thule Culture," *American Antiquity* 28 (April 1963) : 456–64.

———. "Interim Report of an Archaeological Survey in the Central Arctic," *Anthropological Papers of the University of Alaska* 12, no. 1 (Winter 1964) : 46–55.

Tolstoi, Edward. "The Effect of an Exclusive Meat Diet Lasting One Year on the Carbohydrate Tolerance of Two Normal Men," *The Journal of Biological Chemistry* 83 (September 1929) : 747–52.

Velichko, M. "On Wrangel Island," *Soviet Woman* (1948) : 26–28.

White, J. H. "The Geographical Work of the Canadian Arctic Expedition," *Geographical Journal* 63 (June 1924) : 508–11; 65 (April 1925) : 340–42.

Williams, Charles H. M. "An Investigation Concerning the Dentitions of the Eskimos of Canada's Eastern Arctic," *The American Academy of Periodontology* (1942), pp. 34–38.

Wright, Quincy. "Territorial Propinquity," *American Journal of International Law* 12 (July 1918) : 519–61.

Zaslow, Morris. "The Frontier Hypothesis in Recent Historiography," *Canadian Historical Review* 29 (June 1948) : 153–67.

Zubov, N. N. "Arctic Ice Islands and How They Drift," *Priroda* no. 2 (1955) : 37–45. Translated by E. R. Hope, Defence Research Board of Canada.

UNPUBLISHED STUDIES

McGhee, Robert J. "Copper Eskimo Prehistory." Unpublished Ph.D. thesis, University of Calgary, 1968.

Plischke, Elmer. "Jurisdiction in the Polar Regions." Unpublished Ph.D. thesis, Clark University, 1943.

————. "Territorial Sovereignty in the Arctic." Unpublished manuscript specially prepared for the "Encyclopedia Arctica," also unpublished, compiled under Contract N50NR–265, NR162–218 between the Office of Naval Research in the United States Navy Department and the Stefansson Library.

Smith, Gordon W. "The Historical and Legal Background of Canada's Arctic Claims." Unpublished Ph.D. thesis, Columbia University, 1952.

INDEX